T0180539

Communications
in Computer and Information Science

2049

Rationale

The CCIS series is devoted to the publication of proceedings of computer science conferences. Its aim is to efficiently disseminate original research results in informatics in printed and electronic form. While the focus is on publication of peer-reviewed full papers presenting mature work, inclusion of reviewed short papers reporting on work in progress is welcome, too. Besides globally relevant meetings with internationally representative program committees guaranteeing a strict peer-reviewing and paper selection process, conferences run by societies or of high regional or national relevance are also considered for publication.

Topics

The topical scope of CCIS spans the entire spectrum of informatics ranging from foundational topics in the theory of computing to information and communications science and technology and a broad variety of interdisciplinary application fields.

Information for Volume Editors and Authors

Publication in CCIS is free of charge. No royalties are paid, however, we offer registered conference participants temporary free access to the online version of the conference proceedings on SpringerLink (http://link.springer.com) by means of an http referrer from the conference website and/or a number of complimentary printed copies, as specified in the official acceptance email of the event.

CCIS proceedings can be published in time for distribution at conferences or as post-proceedings, and delivered in the form of printed books and/or electronically as USBs and/or e-content licenses for accessing proceedings at SpringerLink. Furthermore, CCIS proceedings are included in the CCIS electronic book series hosted in the SpringerLink digital library at http://link.springer.com/bookseries/7899. Conferences publishing in CCIS are allowed to use Online Conference Service (OCS) for managing the whole proceedings lifecycle (from submission and reviewing to preparing for publication) free of charge.

Publication process

The language of publication is exclusively English. Authors publishing in CCIS have to sign the Springer CCIS copyright transfer form, however, they are free to use their material published in CCIS for substantially changed, more elaborate subsequent publications elsewhere. For the preparation of the camera-ready papers/files, authors have to strictly adhere to the Springer CCIS Authors' Instructions and are strongly encouraged to use the CCIS LaTeX style files or templates.

Abstracting/Indexing

CCIS is abstracted/indexed in DBLP, Google Scholar, EI-Compendex, Mathematical Reviews, SCImago, Scopus. CCIS volumes are also submitted for the inclusion in ISI Proceedings.

How to start

To start the evaluation of your proposal for inclusion in the CCIS series, please send an e-mail to ccis@springer.com.

Miguel Botto-Tobar ·
Marcelo Zambrano Vizuete ·
Sergio Montes León · Pablo Torres-Carrión ·
Benjamin Durakovic
Editors

International Conference on Applied Technologies

5th International Conference on Applied Technologies, ICAT 2023
Samborondon, Ecuador, November 22–24, 2023
Revised Selected Papers, Part I

 Springer

Editors
Miguel Botto-Tobar
Eindhoven University of Technology
Eindhoven, The Netherlands

Marcelo Zambrano Vizuete
Universidad Técnica del Norte
Ibarra, Ecuador

Sergio Montes León
Universidad Rey Juan Carlos
Madrid, Spain

Pablo Torres-Carrión
Universidad Técnica Particular de Loja
Loja, Ecuador

Benjamin Durakovic ⓘD
International University of Sarajevo
Sarajevo, Bosnia and Herzegovina

ISSN 1865-0929   ISSN 1865-0937 (electronic)
Communications in Computer and Information Science
ISBN 978-3-031-58955-3   ISBN 978-3-031-58956-0 (eBook)
https://doi.org/10.1007/978-3-031-58956-0

This Springer imprint is published by the registered company Springer Nature Switzerland AG
The registered company address is: Gewerbestrasse 11, 6330 Cham, Switzerland

If disposing of this product, please recycle the paper.

Preface

The 5th International Conference on Applied Technologies (ICAT) was held on the main campus of the Universidad Espíritu Santo, in Samborondón, Ecuador during November 22 until 24, 2023, and it was organized jointly by Universidad Espíritu Santo in collaboration with GDEON. The ICAT series aims to bring together top researchers and practitioners working in different domains in the field of computer science to exchange their expertise and to discuss the perspectives of development and collaboration. The content of this volume is related to the following subjects:

- Intelligent Systems

ICAT 2023 received 250 submissions written in English by 435 authors coming from 12 different countries. All these papers were double-blind peer-reviewed by the ICAT 2023 Program Committee consisting of 183 high-quality researchers. To assure a high-quality and thoughtful review process, we assigned each paper at least three reviewers. Based on the peer reviews, 66 full papers were accepted, resulting in a 26% acceptance rate, which was within our goal of less than 40%.

We would like to express our sincere gratitude to the invited speakers for their inspirational talks, to the authors for submitting their work to this conference, and to the reviewers for sharing their experience during the selection process.

November 2023

Miguel Botto-Tobar
Marcelo Zambrano Vizuete
Sergio Montes León
Pablo Torres-Carrión
Benjamin Durakovic

Organization

General Chair

Miguel Botto-Tobar   Eindhoven University of Technology,
                             The Netherlands

Program Committee Chairs

Miguel Botto-Tobar   Eindhoven University of Technology,
                             The Netherlands
Marcelo Zambrano Vizuete   Universidad Técnica del Norte, Ecuador
Sergio Montes León   Universidad Rey Juan Carlos, Spain
Pablo Torres-Carrión   Universidad Técnica Particular de Loja, Ecuador
Benjamin Durakovic   International University of Sarajevo,
                             Bosnia and Herzegovina

Organizing Chairs

Miguel Botto-Tobar   Eindhoven University of Technology,
                             The Netherlands
Marcelo Zambrano Vizuete   Universidad Técnica del Norte, Ecuador
Sergio Montes León   Universidad Rey Juan Carlos, Spain
Pablo Torres-Carrión   Universidad Técnica Particular de Loja, Ecuador
Benjamin Durakovic   International University of Sarajevo,
                             Bosnia and Herzegovina

Steering Committee

Miguel Botto-Tobar   Eindhoven University of Technology,
                             The Netherlands
Angela Díaz Cadena   Universitat de València, Spain

Program Committee

A. Bonci	Marche Polytechnic University, Italy
Ahmed Lateef Khalaf	Al-Mamoun University College, Iraq
Aiko Yamashita	Oslo Metropolitan University, Norway
Alejandro Donaire	Queensland University of Technology, Australia
Alejandro Ramos Nolazco	Instituto Tecnólogico y de Estudios Superiores Monterrey, Mexico
Alex Cazañas	University of Queensland, Australia
Alex Santamaria Philco	Universitat Politècnica de València, Spain
Allan Avendaño Sudario	Escuela Superior Politécnica del Litoral, Ecuador
Alexandra González Eras	Universidad Politécnica de Madrid, Spain
Ana Núñez Ávila	Universitat Politècnica de València, Spain
Ana Zambrano	Escuela Politécnica Nacional, Ecuador
Andres Carrera Rivera	University of Melbourne, Australia
Andres Cueva Costales	University of Melbourne, Australia
Andrés Robles Durazno	Edinburgh Napier University, UK
Andrés Vargas Gonzalez	Syracuse University, USA
Angel Cuenca Ortega	Universitat Politècnica de València, Spain
Ángela Díaz Cadena	Universitat de València, Spain
Angelo Trotta	University of Bologna, Italy
Antonio Gómez Exposito	University of Sevilla, Spain
Aras Can Onal	TOBB University of Economics and Technology, Turkey
Arian Bahrami	University of Tehran, Iran
Benoît Macq	Université Catholique de Louvain, Belgium
Benjamin Durakovic	International University of Sarajevo, Bosnia and Herzegovina
Bernhard Hitpass	Universidad Federico Santa María, Chile
Bin Lin	Università della Svizzera italiana, Switzerland
Carlos Saavedra	Escuela Superior Politécnica del Litoral, Ecuador
Catriona Kennedy	University of Manchester, UK
César Ayabaca Sarria	Escuela Politécnica Nacional, Ecuador
Cesar Azurdia Meza	University of Chile, Chile
Christian León Paliz	Université de Neuchâtel, Switzerland
Chrysovalantou Ziogou	Chemical Process and Energy Resources Institute, Greece
Cristian Zambrano Vega	Universidad de Málaga, Spain/Universidad Técnica Estatal de Quevedo, Ecuador
Cristiano Premebida	University of Coimbra, Portugal
Daniel Magües Martinez	Universidad Autónoma de Madrid, Spain
Danilo Jaramillo Hurtado	Universidad Politécnica de Madrid, Spain

Miguel Botto-Tobar	Eindhoven University of Technology, The Netherlands
Miguel Gonzalez Cagigal	Universidad de Sevilla, Spain
Miguel Murillo	Universidad Autónoma de Baja California, Mexico
Miguel Zuñiga Prieto	Universidad de Cuenca, Ecuador
Mohamed Kamel	Military Technical College, Egypt
Mohammad Al-Mashhadani	Al-Maarif University College, Iraq
Mohammad Amin	Illinois Institute of Technology, USA
Muneeb Ul Hassan	Swinburne University of Technology, Australia
Nam Yang	Technische Universiteit Eindhoven, The Netherlands
Nathalie Mitton	Inria, France
Nayeth Solórzano Alcívar	Escuela Superior Politécnica del Litoral, Ecuador/Griffith University, Australia
Noor Zaman	King Faisal University, Saudi Arabia
Omar S. Gómez	Escuela Superior Politécnica del Chimborazo, Ecuador
Óscar León Granizo	Universidad de Guayaquil, Ecuador
Oswaldo Lopez Santos	Universidad de Ibagué, Colombia
Pablo Lupera	Escuela Politécnica Nacional, Ecuador
Pablo Ordoñez Ordoñez	Universidad Politécnica de Madrid, Spain
Pablo Palacios	Universidad de Chile, Chile
Pablo Torres-Carrión	Universidad Técnica Particular de Loja, Ecuador
Patricia Ludeña González	Universidad Técnica Particular de Loja, Ecuador
Paulo Chiliguano	Queen Mary University of London, UK
Pedro Neto	University of Coimbra, Portugal
Praveen Damacharla	Purdue University Northwest, USA
Priscila Cedillo	Universidad de Cuenca, Ecuador
Radu-Emil Precup	Politehnica University of Timisoara, Romania
Ramin Yousefi	Islamic Azad University, Iran
René Guamán Quinche	Universidad de los Paises Vascos, Spain
Ricardo Martins	University of Coimbra, Portugal
Richard Ramirez Anormaliza	Universitat Politècnica de Catalunya, Spain
Richard Rivera	IMDEA Software Institute, Spain
Richard Stern	Carnegie Mellon University, USA
Rijo Jackson Tom	SRM University, India
Roberto Murphy	University of Colorado Denver, USA
Roberto Sabatini	RMIT University, Australia
Rodolfo Alfredo Bertone	Universidad Nacional de La Plata, Argentina
Rodrigo Barba	Universidad Técnica Particular de Loja, Ecuador
Rodrigo Saraguro Bravo	Universitat Politècnica de València, Spain

Ronnie Guerra	Pontificia Universidad Católica del Perú, Peru
Ruben Rumipamba-Zambrano	Universitat Politècnica de Catalanya, Spain
Saeed Rafee Nekoo	Universidad de Sevilla, Spain
Saleh Mobayen	University of Zanjan, Iran
Samiha Fadloun	Université de Montpellier, France
Sergio Montes León	Universidad Rey Juan Carlos, Spain
Stefanos Gritzalis	University of the Aegean, Greece
Syed Manzoor Qasim	King Abdulaziz City for Science and Technology, Saudi Arabia
Tenreiro Machado	Polytechnic of Porto, Portugal
Thomas Sjögren	Swedish Defence Research Agency (FOI), Sweden
Tiago Curi	Federal University of Santa Catarina, Brazil
Tony T. Luo	A*STAR, Singapore
Trung Duong	Queen's University Belfast, UK
Vanessa Jurado Vite	Universidad Politécnica Salesiana, Ecuador
Waldo Orellana	Universitat de València, Spain
Washington Velasquez Vargas	Universidad Politécnica de Madrid, Spain
Wayne Staats	Sandia National Labs, USA
Willian Zamora	Universidad Laíca Eloy Alfaro de Manabí, Ecuador
Yessenia Cabrera Maldonado	University of Cuenca, Ecuador
Yerferson Torres Berru	Universidad de Salamanca, Spain/Instituto Tecnológico Loja, Ecuador
Zhanyu Ma	Beijing University of Posts and Telecommunications, China

Organizing Institutions

Sponsoring Institutions

Collaborators

Contents – Part I

Contents – Part II

Contents – Part III

Electronics

Machine Vision

Security

Technology Trends

Z AT for Engineering Applications

Intelligent Systems

Mobile Application for Calorie Control Using Machine Learning

Kelly Rocio Huamani-Tito(✉) ⓘ, Gerardo Francisco Huaman-La Cruz ⓘ,
and Emilio Antonio Herrera-Trujillo ⓘ

Faculty of Engineering, Universidad Peruana de Ciencias Aplicadas, Lima, Perú
{u201915358,u201817801,pcsieher}@upc.edu.pe

Abstract. Overweight is a serious problem in Peru, and compliance with a healthy and balanced diet is essential for its management. Despite the existence of different types of diets and meal plans, people still find it difficult to comply with the treatment. Also, lack of access to adequate nutritional information and lack of follow-up in implementing a low-calorie diet can demotivate people and reduce the effectiveness of the process. To reduce this problem, a mobile application is presented that allows the control of the caloric intake of food, based on food suggestions using Machine Learning. For this purpose, the Support Vector Machine algorithm is applied to train a model that recommends personalized food to users according to their preferences. This is how the application allows users to easily access personalized food recommendations by analyzing their preferences and caloric needs individually. As a result, it has achieved a Percentage of Caloric Recommendation Satisfaction of 90.5%, a Percentage of Accepted Recommendations of 94.2%, and a Percentage of Usage Satisfaction of 92.6%. These results support its effectiveness and ease of use. It is expected that this proposal will have a positive impact on the fight against overweight in Peru.

Keywords: Mobile solution · Support vector machine · Excess weight · Food recommendation

1 Introduction

Nowadays, nutrition plays a crucial role in daily life; poor nutrition can lead to the development of pathologies and adversely affect health [1]. In this context, it is noteworthy that overweight in Peru is a growing public health concern, affecting 62.7% of the population [2]. This condition is closely linked to chronic diseases, such as type 2 diabetes and heart disease [3]. One of the key elements in the efficient management of overweight is proper nutrition. However, overweight individuals often face considerable obstacles when trying to find dietary options. Because most Peruvian citizens do not receive education on healthy lifestyles due to a lack of public programs [4]. Consequently, more than half of adult overweight patients drop out of dietary treatment before achieving their goals [5].

M. Botto-Tobar et al. (Eds.): ICAT 2023, CCIS 2049, pp. 3–16, 2024.
https://doi.org/10.1007/978-3-031-58956-0_1

Given the evidence related to overweight, it generates motivation to address this issue through a mobile application for caloric food recommendations based on Machine Learning. In this context, the Support Vector Machine (SVM) algorithm is employed, aiming to create a hyperplane to separate two categories, seeking to maximize the margin of separation between them to achieve a more precise classification [6]. It has also demonstrated its effectiveness in various medical areas; for instance, a study used SVM to predict surgical outcomes in patients with cervical degenerative myelopathy, achieving an accuracy of 86.4% [7]. Another study proposed its application in personalized medicine, specifically for the segmentation of breast cancer subtypes, highlighting the efficacy of SVM [8]. These studies highlighted the predictive capability of the algorithm, which is why its application was chosen for the development of the current proposal.

On the other hand, there are similar solutions to the proposed one aiming to assist individuals in making dietary decisions utilizing different algorithms [9–11]. However, based on prior research on the algorithm, it is expected to enhance the precision of recommendations. It is crucial to emphasize that the implementation of recommendation systems plays a pivotal role in modern applications [10].

In addition, the application faces the challenge of accommodating the diverse preferences and caloric needs of each user. Furthermore, the presented proposal is accessible and convenient, thanks to a user-friendly interface, and is anticipated to contribute to addressing current challenges related to overweight, thereby improving the quality of life for those affected by this issue. However, it is crucial to highlight that the accuracy and effectiveness of this solution may be influenced by the quantity and quality of the available data. If the data is limited, unbalanced, or not representative, the solution may not reach its maximum potential in terms of efficacy.

2   Related Works

In the literature review, various studies on food recommendation utilizing Machine Learning algorithms have been identified.

2.1   Machine Learning Algorithms

In the literature analysis related to the proposal, common Machine Learning algorithms were employed for food recommendation, considering various factors related to suggestion accuracy [12]. It is noted that algorithms such as Naive Bayes, Multilayer Perceptron (MLP), Recurrent Neural Network (RNN), Long Short-Term Memory (LSTM), and Gated Recurrent Units (GRU) were included, with results revealing that both LSTM and GRU achieved notable levels of precision and recall, with an accuracy of 98% and 99%, respectively [12]. Additionally, the RNN model demonstrated an accuracy of 99.4% [13].

In [14], it was mentioned that the SVM algorithm provided more accurate predictions for users. Furthermore, according to [15], indicates that SVM outperformed approaches such as Nearest Neighbors (K-NN), Logistic Regression (LR), and Decision Tree (DT) by 92%. This is because the SVM algorithm requires labeled data to train the model and aims to find a hyperplane that optimizes the separation of different data classes [16].

Despite K-NN and LR being widely used in the field of machine learning, especially in the analysis of large datasets or Big Data [10], the SVM algorithm demonstrates significant generalization capability, robustness, and high precision [17]. Moreover, this algorithm employs a structural risk minimization method, allowing it to make fewer errors when faced with new data [18].

2.2 Similar Solutions

In the article [9], a tool called the "Food Frequency Questionnaire" is introduced, employing the LR approach. This method is based on providing recommendations to users using data collected through questionnaires. The tool was designed to offer suggestions for adopting a healthier lifestyle. At the end of the study, 89% accuracy in recommendations that aligned with the established goal was achieved.

In [10], a healthy diet recommendation system is presented using machine learning techniques and big data analysis. The Intelligent Recommender for Healthy Diet (IR-HD) algorithm and a combination of matrix decomposition techniques and the K-NN method were employed to provide healthy diet recommendations. The primary result of the experimental study is that the proposed framework can provide healthy diet recommendations with high precision, ranging between 85–90%.

In the study [11], a system leveraging genomic associations concerning care and weight loss recommendations is introduced. This system employs data classification through Machine Learning, and the results show that 72% of the participants accepted and benefited from the recommendations, successfully reducing their body mass.

3   Material and Method

In this section, we will delineate the method employed to validate the proposed approach. The approach is segmented into five primary stages, providing a structured guide for the entire process (see Fig. 1). Here is an overview of these steps, spanning from data preparation to experiment analysis.

3.1   Data Preparation

Data Collection. The initial step in this process entailed conducting large-scale surveys to identify the individual food preferences of various user profiles. Consequently, data was gathered from a total of 320 participants. The survey form prompted respondents to disclose their favorite foods for breakfast, lunch, and dinner.

Data Processing. The collected data undergo an exhaustive preprocessing process to ensure their quality and applicability. This process involves several crucial stages, including:

Data Normalization. This was conducted to eliminate any differences in the variables, thereby ensuring sufficient comparability between them. This measure is essential to guaranteeing the validity of the results derived from subsequent analyses.

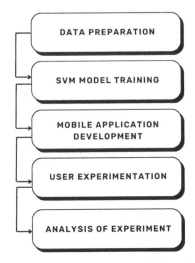

Fig. 1. Sequential Breakdown of the Five Phases of the Validation Method: From Data Preparation to Experiment Analysis. Author's Own Work.

Imputation Techniques. The imputation was carried out carefully and accurately, preserving the integrity of the data and minimizing potential bias in the results.

Codification. Numeric identifiers were assigned to the foods and identified groups, which facilitated the analysis. Within the food categories, groups with unique identifiers were established. For example, the legume group was designated with ID 3. Therefore, if you have a lentil stew with ID 36, it is classified in the legume group.

Overall, this data preprocessing process is essential to ensuring the reliability and usefulness of the collected data, thereby significantly contributing to the robustness and reliability of our analysis within the context of our study.

Data Division. After the data has been properly prepared and processed, it is then subdivided into three categories corresponding to the main meals of the day: breakfast, lunch, and dinner. In organizing the dataset, specific columns were created for each day of the week, assigning identifiers to the consumed dishes. Additionally, seven more columns were incorporated, containing identifiers for the groups to which each meal belongs based on the day of the week.

3.2 SVM Model Training

During the training phase, the SVM algorithm is employed to classify foods based on specific characteristics, aiming to predict foods according to both the day of the week and the preferred food group.

In this phase, the Scikit-Learn Python library is utilized to construct an SVM model. Specifically, the Support Vector Classifier (SVC) class from the library is employed, enabling the implementation of the SVM algorithm in the language. The model is trained using features (x) and labels (y), where features represent attributes extracted from the foods and labels denote the corresponding food categories.

Throughout the training process, the model endeavors to identify a hyperplane in a multidimensional space, effectively segregating foods into distinct categories. In simpler terms, the model learns to differentiate between various types of food based on the provided features. Additionally, the linear kernel plays a crucial role in finding a straight line in the feature space to adeptly classify foods according to both "day of the week" and "type of food". Given that the application focuses on classification, the algorithm is trained to assign foods to different categories based on the provided features. Once the model is trained, it can be utilized to predict food recommendations.

3.3   Mobile Application Development

At this stage, the mobile application was designed and developed based on the trained SVM model, enabling users to input their preferences and receive personalized recommendations. To achieve this, the following architecture was implemented (see Fig. 2), which is grounded in a logical and physical structure. The mobile application, built for Android using React Native, connects to Azure Functions to access various services, including one utilizing the trained model. Additionally, other services such as Azure Database for PostgreSQL and Azure Blob Storage are employed for structured data storage and datasets, respectively.

The functionality of the application begins when the user accesses it from their mobile device with the Android operating system. Upon completing the registration or login process, the user is then directed to the main screen (see Fig. 3). Here, you will have the ability to choose your food preferences by selecting your preferred food group, and the corresponding day of the week will be considered. This information will be transmitted to the backend of the system through an Application Programming Interface (API). Once the model has made the prediction, it proceeds to the next process, where the database is searched for the healthiest and most equitable option based on the obtained prediction. For example, if the result is "fried chicken", the application searches for the healthiest alternative, such as "baked chicken". Additionally, it adjusts the amount of ingredients in the meal preparation according to the caloric amount required for the user's profile. This is done to ensure that the total caloric content of the meal meets the specific needs of each user, allowing them to effectively reduce their caloric intake. Additionally, the application takes into account the appropriate amount of macronutrients. In this way, users can enjoy a culinary experience tailored to their dietary needs and preferences.

3.4   User Experimentation

To assess the effectiveness of the mobile application, the following experiment was conducted with end users. Below, we will describe the experimental protocol that we followed:

Study Design. The study was conducted over 15 days to evaluate the proposal.

Participant Group. The study selected a total of 31 participants, consisting of 17 males and 14 females with ages ranging from 20 to 53 years. All participants had a body mass index (BMI) equal to or greater than 25, indicating overweight.

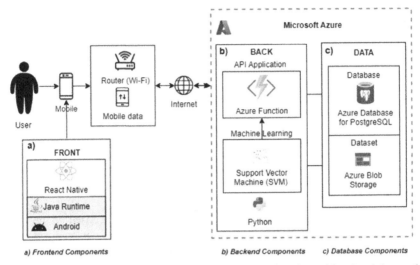

Fig. 2. Representation of the architecture of the mobile application with a breakdown of the Frontend (a), Backend (b), and Data (c) components. Author's Own Work.

Fig. 3. Main Caloric Recommendation Interface in NutriSage, displaying food suggestions for breakfast, lunch, and dinner, along with the total recommended calorie amount. Author's Own Work

Procedure. It commenced with an informative meeting held one day before the start of the experimentation. During this session, the proposal was introduced, and the experiment procedure was outlined. Additionally, participants were informed that the collected data would be solely used for academic purposes, underscoring the application's assurance of the confidentiality of personal information. Subsequently, consent for participation was obtained from the attendees. Finally, participants were provided with the Android Application Package (APK) file for installation on their mobile devices.

Throughout the experiment, users recorded their daily progress and used the "like" or "dislike" function for each food recommendation to gauge the acceptance of the provided suggestions. Additionally, they were given a daily survey to record their caloric satisfaction for each food consumed during the day. After the experiment, participants received a survey to measure satisfaction with their experience using the application.

3.5 Analysis of Experiment

After the experimental period, data collection was carried out to assess the effectiveness of the solution. These were measured using three indicators, which are:

Percentage of Caloric Recommendation Satisfaction (PCRS). To assess this indicator, a daily process was implemented in which users completed a form, registering their satisfaction level for each meal of the day. To calculate this indicator, the Average of the Total Caloric Satisfaction Responses (ATCSR) was obtained, then divided by the Maximum Satisfaction Value (MSV), set at 5, and multiplied by 100.

$$PCRS = (ATCSR / MSV) \times 100 \tag{1}$$

Percentage of Accepted Recommendations (PAR). This indicator allows identifying which recommendations provided by the application were liked by the user. To measure its effectiveness, the "like" button was used to collect the Total Accepted Recommendations (TAR), which was then divided by the Total Recommendations Given (TRG), and the result was multiplied by 100.

$$PAR = (TAR / TRG) \times 100 \tag{2}$$

Percentage of Usage Satisfaction (PSU). To calculate this indicator, a Satisfaction of Use survey of the application was used to obtain the Average Response Satisfaction of Use (ARSU). The average is then divided by the Maximum Rating Value (MRV), set at 5, and multiplied by 100.

$$PSU = (ARSU / MRV) \times 100 \tag{3}$$

4 Result and Discussion

In this section, we present the results obtained from three indicators that assessed the effectiveness of the application.

4.1 Percentage of Caloric Recommendation Satisfaction (PCRS)

As a result, participants reported a satisfaction level of 90.5% regarding the calories consumed per meal (see Table 2). Furthermore, upon a more detailed analysis by participant and meal type, averages were obtained, revealing that breakfast exhibits a higher percentage (see Table 1). Despite some participants not feeling entirely satisfied at the beginning of the experiment due to changes in their eating habits, the analysis demonstrates that, over time, they adapt to the caloric recommendations. Consequently, the progressive adaptation of users to caloric recommendations indicates that the application successfully generated consistent levels of satisfaction.

Table 1. Summary of Average Calorie Recommendation Satisfaction by Participant and Category.

N° Participant	Breakfast	Lunch	Dinner
P01	4.67	4.67	4.67
P02	4.60	4.53	4.53
P03	4.53	4.60	4.53
P04	4.73	4.40	4.47
P05	4.67	4.13	4.20
P06	4.47	4.47	4.33
P07	4.47	4.53	4.53
P08	4.47	4.53	4.53
P09	4.53	4.53	4.40
P10	4.53	4.27	4.33
P11	4.47	4.40	4.33
P12	4.53	4.33	4.47
P13	4.73	4.60	4.73
P14	4.80	4.47	4.47
P15	4.47	4.40	4.33
P16	4.60	4.60	4.47
P17	4.67	4.60	4.53
P18	4.60	4.53	4.53
P19	4.60	4.33	4.47
P20	4.80	4.47	4.47
P21	4.53	4.27	4.53
P22	4.80	4.60	4.73
P23	4.53	4.60	4.60
P24	4.60	4.60	4.67

(*continued*)

Table 1. (*continued*)

N° Participant	Breakfast	Lunch	Dinner
P25	4.53	4.20	4.40
P26	4.73	4.13	4.53
P27	4.67	4.60	4.67
P28	4.67	4.27	4.33
P29	4.73	4.13	4.53
P30	4.80	4.60	4.60
P31	4.80	4.60	4.73
Average	**4.62**	**4.45**	**4.51**

Table 2. Final Result of Caloric Recommendation Satisfaction.

Total Average	% in decimal	% PCRS
4.53	0.905	90.5%

4.2 Percentage of Accepted Recommendations (PAR)

The collected data reveals that 94.2% of the food recommendations elicited a positive response (see Table 4). This finding reflects an outstanding level of acceptance for the recommendations generated by the trained model. Furthermore, delving into the analysis (see Table 3), it is highlighted that breakfast recommendations were the most accepted by the participants. Additionally, we observe a greater inclination towards traditional Peruvian cuisine. This underscores the importance of incorporating more of these foods while maintaining a healthy focus.

Table 3. Summary of Accepted Recommendations by Participant and Category

N° Participant	Breakfast	Lunch	Dinner
P01	1.00	0.84	1.00
P02	1.00	0.89	0.94
P03	1.00	0.89	1.00
P04	1.00	0.74	0.89
P05	1.00	0.86	1.00
P06	1.00	0.89	0.94
P07	1.00	0.94	0.94
P08	1.00	0.88	0.94

(*continued*)

Table 3. (*continued*)

N° Participant	Breakfast	Lunch	Dinner
P09	1.00	0.93	0.93
P10	1.00	0.93	0.93
P11	1.00	0.93	0.94
P12	0.94	1.00	0.91
P13	0.93	0.92	0.93
P14	0.94	0.93	0.93
P15	0.94	1.00	1.00
P16	0.94	0.88	0.94
P17	1.00	0.83	1.00
P18	1.00	1.00	1.00
P19	1.00	0.94	0.88
P20	0.93	1.00	0.88
P21	1.00	0.94	0.94
P22	1.00	1.00	1.00
P23	1.00	0.94	0.83
P24	0.94	0.94	0.94
P25	0.94	0.79	0.94
P26	1.00	0.94	0.94
P27	1.00	0.79	1.00
P28	1.00	1.00	0.94
P29	1.00	0.88	1.00
P30	1.00	0.88	0.94
P31	1.00	0.88	0.94
Average	**0.98**	**0.91**	**0.95**

Table 4. Final Result of Accepted Recommendations.

Total Recommendations Given	Total Accepted Recommendations	% PAR
1490	1404	94.2%

4.3 Percentage of Usage Satisfaction (PUS)

The results showed that 92.6% of the participants expressed satisfaction with the use of the application (see Table 6). For a more detailed analysis, the averages per question were calculated, covering the following characteristics: Design (C01), Distribution (C02), Functionality (C03), General Comprehension (C04), Comprehension with Images and Icons (C05), Eating Habits (C06), Motivation (C07) and Recommendation (C08). The results show that General Comprehension was the characteristic with the highest score (see Table 5). Overall, the positive result of this indicator shows that most users found the application easy to understand and that it met their expectations.

Table 5. Summary of Usage Satisfaction by Participant and Main Question Characteristic

N° Participant	C01	C02	C03	C04	C05	C06	C07	C08
P01	4	5	4	5	4	4	4	4
P02	5	4	4	5	5	4	4	4
P03	5	5	5	5	5	4	4	5
P04	5	4	4	5	5	5	5	5
P05	5	4	5	5	5	5	5	5
P06	5	4	5	5	5	4	4	5
P07	5	4	5	4	5	5	5	5
P08	5	5	5	5	5	5	4	5
P09	5	4	5	5	5	5	5	5
P10	5	4	5	5	5	5	5	5
P11	5	5	5	5	5	4	4	5
P12	5	5	5	5	5	5	5	5
P13	5	5	4	5	5	5	5	5
P14	4	5	5	5	4	5	5	5
P15	5	5	5	5	5	5	5	5
P16	4	5	3	4	4	4	4	4
P17	5	5	4	5	5	5	5	5
P18	4	4	5	4	5	4	5	5
P19	4	4	4	4	4	4	4	4
P20	4	4	4	5	5	5	5	5
P21	4	4	4	5	5	4	4	4
P22	4	4	4	5	4	4	4	4
P23	4	4	5	5	5	5	5	5

(continued)

Table 5. (*continued*)

N° Participant	C01	C02	C03	C04	C05	C06	C07	C08
P24	5	4	5	5	5	4	4	4
P25	5	5	5	5	5	5	5	5
P26	5	4	5	5	5	5	5	5
P27	4	4	4	5	3	5	5	4
P28	5	5	5	5	5	5	5	5
P29	4	5	4	4	5	4	4	4
P30	5	5	5	5	5	5	5	5
P31	4	5	4	4	4	4	4	4
Average	**4.61**	**4.48**	**4.55**	**4.81**	**4.74**	**4.58**	**4.58**	**4.68**

Table 6. Final Result of Usage Satisfaction

Total Average	% in decimal	% PSU
4.63	0.926	92.6%

4.4 General Results

In this section, a comprehensive summary has been prepared, concisely presenting the results associated with each experiment indicator (see Table 7).

Table 7. Results of Indicators from the Experimental Group

Indicator	Results
Percentage of Caloric Recommendation Satisfaction	90.5%
Percentage of Accepted Recommendations	94.2%
Percentage of Usage Satisfaction	92.6%

4.5 Discussion of the Results

Following an analysis of the results obtained from the indicators, it is evident that the application has succeeded in terms of Caloric Recommendation Satisfaction, Accepted Recommendations, and App Usage Satisfaction. This demonstrates the effectiveness of the proposal for controlling caloric intake in individuals with overweight. It is worth noting that the findings support the innovation and positive impact of this application. Additionally, it was demonstrated that the mobile application can adapt appropriately to the needs of each user. Furthermore, an intuitive interface was ensured, facilitating an optimal experience and making it easier to improve healthy habits. Despite the positive results, it is important to note some limitations in the validation process, such as the small sample size, the short evaluation period, and potential biases. These limitations could impact the generalization of the results and the robustness of the conclusions drawn from the study.

5 Conclusions

In this study, we introduce an innovative mobile application based on machine learning that addresses the challenge of caloric intake control through personalized recommendations for individuals with overweight. The results obtained support the effectiveness and user-friendliness of the application. This demonstrates that focusing on each user's preferences and providing precise recommendations allows them to feel comfortable and motivated to follow a low-calorie diet. This is how the application helps improve the healthy lifestyle of these individuals, contributing to their overall health improvement.

Moreover, the proposal not only effectively reduces calorie intake but also showcases the value of SVM in providing accurate recommendations.

On the other hand, it is recommended to expand the application to include more features, such as physical activity tracking, to provide users with a more comprehensive experience. Additionally, it is advised to stay in constant contact with nutrition professionals to assess potential updates to the dietary regimen.

Finally, as a team, we are committed to the continuous improvement of our solution. Our mission is to expand its positive impact on the quality of life for individuals with overweight through the constant application of technology and innovation.

Financing. Universidad Peruana de Ciencias Aplicadas/UPC-EXPOST-2023-2.

Gratitude. The authors thank the evaluators for their important suggestions that have allowed a significant improvement of this work. Likewise, to the Rescarch Departament of the Universidad Peruana de Ciencias Aplicadas for the support provided to carry out this rescarch work through the UPC-EXPOST-2023-2 incentive.

References

1. Pereira, G.Q., Jiménez, K.P., Arcos-Medina, G., Pesantez, M.A., et al.: Gestión y seguimiento de pacientes en sus dietas nutricionales utilizando un sitio web. Ecuad. Sci. J. **5**(2), 15–30 (2021)
2. Ministerio de Salud: En el Perú, el 62.7% de personas de 15 años de edad a más padece de exceso de peso (2022). https://www.gob.pe/institucion/minsa/noticias/619520. Accessed 11 Oct 2023
3. World Health Organization: WHO: Obesidad y sobrepeso (2021). https://www.who.int/es/news-room/fact-sheets/detail/obesity-and-overweight. Accessed 18 Nov 2023
4. Hernández, G.: El incremento del sobrepeso y la obesidad es un problema de salud pública (2022). https://www.udep.edu.pe/hoy/2022/08/incremento-de-sobrepeso-y-obesidad-es-un-problema-de-salud-publica/. Accessed 12 Oct 2023

5. Mendoza, F.G., Ledezma, J.C.R., Lezama, M.P., Hermenegild, A.Y.I., Saldaña, R.G.: Adherencia al tratamiento en personas con sobrepeso y obesidad. Enseñanza e Investigación en Psicología **2**(1), 127–138 (2020)

6. Jahed Armaghani, D., Asteris, P.G., Askarian, B., Hasanipanah, M., Tarinejad, R., Huynh, V.V.: Examining hybrid and single SVM models with different kernels to predict rock brittleness. Sustainability **12**(6), 2229 (2020)

7. Song, J., Li, J., Zhao, R., Chu, X.: Developing predictive models for surgical outcomes in patients with degenerative cervical myelopathy: a comparison of statistical and machine learning approaches. Spine J. (2023)

8. Ozer, M.E., Sarica, P.O., Arga, K.Y.: New machine learning applications to accelerate personalized medicine in breast cancer: rise of the support vector machines. OMICS J. Integr. Biol. **24**(5), 241–246 (2020)

9. Reščič, N., Mayora, O., Eccher, C., Luštrek, M.: Food frequency questionnaire personalisation using multi-target regression. Nutrients **14**(19), 3943 (2022)

10. Lambay, M.A., Mohideen, S.P.: A hybrid approach based diet recommendation system using ml and big data analytics (2022)

11. Sinha, R., et al.: Leveraging genomic associations in precision digital care for weight loss: cohort study. J. Med. Internet Res. **23**(5), e25401 (2021)

12. Iwendi, C., Khan, S., Anajemba, J.H., Bashir, A.K., Noor, F.: Realizing an efficient IoMT-assisted patient diet recommendation system through machine learning model. IEEE Access **8**, 28462–28474 (2020)

13. Boppana, V., Sandhya, P.: Web crawling based context aware recommender system using optimized deep recurrent neural network. J. Big Data **8**, 1–24 (2021)

14. Kothari, A.A., Patel, W.D.: A novel approach towards context based recommendations using support vector machine methodology. Procedia Comput. Sci. **57**, 1171–1178 (2015)

15. Jamil, F., Kahng, H.K., Kim, S., Kim, D.H.: Towards secure fitness framework based on IoT-enabled blockchain network integrated with machine learning algorithms. Sensors **21**(5), 1640 (2021)

16. Loosli, G., Canu, S., Ong, C.S.: Learning SVM in Kreĭn spaces. IEEE Trans. Pattern Anal. Mach. Intell. **38**(6), 1204–1216 (2015)

17. Ma, Y., Yao, J., Ma, C., Xiao, X.: Pattern recognition of rigid hoist guides based on support vector machine. Adv. Mech. Eng. **10**(12), 1687814018812307 (2018)

18. Rajaee, T., Khani, S., Ravansalar, M.: Artificial intelligence-based single and hybrid models for prediction of water quality in rivers: a review. Chemom. Intell. Lab. Syst. **200**, 103978 (2020)

Application of Machine Learning for Air Quality Analysis

Jesús Ocaña[1] ![ORCID], Guillermo Miñan[1(✉)] ![ORCID], Luis Chauca[1] ![ORCID], Karina Espínola[1] ![ORCID], and Luis Leiva[2] ![ORCID]

[1] Universidad Tecnológica del Perú, Km 424 Panamericana Norte - Calle 56, Chimbote, Perú
{c25777,c20342,jchauca,C24051}@utp.edu.pe
[2] Universidad Nacional del Santa, Av. Pacifico 508 Urb. Buenos Aires – Nvo., Chimbote, Perú
lleiva@uns.edu.pe

Abstract. The main objective of this research work is to apply Machine Learning to gas sensors, to analyze air quality and transmit the data to a server through the Internet of Things (IoT). The Arduino MEGA 2560 was used, the Ethernet shield module and four gas sensors, MQ2, MQ5, MQ7 and MQ135, were placed; Machine Learning was designed with Artificial Neural Networks (ANN) and greater effectiveness was obtained using the backpropagation training algorithm. The CRISP-DM methodology was used, which contains seven stages, first the problem was identified, in the second stage the data understanding, the third data preparation, in the fourth the Machine Learning with artificial neural networks was designed, the fifth was the modeling, the sixth is the implementation of the model and the seventh is the validation by performing the most common gas tests, resulting in the recognition of the gases in its environment, obtaining a functional system. In conclusion, it was verified and confirmed that Machine Learning with Artificial Neural Networks and the use of the Backpropagation algorithm can automatically detect gases and show the Air Quality Analysis. This research is exclusive for those interested who are beginning their investigation into the world of Machine Learning.

Keywords: Machine Learning · Artificial Neural Networks · Backpropagation · air quality

1 Introduction

Environmental pollution is mainly due to the presence of a diversity of chemical and biological components present in the air we breathe and mobile sources, which affects the main cities of the country [1, 2]. Furthermore, it has pollution concentrations high enough to have a negative impact on human health [3–5]. The perceived health impacts are chronic airway diseases [6, 7]. In relation to this, the negative effects also exacerbate respiratory, cardiovascular, dermatological diseases and cancer, among others [8–10]. Climate change has as a consequence the greenhouse effect, it is produced by certain gases and the largest emission is carbon dioxide CO_2, 60% of which is generated mainly by the combustion of fossil fuels, such as coal or oil; Transportation emits 14% and industry generates 9% of CO_2 emissions [11].

© The Author(s), under exclusive license to Springer Nature Switzerland AG 2024
M. Botto-Tobar et al. (Eds.): ICAT 2023, CCIS 2049, pp. 17–30, 2024.
https://doi.org/10.1007/978-3-031-58956-0_2

The number of vehicles in cities increases and polluting emissions decrease air quality [2, 12, 13]. Automotive pollution comes from the gases generated by the combustion of gasoline. These pollutants have the ability to affect human health, such as: carbon monoxide (CO), sulfur dioxide (SO2), nitrogen oxides (NOx), unburned hydrocarbons, ozone (O3), volatile organic compounds (VOCs) and suspended particles (PM10) and (PM2.5), these suspended particles, such as mist, smoke and dust, are main ingredients that contribute to air quality problems. Pollution by particles can cause serious health problems, even the concentrations are found in many cities [5, 14–17], these pollutants are emitted by vehicles in general. Carbon monoxide (CO) is a colorless and odorless gas that is expelled into the atmosphere as a result of the combustion process of gas stoves, as well as the oxidation of hydrocarbons and other organic compounds; CO emission is affected by the gas components, which is composed of natural gas, propane, butane, liquefied petroleum gas or other flammable gas [18]. Scientists at the University of Colorado at Boulder have found that cooking, cleaning, and other routine activities generate considerable levels of volatile chemicals in a home, producing environmental pollution similar to that of polluted cities [19].

Air quality is one of the phenomena where a large amount of data is collected and the air quality index is evaluated based on the main pollutants [20, 21], in some cities in the world the air quality is monitored air [22].

Artificial intelligence perceives its environment, which allows it to understand and solve problems [23, 24]. The development of artificial intelligence in the health field can help prevent some environmental diseases [25].

Machine Learning is an application of AI, it creates systems that automatically learn and can predict more accurately [26–28]. The type of Machine Learning algorithm to use for air quality analysis is Artificial Neural Networks (ANN), which learn by example and experience. To obtain the best results, the back-propagation training method is used, which has 3 layers: input layer, hidden layer and output layer.

The Internet of Things (IoT) allows sensors to be interconnected and data transmitted over the Internet, [29, 30], and also allows devices to connect in real time, generating a series of applications [31, 32].

With respect to other similar and more recent research on the applications of Machine Learning related to environmental pollution, we find it in the project of Martínez and López [33], they developed an application that uses Machine Learning to analyze, interpret and predict environmental pollution data.

Li et al. [34] used artificial intelligence techniques, such as artificial neural networks (ANN) and the Machine Learning model, achieving air quality forecasting and controlling pollution levels.

Cabaneros et al. [35], in their research, used artificial neural networks to predict and forecast ambient air pollutants from 2001 to 2019. The data was entered and after training the ANN, the results were that environmental pollution has increased drastically in recent years. De Caso [36], in his result indicates that the prediction of the component PM10 increases with the number of hidden layers, models with three hidden layers were used. This has allowed us to obtain a predictive model of the level of air pollution.

Livingston et al. [37] implemented Machine Learning using sensors connected to a controller, these collected data were entered into Machine Learning, allowing air quality to be predicted.

Ruiz and Velásquez [29] developed Machine Learning focused on supervised learning, from a set of data that was applied to the machine learning algorithm, resulting in an effective and accurate measure.

As background, Pasic et al. [21], in their article "Modeling of Nonlinear Autoregressive Neural Network for Multi-Step Ahead Air Quality Prediction", mentions that the problem found regarding poor air quality is associated with various diseases, both acute and chronic. Used the NARXSP neural network type methodology to develop the neural network model and the data were obtained from the Federal Meteorological Institute of BiH. The results show that the optimal neural network model can predict the pollutant concentrations of the air for the next 72 h. They concluded that the NARXSP neural network has proven to be a powerful tool that highly accurately predicts sudden changes in the concentration of air pollutants.

According to Yanto et al. [25], in their research "Hybrid Method Air Quality Classification Analysis Model", the problem found is that air pollution has a significant impact on environmental pollution and human health. It used the hybrid model that it has, the analysis stages that begin with data preprocessing, then multiple linear regression (MRL) is used to measure the correlation between the variables in the obtained pattern, then the process is used of artificial neural networks (ANN) learning, finally, classification is performed using the decision tree method. The results obtained from the artificial neural network (ANN) showing an MSE (mean square error) value and an output accuracy of 99.99%. In conclusion, it was determined that the learning of the artificial neural network using backpropagation algorithms was highly accurate in determining air quality.

In the research of Rubio et al. [38], in their article titled "Sensor System Based in Neural Networks for the Environmental Monitoring", one of the problems associated with waste is the contamination of land, air and water. This research focuses on the use of electronic nose technology to monitor volatile organic compounds present in the air. The results obtained were efficient, achieving 100% accuracy in the classification of odors. He concludes that the neural network is a powerful tool to predict the accumulation of pollutants in the air.

Also in their project by Paz, Moreno and Poveda [39], they present "Air Quality Measurement Using an IoT Network: a Case Study". This work addresses the problem of determining the level of contamination and the population affected by the risk for human health due to exposure to atmospheric pollutants at the Guaymaral climatological station. The methodological approach of this research is classified as Top-Down and qualitative, since it seeks to explain and predict the phenomena investigated. The results indicate that a concentration of PM10, PM2.5, O3, NO2 CO and SO2 was recorded in the buildings. It was concluded that the implemented IoT network complies with the correct transmission and reception of data in real time.

Because there is little research on the use of Machine Learning that verifies air quality, it was decided to carry out this research, building a prototype that focuses on the use of the Arduino MEGA 2560 because it has more memory and four gas sensors of the family. MQ (MQ2, MQ5, MQ7 and MQ135), these sensors detect different chemical components of the air, which is normally in ppm (parts per million).

A table record of data obtained from each sensor was made, with 160 data each, these data were obtained by connecting each sensor to the Arduino and different gases such as CO2, CO, ALCOHOL, SMOKE, BUTANE and LPG were introduced, these data were displayed on a 16 × 2 LCD screen and the total data obtained was 480 data, for this we objectively and precisely carried out the data obtained, ready to enter the artificial neural networks.

This work focuses on the use of Machine Learning technology with Artificial Neural Networks to detect gases and verify air quality. Our research provides a search strategy in this field, benefiting relevant researchers and practitioners. Our findings help identify current advances in Machine Learning research and build new work in this active field. The availability of data provided by the sensors allows us to verify air quality with the use of Machine Learning techniques that are constantly growing, which predicts a promising future.

The main objective of this research is to apply Machine Learning to detect the chemical components found in the environment, and thus show the analysis of air quality as a result.

The main contribution of this work is an inexpensive gas detection prototype that can detect and classify polluting gases in the air. Testing was conducted using common household items, demonstrating a rapid response solution that can be developed as a portable solution.

The purpose of this research is to measure and report air quality, and then that information is sent through the Internet of Things (IoT) to a server, when the allowed air quality limits are exceeded, an alarm is activated. This work is divided into five sections. The first section describes the Materials and methods, then in section two the results are shown, in section three the discussion is shown, in section four the limitations and future work are mentioned, and finally the conclusions are detailed.

2   Materials and Methods

The CRISP-DM methodology was used, which contains six stages, first the problem is identified, in the second the data understanding, the third data preparation, in the fourth the Machine Learning was designed, the fifth the modeling and the Sixth is model implementation and validation [40].

2.1   Problem Analysis

Air quality is one of the main problems within an urban area, which affects the environment and people's health conditions. Therefore, it is crucial to develop a system that allows air quality to be accurately analyzed.

2.2   Understanding Data

It involves a descriptive analysis and search for patterns, 160 data were collected from each sensor and different gases such as CO2, CO, ALCOHOL, SMOKE, BUTANE and LPG were inserted, the total information obtained was 640 data called patterns.

2.3 Data Preparation

The preparation of the gas data must be ready to enter the neural networks, this implies that the data is in a suitable format for the training of the neural network, then the data is coded into categories and can be used for training and prediction.

2.4 Machine Learning Design

In the Machine Learning design, the classification metric, the accuracy or precision metric (ACC), was selected. Precision is a simple metric to understand and communicate, it is intuitive and easy to interpret. It represents the proportion of correct predictions made by the model in relation to the total samples. Also, Supervised Learning was selected, which allows creating outputs that are as closely aligned as possible with the desired result. Also, artificial neural networks were selected.

There are several algorithms used in artificial neural networks such as: back-propagation, Stochastic Gradient Descent (SGD), Gradient Descent with Momentum, Genetic Algorithm and Resilient Error Propagation Algorithm.

The backpropagation algorithm was selected because it has proven to be effective in learning complex models from data. The backpropagation algorithm allows training artificial neural networks, adjusting the weights of the connections between the neurons of the network based on the difference between the outputs predicted by the network and the desired outputs.

2.5 Modeling

The number of neurons and the number of hidden layers were established. Eight neurons were connected in the input layer and three neurons in the output layer. To calculate the number of neurons in the hidden layer, the approximate rules that are recommended to be used have been used. The Matlab NNTool tool was used to create, train and simulate the ANN, the test was done with four hidden layers, the 1st hidden layer had 42 neurons, the 2nd layer 11 neurons, the 3rd layer 6 neurons and the 4th layer 4 neurons. It was trained and when comparing the target data with the output, they do not match and show a high error, the Train NetWork was performed several times and it did not improve. Also in the 1st layer it was reduced to 30 neurons, then to 20 neurons and the expected result did not improve.

It was implemented with three hidden layers, the 1st hidden layer with 11 neurons, the 2nd layer with 6 neurons and the 3rd layer with 4 neurons, the Train NetWork was performed repeatedly, showing an epoch of 213 iterations and comparing the target data with the network output, showed the desired output and with less error.

2.6 Model Implementation and Validation

The hardware and software design was carried out. The electronic board was developed, taking into account the dimensions of the Arduino MEGA 2560, the Ethernet shield module, 4 gas sensors, the LCD screen, the power supply and others were installed. The Arduino was also programmed with the neural networks described above.

In the validation, all the corresponding tests were carried out, with the neural networks implanted in the Arduino Mega board.

3 Results

The tests were carried out with each of the sensors and the Arduino Mega, without using the ANN, different types of gases were used such as CO2, CO, alcohol, Smoke, Butane and LPG.

Table 1. Measurement of sensors with three neurons and the types of gas detected.

MQ2 ppm	MQ5 ppm	MQ7 ppm	MQ135 ppm	Neurons			Gas type
				n3	n2	n1	
50–110	60–150	30–85	10–149	0	0	0	REGULAR AIR
100–250	150–650	90–310	150–900	0	0	1	CO2
140–320	180–450	200–500	280–450	0	1	0	CO
320–1500	200–330	100–400	180–280	0	1	1	ALCOHOL
200–1000	150–600	220–1000	250–600	1	0	0	SMOKE
300–2500	500–2000	500–1800	350–800	1	0	1	BUTANE
330–2100	600–2500	600–1964	400–900	1	1	0	LPG

From Table 1 we can indicate a summary of 640 data, which were carried out with the tests of the mentioned gases. When carrying out the measurements we realize that each gas sensor has a different value of Parts per million (ppm), for example, in the CO2 test, each sensor shows us a different value of ppm. After testing each sensor with the Arduino Mega, different values were obtained and the minimum and maximum values of each gas were considered. For example, the LPG test was carried out, the MQ2 sensor on the LCD screen showed several values that ranged between 330 ppm to 2100 ppm, the MQ5 sensor showed the values from 600 to 2500 ppm, the MQ7 sensor showed the values from 600 to 1964 ppm and the MQ135 sensor showed the values from 400 to 900 ppm, in this way the tests on the six types of gases, mentioned in Table 1. To analyze the six types of gases, three output neurons were needed, called n1, n2 and n3, the combinations of these three neurons will define the type of gas detected, if the neurons show us n1 = 0, n2 = 0 and n3 = 0 it should show us normal air, if n1 = 0, n2 = 0 and n3 = 1 it should show us what CO2 is in the environment, and so on, it detects the type of gas, as indicated in Table 1.

We can also observe that in Table 1, there is data that is within several regions, that is, the sensor data in ppm is in several regions, for example, in the measurements made of butane, the MQ2 sensor showed us between 300 ppm to 2500 ppm and the smoke showed between 200 ppm to 1000 ppm and these data are within the values of butane just like butane gas, the MQ5 sensor showed the values between 500 ppm to 2000 ppm and the smoke showed values between 150 ppm to 600 ppm, some data is also within the butane values and so we can visualize them with the other sensors. When this type of problem occurs, it is recommended to develop the Backpropagation algorithm [41]. Therefore, Machine Learning with Artificial Neural Networks (ANN) was designed and the backpropagation training method was chosen, one input layer, three hidden layers and one output layer. The input layer was considered to have eight neurons and the output layer according to Table 1 has three neurons. To calculate the number of neurons to use, there is no specific formula, but some approximate rules have been used that are recommended to be used to assign the number of neurons that the hidden layer will have.

Calculation of the ratio between the input neuron and the output neuron (Fig. 1).

$$R = \left(\frac{IN}{ON} \right)^{\frac{1}{3}} \tag{1}$$

Where:

R: Ratio
IN: Input Neuron $= 8$ neurons
ON: Output Neuron $= 3$ neurons

$$R = \left(\frac{8}{3} \right)^{\frac{1}{3}}$$

$$R = 1.39$$

Calculation of the first hidden layer

$$C_1 = ON * R^4$$
$$C_1 = 3 * 3.73 \tag{2}$$
$$C_1 = 11 \text{ neurons}$$

Calculation of the second hidden layer

$$C_2 = ON * R^2$$
$$C_2 = 3 * 1.93 \tag{3}$$
$$C_2 = 6 \text{ neurons}$$

Calculation of the third hidden layer

$$C_3 = ON * R$$
$$C_3 = 3 * 1.39 \tag{4}$$
$$C_3 = 4 \text{ neurons}$$

Control Circuit

The electronic card was implemented with the Arduino MEGA 2560 because it had more memory, the 4 gas sensors were installed, MQ2, MQ5, MQ7 and MQ135, and the Ethernet shield module was placed on top of the Arduino MEGA 2560, the Arduino IOT Cloud was used to send the data to the cloud to a server. The new Arduino IoT Cloud platform can be programmed more easily and quickly for all types of Arduino projects [42]. Arduino IoT Cloud also makes it easy to communicate with all types of sensors.

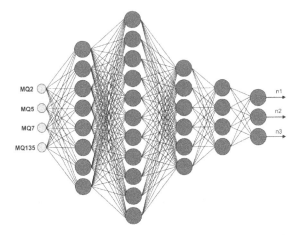

Fig. 1. Design of Artificial Neural Networks, backpropagation

To transmit information over the network, HTTP was used, which is an information transmission protocol, and the programming language used to create the website was CSS and Javascript.

To power the MQ family sensors, different power supplies were tested. The first one that began to be used was an economical and unregulated source, which produced noticeable noise. To reduce the noise, a regulated 5 V power supply was implemented (Fig. 2).

The Matlab program was used to train the artificial neural network. All data from the tests carried out on each gas sensor were entered into the Artificial Neural Network, which consisted of 160 data for each sensor, making a total of 640 input data.

For the simulation, the Matlab neural network tool nntool was used, which allows creating, training and simulating this type of Artificial Neural Network (ANN) [44].

The Neural Network was trained, as shown in Fig. 3, with its respective weights (w) and polarization (b). About 12 trainings were performed until the Neural Network can learn. With the result, it was programmed in the Arduino IDE development environment and then uploaded to the Arduino MEGA 2560, the data was sent to the Arduino IoT Cloud internet platform and thus report information on air quality through IoT networks; the project activates an alarm when standard air quality levels are exceeded. As a result, it was obtained that the system detects gases automatically.

Figure 4 illustrates actual butane measurements, with approximately up to 950 ppm. The system perceives the gas, showing us on the LCD screen that the detected gas is Butane and this information is sent to the Arduino IoT Cloud internet platform.

Figure 5 shows actual measurements of the gas emitted by cars, reaching approximately 192 ppm. The Artificial neural network perceives the gas and shows us on the LCD screen that the detected gas is carbon dioxide CO2, the information is sent to the Arduino IoT Cloud platform.

Figure 6 illustrates actual measurements of oil combustion, reaching approximately 182 ppm. The Artificial neural network perceives the gas and shows us on the LCD

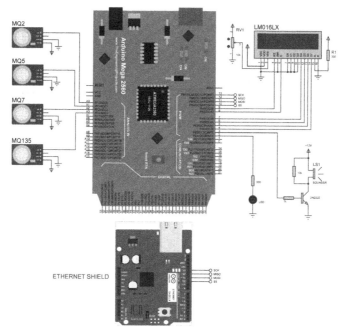

Fig. 2. Electronic card design

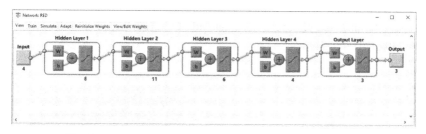

Fig. 3. Training with the Backpropagation algorithm in Matlab

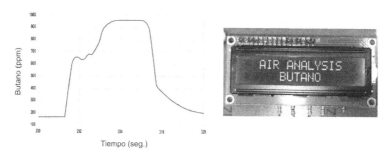

Fig. 4. Test with the gas from lighters

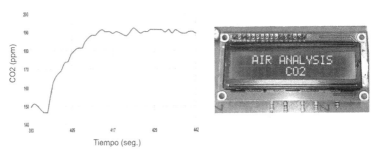

Fig. 5. Test of the gas emitted by cars

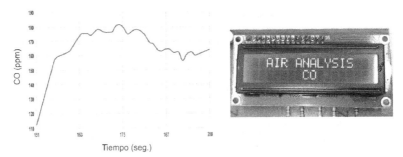

Fig. 6. Test with the gas emitted by the combustion of oil.

screen that the detected gas is carbon monoxide CO. This information is sent to the Arduino IoT Cloud platform.

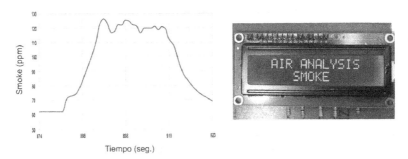

Fig. 7. Test with the gas emitted by burning paper smoke

Figure 7 shows the actual measurements of the gas emitted by the smoke from burning paper, reaching approximately up to 128 ppm. The Artificial neural network perceives the smoke and shows us on the LCD screen that the detected gas is smoke. This information is sent to the Arduino IoT Cloud platform.

4 Discussion

Pasic et al. [21], in the article "Modeling of Nonlinear Autoregressive Neural Network for Multi-Step Ahead Air Quality Prediction", mentions that the neural network is a powerful tool to predict the accumulation of pollutants in the air with very high precision. The neural network is great because it can accurately forecast unexpected changes in the accumulation of air pollutants. The neural network must be nonlinear between inputs and outputs. The results obtained show that the measured data are found within several regions, that is, the sensor data in ppm are found in several regions, therefore it must be carried out in a non-linear neural network. In this research, the ANN algorithm was improved with the use of Machine Learning and to obtain better results, the backpropagation training method was used, resulting in a high-precision system that is perfectly adaptable to reality, and can be placed in various environments.

Ruiz and Velásquez [29], in their research work "Artificial intelligence at the service of the health of the future", mention that Artificial Intelligence, through data processing, can help people's health. The results obtained in our research show that the use of artificial intelligence allows us to contribute to the prevention of diseases caused by gases. If the air quality exceeds the permitted limits, it will notify people through an alarm warning that there are dangerous gases.

On the other hand, in the research of Rubio et al. Alabama [38], "Neural network-based sensor system for environmental monitoring" notes that it used a series of tin oxide gas sensors, worked with a neural network to detect common chemicals found in the home, The card The electronics are developed in a compact and portable way, facilitating the analysis and recognition of air gases in real time. In this research, it was possible to improve the design of Machine Learning with Artificial Neural Networks, the Arduino Mega was used and the operation of the five gas sensors, the MQ2, MQ5, MQ7 and MQ135, which are low cost, was verified. In addition, a compact prototype was implemented to install all the mentioned components.

For their part, Paz, Moreno and Poveda [39], present "Measuring Air Quality Using an IoT Network: A Case Study", concluded that the IoT network executes the precise conditions in the transmission of information in real time. In this research, it was enhanced to transmit and receive data to a cloud server, the Arduino IOT Cloud. Likewise, to transmit information from the sensors, the HTTP transmission protocol was used and CSS and Javascript were used to develop the website.

5 Limitations and Future Work

Certain limitations are considered regarding this research. There is little information and research on projects related to this topic using Machine Learning, with the Artificial Neural Networks (ANN) algorithm and very little information on the use of the backpropagation training method, thus obtaining better results in gas detection.

For future projects, it is proposed to use more sensors to detect all types of gases in the air, and if Machine Learning is the case, the number of neurons that each layer of the Artificial Neural Network will have must be recalculated and it is recommended to use the training method of backpropagation, because it results in an excellent system for learning.

6 Conclusion

In this research, Machine Learning was used, the type of algorithm was Artificial Neural Networks (ANN) and the best results were obtained using the backpropagation training algorithm, resulting in a system perfectly adaptable in real places, detecting exhaust gases automatically, thanks to its learning from artificial neural networks.

Artificial intelligence was used to analyze air quality, obtaining the expected results, which contributes to the prevention of diseases caused by gases and if it exceeds the permitted limits, it notifies the user through an alarm warning of the danger.

A compact prototype was implemented to install the Arduino MEGA 2560, the Ethernet shield module, the 16x2 LCD screen and the four gas sensors, MQ2, MQ5, MQ7 and MQ135, were installed on the same board. In addition, it could be improved with the design of Machine Learning with Artificial Neural Networks and all gas tests were carried out, resulting in an excellent air quality analysis system.

It was possible to transmit and receive the data from the sensor readings and their gas detection to the Arduino IOT Cloud platform, resulting in this platform providing communication with the four sensors in an easy way, to transmit information from the sensors. The HTTP information transmission protocol was used and the programming language used to create the website was CSS and Javascript.

References

1. Martín, P., Sánchez, M.: Impact of environmental contamination in pediatric Primary Care consultations: an ecological study. Analesdepediatria **89**(2), 80–85 (2017)
2. Hernández, C., Ávila, A., Cerda, D.: Impact of urban mobility on air quality in the metropolitan area of San Luis Potosí, Mexico. Environ. Sci. Mag. **57**(1), 1–27 (2023)
3. Adigun, O., Kosko, B.: Bidirectional backpropagation. IEEE Trans. Syst. Man Cybern. Syst. **50**(5), 1–13 (2020)
4. Salas, D.: Complex index for air quality and sustainability management. Adm. Investig. **52**(131), 1–15 (2023)
5. Sunyer, J., Rivas, I.: Air pollution and health, 20 years later. Clin. Med. **159**(7), 334–335 (2022)
6. Clofent, D., Culebras, M., Loor, K., Cruz, M.: Environmental pollution and lung cancer: the carcinogenic power of the air we breathe. Arch. Bronconeumol. **57**(5), 317–318 (2021)
7. Raherison, C.: Atmospheric and environmental pollution and expiratory pathology. EMC Treatise Med. **24**(3), 1–9 (2020)
8. Rodríguez, P., Prat, C., Domínguez, J.: Interaction between environmental pollution and respiratory infections. Bronconeumol. Arch. **55**(7), 351–352 (2019)
9. Ortega, J., et al.: Urban air pollution and hospital admissions for asthma and acute respiratory disease in Murcia city (Spain). Ann. Pediatr. **93**(2), 95–102 (2020)
10. Soldevilla, N., Vinyoles, E., Agudo, J., Camps, L.: Air pollution, cardiovascular risk and hypertension. Hypertens. Vasc. Risk **35**(4), 177–184 (2018)
11. Roca, B., Beltrán, M., Gómez, R.: Change climate and health. Span. Clin. Mag. **219**(5), 260–265 (2019)
12. Cerqueira, L., Barreto, V., Bolzan, F., Toledo de Almeida, T.: Patterns related to pollutant concentrations in the Metropolitan Area of Belo Horizonte, Brazil. Atmosphere **36**(2), 329–341 (2023)

13. Aquise, E., Chirinos, K.: Photocatalytic mortar with tiO2 for the reduction of air pollutants produced by vehicular emissions. Constr. Eng. Mag. **17**(1), 26–34 (2022)
14. Rivas, M., Suárez, A., Serebrisky, T.: Stylized facts of urban transport in Latin America and the Caribbean. Inter-American Development Bank, 1–14 (2019)
15. Letyagina, E.: On assessing the impact of automotive transport on the environment of urban agglomerations using the Krasnoyarsk territory as an example. Transp. Res. Procedia **68**, 505–510 (2023)
16. Yang, X., Liu, H., Man, H., He, K.: Characterization of road freight transportation and its impact on the national emission inventory in China. Atmos. Chem. Phys. **15**(4), 2105–2118 (2015)
17. Singh, D., et al.: GIS-based onroad vehicular emission inventory for Lucknow, India. J. Hazard. Toxic Radioact. Waste **20**(4), 1–10 (2016)
18. Mat, A., Wan, W., Muhammud, A., Ahmad, F., Petra, R.: Spatial and temporal CO concentration over Malaysia and Indonesia using 4 decade. TEM J. **8**(3), 836–841 (2019)
19. Yitong, X., Chaokui, Q., Pengfei, D., Zhiguang, C.: Prediction of CO emission from partially-premixed gas cooker. Case Stud. Therm. Eng. **31**, 101833 (2022)
20. Liu, H., Li, Q., Yu, D., Gu, Y.: Air quality index and air pollutant concentration prediction based on machine learning algorithms. Appl. Sci. **9**(19), 1–9 (2019)
21. Pasic, M., Bijelonja, I., Kadric, E., Bajric, H.: Modeling of nonlinear autoregressive neural network for multi-step ahead air quality prediction. TEM J. **9**(3), 852–861 (2020)
22. Hernández, C., Ávila, A., Cerda, D.: Impact of urban mobility on air quality in the metropolitan area of San Luis Potosí, Mexico. J. Environ. Sci. **57**(1), 1–27 (2022)
23. León, B., Moreno, E., Carrasco, L., Violán, C., Liutsko, L.: Challenges and obstacles of artificial intelligence in health research. Sanit. Gaz. **37** (2023)
24. Dihlac, M., Mai, V., Mörch, C., Noiseau, P., Voarino, N.: Thinking Responsible Artificial Intelligence: A Deliberation Guide. University of Montreal, Quebec (2020)
25. Yanto, M., Arlis, S., Na'am, J., Yuhandri, Y., Marse, D.: Hybrid method air quality classification analysis model. TEM J. **11**(2), 829–836 (2022)
26. Molina, A., Pichunman, C., Martínez, B., Remior, A.: Water quality monitoring in rural drinking water system. Electron. Eng. Autom. Commun. Mag. **42**(3), 60–70 (2021)
27. Kiryakova, G., Yordanova, L., Angelova, N.: Can we make Schools and Universities smarter with the Internet of Things? TEM J. **6**(1), 80–84 (2017)
28. Atalay, M., Çelik, E.: Artificial intelligence and machine learning applications in big data analysis. J. Mehmet Akif Ersoy Univ. Inst. Soc. Sci. **9**(22), 155–172 (2017)
29. Ruiz, R., Velásquez, J.: Artificial intelligence at the service of the health of the future. Condes Clin. Med. J. **34**(1), 84–91 (2023)
30. Gómez, J., Marcillo, F., Triana, F., Gallo, V., Oviedo, B., Hernández, V.: IoT for environmental variables in urban areas. Procedia Comput. Sci. **109C**, 67–74 (2017)
31. Duque, J.: The IoT to smart cities - a design science research approach. Procedia Comput. Sci. **219**, 279–285 (2023)
32. Mrzic, E., Zaimovic, T.: Data science methods and machine learning algorithm implementations for customized pratical usage. TEM J. **9**(3), 1179–1185 (2020)
33. Martínez, E., López, R.: Telematic air quality monitoring system in remote areas. Development of a platform for data analysis and model generation through big data and machine learning techniques. ITCA Fepade, Universidad Tecnológica de El Salvador (2020)
34. Li, Y., Guo, J., Sun, S., Li, J., Wang, S., Zhang, C.: Air quality forecasting with artificial intelligence techniques: a scientometric and content analysis. Environ. Model. Softw. **149**(3), 105329 (2022)
35. Cabaneros, S., Calautit, J., Hughes, B.: A review of artificial neural network models for ambient air pollution prediction. Environ Model Softw. **119**, 285–304 (2019)

36. De Caso, M.: Prediction of air quality in the city of Madrid using machine-learning techniques. Open University of Catalonia (2020)
37. Livingston, S., Kanmani, S., Ebenezer, A., Sam, D., Joshi, A.: An ensembled method for air quality monitoring and control using machine learning. Meas. Sens. **30**, 101914 (2023)
38. Rubio, J., Hernández, J., Ávila, F., Stein, J., Meléndez, A.: Sensor system based in neural networks for the environmental monitoring. In: Engineering Research and Technology, vol. XVII, no. 2, 211–222 (2016)
39. Paz, H., Moreno, A., Poveda, J.: Air measuring quality using an IoT network: a case study. Eng. Mag. **26**(3), 401–418 (2021)
40. Inicio, F., Capuñay, D., Estela, R., Delgado, J., Vergara, S.: Design and implementation of an artificial neural network to predict academic performance in civil engineering students from UNIFSLB. Veritas Scientia **10**(1), 107–117 (2021)
41. Wu, Y., Li, L., Xin, B., Hu, Q., Dong, X., Li, Z.: Application of machine learning in personalized medicine. Intell. Pharm., 1–5 (2023)
42. CEAC, What is Arduino IoT Cloud? https://www.ceac.es/blog/que-es-arduino-iot-cloud/. Accessed 22 June 2023

Unsupervized Techniques to Identify Patterns in Gynecologic Information

Marco Chacaguasay, Ruth Reátegui$^{(\boxtimes)}$ ⓘ, Priscila Valdiviezo-Diaz ⓘ, and Janneth Chicaiza ⓘ

Universidad Técnica Particular de Loja, Loja 08544, Ecuador
{mvchacaguasay,rmreategui,pmvaldiviezo,jachicaiza}@utpl.edu.ec

Abstract. Medical records are a source of valuable information. Processing enormous amounts of data effectively while looking for patterns of interest is made feasible by utilizing artificial intelligence and machine learning techniques. In this research, we apply clustering methods to identify patterns in the health records of women, including age, medical condition, illness, contraceptive methods, and gynecologic features. The methodology used includes data understanding, preprocessing, modeling, and evaluation. For data clustering, three unsupervised algorithms -k-means, DBSCAN, and hierarchical clustering-were applied. To evaluate each technique's effectiveness, the silhouette metric was used. The experiment results highlight that the optimal silhouette value of 0.73 was achieved with the DBSCAN algorithm by grouping data into 9 clusters. These findings greatly advance our understanding of the most common genital infections and improve our capacity to identify unique patterns within each cluster.

Keywords: machine learning · cluster analysis · gynecologic data

1 Introduction

The vast amount of data produced by healthcare institutions has become an essential input for data analysis. Results can reveal insights that benefit both patients and healthcare professionals. In recent decades, artificial intelligence methods have emerged as a reliable tool for healthcare data analysis [1].

Within the field of women's health, gynecological infections stand out as a prevalent cause for medical consultations. Women's propensity to experience genital infections, often attributed to hormonal and functional fluctuations [2], is particularly pronounced during their reproductive years. In Ecuador, in 2019, gynecology and obstetrics occupied the second-highest allocation of hospital beds, using 15.8% of the available capacity [3]. Accordingly, the goal of this study is to analyze these conditions using unsupervised learning algorithms to discover unknown patterns in women's medical data.

Research related to the application of cluster analysis within the context of medical information includes [4], where the potential of unsupervised learning

M. Botto-Tobar et al. (Eds.): ICAT 2023, CCIS 2049, pp. 31–43, 2024.
https://doi.org/10.1007/978-3-031-58956-0_3

to analyze data related to primary breast cancer is demonstrated. In this study, clinical records from women with breast cancer were analyzed using k-means [4], self-organizing maps, hierarchical agglomerative clustering, and Gaussian mixture model clustering. The first two algorithms showed superior grouping and classification outcomes in defining treatments for patients.

Furthermore, in *Ref.* [5], a hybrid machine learning framework to analyze risk factors for breast cancer patients with diabetes mellitus is proposed. This study leverages health insurance data from the Taiwanese population and the synergy between SBS, k-means, and XGBoost algorithms.

In the domain of ovarian carcinomas, [6] employs machine learning to effectively stratify patients and evaluate their survival. Hierarchical clustering is chosen as the analytical method, successfully identifying distinct patient groups across two datasets.

To analyze other medical conditions with clustering algorithms, we find studies like [7] that reveal potential phenotypes based on dietary macronutrients in women, phenotypes among patients with type 2 diabetes [8], obesity [9] and pelvic organ prolapse [10].

Overall, according to the review, the convergence of advanced machine learning algorithms and medical data opens new avenues for comprehending health phenomena. In particular, in this study, we analyze gynecologic infections from health systems data to make well-informed decisions that will improve patient treatment and health outcomes.

2 Methodology

This section outlines the sequential steps undertaken to formulate this study.

2.1 Dataset

The dataset utilized in this study comprises 4,505 records of female patients who received gynecological attention between 2016 and 2021 at a healthcare institution situated in Loja, southern Ecuador. Extracted from the computerized system, the dataset encompasses 30 features about women's health conditions. Importantly, the extraction and subsequent anonymization of this dataset received official endorsement from the Ethics Committee for Research on Human Beings at the Universidad Técnica Particular de Loja.

It is essential to emphasize that although the dataset is not publicly accessible, the University has the prerogative to use it following proper advance notification and obtaining the necessary consent from the relevant healthcare institution.

2.2 Preprocessing

With the guidance of a physician, a thorough selection process was conducted for patients treated for genital infections, leading to the identification of a total of 11 infections. The CIE-10 codes utilized in the computerized system for diagnostic reference were employed to filter and categorize these infections. Table 1 shows more details of the infections names and codes.

Table 1. Infections and codes

Infections	Code
Vulvar abscess	N764
Yeast infection (candidiasis)	B37
Vulvar and vaginal candidiasis	B373
Gonococcal infections	A540
Acute vaginitis	N760
Atrophic vaginitis	N95.2
Subacute and chronic vaginitis	N761
Bacterial vaginosis	N76.8
Viral warts	B07
Acute vulvitis	N762
Subacute and chronic vulvitis	N763

After the filtration phase, a refined compilation of 1,251 patient records, ranging from 18 to 88 years old, was obtained. Furthermore, through scrutiny, specific features with negligible relevance to the research were identified. Out of the original set of 30 features, 14 have been retained, while 16 have been excluded. For instance, attributes like 'city' were omitted, given that a majority of records originated from the same urban center. Similar redundancy was observed in attributes such as 'blood type', 'medical attention date', 'height', 'weight', and others. Moreover, the dataset includes categorical attributes such as 'marital status', 'disease name', and 'previous contraceptive method', which were subsequently encoded into dummy variables to accommodate the analysis.

To culminate the data preprocessing phase, a uniform normalization with *MinMAxScaler* function of Python was applied to all features, aligning them to a consistent value range. For instance, while the 'age' feature spanned from 18 to 88 years, 'menarche' values oscillated between 0 and 6. In response, a normalization protocol was executed, transforming the data into a coherent numerical scale ranging from 0 to 1. Finally, for the analysis, the next 34 variables were used:

age, allergy, cancer, candidiasis_name, candidiasis_of_vulva_and_vagina, cesarean, control, contraception_previous_use, diabetes, gonococcal_infection_name,

hpv, hypothyroidism, hysterectomy, iud, leucorrhea, divorced_marital_status, single_marital_status, de_facto_union_marital_status, free_union_marital_status, widowed_marital_status, menarche, pregnancy, pruritus, ivsa, total_gravity, tubal_*

ligation, vaginal_discharge, acute_vaginitis_name, bacterial_vaginosis_name, atrophic_vaginitis_name,   subacute_and_chronic_vaginitis_name,   viral_warts_name, acute_vulvitis_name, subacute_and_chronic_vulvitis_name.
    (*) ivsa is the Spanish acronym for age at first sexual intercourse.

2.3   Algorithms

Following contemporary research standards, algorithms commonly employed for cluster analysis comprise K-means, DBSCAN, and hierarchical algorithms. In congruence with this established precedent, the present study proceeded to engage these three unsupervised algorithms.

K-means: It is a prominently utilized unsupervised algorithm in cluster analysis that operates on the principle of partitioning a dataset into k distinct clusters. K-means separates groups with similar characteristics, adjusting them to their position in each iteration. Author [11] presents the following sequence of steps for K-means:

1. Initialization and centroid definition: K centroids are established, each representing a cluster
2. Object Assignment to centroids: Objects within the dataset are allocated to the nearest centroids, determining their cluster affiliations.
3. Centroid Update: Centroids are recalibrated to the average of their constituent objects' attributes.

The iterative process of steps 2) and 3) continues until the centroids reach a state of stability, where they no longer change. Noteworthy advantages of the k-means algorithm encompass its simplicity and expeditious computation, rendering it an efficient tool for clustering purposes.

Hierarchical Clustering: According to [12], this methodology can be executed via two principal strategies: agglomeration and division. In the agglomeration strategy, the algorithm begins by merging the two closest nodes into a single cluster. This merging process is iteratively performed until all nodes coalesce into a solitary cluster. The division strategy begins by merging all nodes as an initial step. Subsequently, this initial cluster is iteratively divided into two distinct clusters, with the division process persisting until each node stands as an independent cluster.

DBSCAN: Standing for Density-Based Spatial Clustering of Applications with Noise, operates on the principle of analyzing regions of high density [13]. The algorithm takes into consideration two pivotal factors: the radius parameter and the minimum number of points required within the vicinity, often referred to as the neighborhood size. A notable attribute of DBSCAN is its capacity to obviate the necessity of designating an initial number of clusters, thus evincing its flexibility in handling diverse datasets and their inherent structures. This feature underscores the algorithm's robustness and adaptability in various clustering scenarios.

2.4 Metrics

Given that the dataset lacks any variable or ground truth labels that can be used as a reference for evaluating the results obtained in the experiments, we have proceeded to assess these results using an intrinsic metric, such as the Silhouette coefficient. The Silhouette coefficient evaluates the group quality obtained, by measuring the object's similarity with its cluster called cohesion, and compares them with the other clusters, this is called separation. The obtained value ranges between −1 to 1, where values close to 1 denote that there is a great separation from its cluster and that it is poorly accommodated to its neighboring clusters. If the values are close to 1, it is considered that the group is appropriately clustered; on the other hand, if the value is close to −1, the obtained agglomeration is not adequate or is not correctly assigned to the cluster. If the value is close to 0 the group is between two clusters [14]. The equation used for Silhouette calculation is the following:

$$S_i = \frac{(b_i - a_i)}{max\,\{a_i, b_i\}} \tag{1}$$

Where:

- a is the average distance from a point related to the other points in the same group
- b is the average distance of the selected point with the other points in the closest group to its group.

2.5 Calculate the Number of Clusters

The elbow method was used to determine the number of clusters (k). This method works with the intra-cluster distances, which are, the mean distance of the observed points to their centroids. The elbow method looks for the k value that keeps after experiencing the curve (elbow of the curve) as the cut-off point to a decreasing performance that does not justify an additional cost o a significant change [13].

2.6 Tools

Python was used as language programming, including the following libraries for preprocessing and data analysis:

- Pandas: It is a library specialized in handling and structured data analysis.
- Numpy: It is a fundamental package for scientific computing in Python, especially for handling matrices.

– Matplotlib: It is a library that allows the creation, personalizing, and plotting of graphics in 2 dimensions.
– Sklearn: It is a useful library for machine learning and provides supervised and unsupervised learning algorithms.

3   Results

Before presenting the findings, it is essential to emphasize that the results derived from the cluster analysis of each algorithm were calculated based on the average values of the following variables: age, IVSA, and menarche. The mode was used to handle the remaining variables. In particular, Tables 6, 7, 8, and 9, exclusively cover infections with a value of 1 in at least one group, while infections with 0 in all groups were excluded to simplify the presentation of information.

3.1   K-means Results

The optimal number of clusters k, was selected using the Elbow method. The plot in Fig. 1 shows the results of this method. The optimal number of clusters could be between 6 and 8.

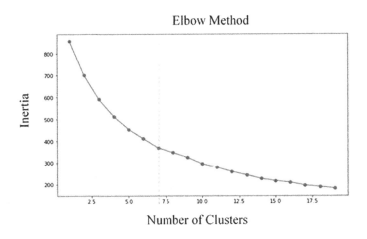

Fig. 1. Estimated cluster number using the Elbow method.

Using the k-means algorithm with 7 clusters the silhouette value was 0.34. Results of the number of patients and silhouette values by clusters are presented in Table 2.

Table 6 presents the outcomes obtained from the application of the k-means algorithm. Notably, the results reveal that an age of 36 is consistently observed across three distinct clusters (0, 1, and 6). This convergence prompts an inference that the average age associated with the occurrence of gynecological infections

Table 2. Silhouette coefficient for cluster results with K-means.

Cluster	Silhouette	Number of patients
0	0.22	143
1	0.38	214
2	0.38	268
3	0.36	134
4	0.32	199
5	0.32	162
6	0.34	131

is approximately 36 years. A similar pattern emerges with the onset of IVSA which is reiterated within three distinct groups, each characterized by an age of 18 years. Moreover, while the count of infections influencing each group varies, it's noteworthy that three clusters (2, 3, and 4) exhibit an association with the same infection, indicated by the N76.8 code.

3.2 Hierarchical Clustering Results

During the utilization of the hierarchical clustering algorithm, the division strategy was employed. Consequently, the implementation led to the formation of five distinct clusters, yielding a silhouette value of 0.41. Detailed insights into the distribution of patients across these clusters, along with their corresponding silhouette values, are expounded in Table 3

Table 3. Silhouette coefficient for cluster results with hierarchical clustering.

Cluster	Silhouette	Number of patients
1	0.44	422
2	0.38	225
3	0.25	180
4	0.46	161
5	0.48	263

Table 7 provides an overview of the algorithm's findings. In a parallel fashion to the k-means algorithm, the age of 36 years recurs within three out of the five identified groups. Moving on to the variable of the number of pregnancies, the value "2" predominates across the majority of the clusters, barring a single exception observed in cluster 5. In terms of infections under consideration, they exhibit a diverse distribution, with no shared ailments evident among the identified groups.

3.3   DBSCAN Results

The DBSCAN algorithm yielded a total of 9 clusters, accompanied by a notable silhouette value of 0.73. The noise objects were 102 instances. Comprehensive details encompassing the distribution of patients across these clusters and the corresponding silhouette values are presented in Table 4.

Table 4. Silhouette coefficient for cluster results with DBSCAN.

Cluster	Silhouette	Number of patients
0	0.07	851
1	0.90	70
2	0.89	53
3	0.88	23
4	0.92	37
5	0.91	35
6	0.85	17
7	0.84	14
8	0.91	49

Table 8 encapsulates the outcomes derived from this algorithm. Two infections emerge as shared factors among two distinct groups: B373 appears in clusters 4 and 8, whereas N761 is present in clusters 6 and 7. Additionally, in cluster 0, none of the five infections that manifest in the other clusters exhibit significance for the patients within this particular group.

3.4   PCA and DBSCAN Results

In the aforementioned series of experiments, the DBSCAN algorithm yielded the most favorable silhouette value. In an attempt to further refine these results, the PCA reduction method was implemented before the application of DBSCAN. In this experiment, a configuration of 5 clusters was derived, accompanied by a silhouette value of 0.60. Details of the distribution of patients across these newly established clusters, alongside the corresponding silhouette values, are systematically presented in Table 5.

Table 9 presents results from the execution of the DBSCAN algorithm incorporating PCA with 4 components. This endeavor culminated in the identification of six distinct groups, inclusive of noise. Subsequently, the investigation led to the exclusion of the noise, thereby yielding five final groups. A meticulous breakdown of these groups is outlined in Table 5.

The results revealed that the B373 infection was predominantly featured in clusters 1 and 4. In contrast, for cluster 2, the N760 infection exerted the most prominent influence. Notably, cluster 3 was primarily influenced by the N95.2. It's worth mentioning that cluster 0 remained devoid of any identified infections.

Table 5. Silhouette coefficient for cluster results with PCA and DBSCAN.

Cluster	Silhouette	Number of patients
0	0.43	805
1	0.51	155
2	0.69	99
3	0.61	76
4	0.73	16

4 Discussion

Eleven gynecological infections were used in the dataset. To explain that our experiments have similar results despite the number of clusters, Fig. 2 shows the coincidence between six representative infections present in clusters of different algorithms. The six infections were identified by the DBSCAN algorithm, namely B373, B37, N760, N761, N76.8, and B95.2. With k-means, 5 infections were identified, and they are related to DBSCAN results. When applying the hierarchical clustering algorithm, there is a similarity with the five infections shown by k-means.

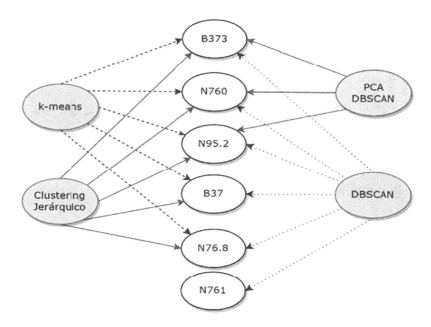

Fig. 2. Relation between algorithms and infections. Each cluster is identified by DBSCAN and some of them are identified by alternative algorithms.

Table 6. Results with K-means algorithm

Cluster	Age	Menarche	ivsa	Total pregnancy	Contra-ceptive	Marital Status Single	B37	N95.2	N76.8	N760	B373	Silhouette	Records
0	36	13	17	2	0	0	0	0	0	0	1	0.22	143
1	36	13	15	2	0	0	0	0	0	1	0	0.38	214
2	43	13	18	3	0	0	0	0	1	0	0	0.38	268
3	40	13	18	3	1	0	0	0	1	0	0	0.36	134
4	29	13	17	1	0	1	0	1	1	0	0	0.32	199
5	58	14	19	4	0	0	0	0	0	0	0	0.32	162
6	36	13	18	2	1	0	1	0	0	0	0	0.34	131
												Total	1251

Table 7. Results with Hierarchical clustering algorithm

Cluster	Age	Menarche	ivsa	Total pregnancy	Contra-ceptive	N95.2	B373	B37	N760	N76.8	Silhouette	Records
1	36	13	18	2	0	0	0	0	0	1	0.44	422
2	36	13	15	2	0	0	0	0	1	0	0.38	225
3	36	13	18	2	1	0	0	1	0	0	0.25	180
4	35	13	17	2	0	0	1	0	0	0	0.46	161
5	54	13	19	4	0	1	0	0	0	0	0.48	263
											Total	1251

Table 8. Results with DBSCAN algorithm

Cluster	Age	Menarche	ivsa	Total pregnancy	Marital Status Single	Contra-ceptive	N761	N95.2	B373	B37	N760	N76.8	Silhouette	Records
0	36	13	17	2	0	1	0	0	0	0	0	0	0.07	851
1	44	13	18	3	0	0	0	0	0	0	0	1	0.90	70
2	46	13	17	3	0	0	0	0	0	0	1	0	0.89	53
3	47	14	19	3	0	0	0	0	0	1	0	0	0.88	23
4	40	13	18	2	0	0	0	0	1	0	0	0	0.92	37
5	64	14	22	5	0	0	0	1	0	0	0	0	0.91	35
6	48	13	15	2	0	0	1	0	0	0	0	0	0.85	17
7	31	13	16	1	1	0	1	0	0	0	0	0	0.84	14
8	28	13	14	1	1	0	0	1	0	0	0	0	0.91	49
													Total	1149

Table 9. Results with PCA and DBSCAN algorithm

Cluster	Age	Menarche	ivsa	Total pregnancy	Marital Status Single	B373	N760	N95.2	Silhouette	Records
0	36	13	18	2	0	0	0	0	0.43	805
1	34	13	18	1	0	1	0	0	0.51	155
2	31	13	13	1	1	0	1	0	0.69	99
3	59	13	19	4	0	0	0	1	0.61	76
4	27	13	13	0	1	1	0	0	0.73	16
								Total		1151

Employing the PCA algorithm for dimensionality reduction in conjunction with the DBSCAN algorithm, our research brings into focus a trio of infections that delineate variations among clusters (B373, N760, and N95.2). Additionally, the results highlight age as a recurring common factor within clusters generated by different algorithms, with the age of 36 consistently surfacing across various clusters. Similarly, the IVSA value accentuates its significance, with a recurring commonality of 15 years across different clusters, further emphasizing the interconnected nature of these clusters.

4.1   Conclusion

Throughout the experimental phase, it was observed that the DBSCAN algorithm exhibited the most favorable Silhouette value of 0.73, while the k-means algorithm yielded the lowest Silhouette value of 0.34. Upon implementing dimensionality reduction through PCA in conjunction with the DBSCAN algorithm, the resultant global Silhouette value converged to 0.60.

A thorough analysis of the results inside every cluster leads to several noteworthy conclusions. All of the identified clusters show a consistent pattern that indicates the persistence of some infections (B373, N760, N95.2, N76.8, and B37). However, applying dimensionality reduction to the dataset, it is interesting to see that the distribution of B373, N95.2, and N760 infections is still similar. This fact provides important information about the illnesses that are most prominent in each algorithmic application. As a result, B373, N95.2, and N760 are identified as the key infectious agents that greatly influence the algorithms' results.

The code N95.2 appears in all experiments within groups that have the highest average age across the entire set of women. This is to be expected since this code corresponds to postmenopausal atrophic vaginitis. The code N760 corresponds to acute vaginitis, while B373 is associated with vulvar and vaginal candidiasis; both conditions are caused by the Candida fungus. Vaginal yeast infection affects up to 3 out of 4 women at some juncture in their lives, with many experiencing at least two episodes. Importantly, a vaginal yeast infection is not classified as a sexually transmitted infection. However, the risk of developing a vaginal yeast infection tends to increase with the onset of regular sexual activity [15].

For future work, the findings outlined in this study merit validation through concerted engagement with healthcare experts, affording a medical vantage point to contextualize the outcomes produced by each algorithm. Moreover, it is required to integrate alternative algorithms such as HDBSCAN or variables such as the spectrum of administered pharmaceutical agents and the temporal aspects underpinning each therapeutic intervention. The factors unaddressed within the present research would hold the potential to discover insight and enrich the overall breadth of research outcomes.

References

1. Balaji, F., Lavanya, K.: Machine learning algorithm for cluster analysis of mixed dataset based on instance-cluster closeness metric. Chemom. Intell. Lab. Syst. **215**, 1–13 (2021)
2. Ministerio de Salud Pública del Ecuador: Diagnóstico y tratamiento de infección vaginal en obstetricia (2014)
3. Herrera, M.: Registro Estadístico de Camas y Egresos Hospitalarios 2019. INEC, no. 2020, pp. 11–13 (2019). www.ecuadorencifras.gob.ec
4. Ferro, S., Bottigliengo, D., Gregori, D., Fabricio, A.S.C., Gion, M., Baldi, I.: Phenomapping of patients with primary breast cancer using machine learning-based unsupervised cluster analysis. J. Personal. Med. **11**(4), 272 (2021)
5. Ye, L., Lee, T.-S., Chi, R.: A hybrid machine learning scheme to analyze the risk factors of breast cancer outcome in patients with diabetes mellitus. J. Univ. Comput. Sci. **24**(6), 665–681 (2018)
6. Grimley, P.M., et al.: A prognostic system for epithelial ovarian carcinomas using machine learning. Acta Obstet. Gynecol. Scand. **100**(8), 1511–1519 (2021)
7. Ramyaa, R., Hosseini, O., Krishnan, G.P., Krishnan, S.: Phenotyping women based on dietary macronutrients, physical activity, and body weight using machine learning tools. Nutrients **11**(7), 1681 (2019)
8. Sharma, A., et al.: Cluster analysis of cardiovascular phenotypes in patients with type 2 diabetes and established atherosclerotic cardiovascular disease: a potential approach to precision medicine. Diab. Care **45**(1), 204–212 (2022)
9. Reátegui, R., Ratté, S., Bautista-Valarezo, E., Duque, V.: Cluster analysis of obesity disease based on comorbidities extracted from clinical notes. J. Med. Syst. **43**(3), 52 (2019)
10. Jelovsek, J.E., et al.: Subgroups of failure after surgery for pelvic organ prolapse and associations with quality of life outcomes: a longitudinal cluster analysis. Am. J. Obstet. Gynecol. **225**(5), 504.e1–504.e22 (2021)
11. Amr, T.: Hands-On Machine Learning with scikit-learn and Scientific Python Toolkits. Packt Publishing, UK (2020)
12. Everitt, B., Landau, S., Leese, M., Stahl, D.: Cluster Analysis, 5th edn. Wiley, UK (2011)
13. Géron, A.: Hands-On Machine Learning with Scikit-Learn, Keras and TensorFlow, 2nd edn. O'Reilly Media Inc., Canada (2019)
14. Han, J., Kamber, M., Pei, J.: Data Mining: Concepts and Techniques, 3rd edn. Morgan Kaufmann Publisher, USA (2012)
15. Mayo Clinic: Yeast infection (vaginal). https://www.mayoclinic.org/diseases-conditions/yeast-infection/symptoms-causes/syc-20378999

Web Application for Early Cataract Detection Using a Deep Learning Cloud Service

Fatima Dayana Galindo-Vilca$^{(\boxtimes)}$ ⓘ, Fredy Daniel Astorayme-Garciaⓘ, and Esther Aliaga-Cernaⓘ

Faculty of Engineering, Universidad Peruana de Ciencias Aplicadas, Lima, Peru
{u202021987,u202022001,pcsieali}@upc.edu.pe

Abstract. Cataracts are a degenerative disease that causes opacity in the crystalline lens. They represent one of the leading causes of blindness worldwide, making early detection crucial to prevent severe damage to patients. Current studies on cataract detection face limitations, particularly due to the high cost of imaging devices and their limited accessibility for users. In this study, we propose a web application that utilizes a Deep Learning service to analyze fundus images and provide a cataract diagnosis. This application aims to assist healthcare personnel in medical centers lacking specialist ophthalmologists or facing limited resources for cataract diagnosis. We designed the physical architecture of the application using Azure services, enabling its deployment and operation in the cloud. Azure Custom Vision facilitated the training of our model with a dataset of 1446 fundus images, encompassing both cataract and non-cataract cases. Subsequently, we implemented the web application using React.js and Express.js technologies, integrating the Deep Learning model to perform diagnoses through the web interface. The results demonstrated that the model achieved sensitivity, specificity, precision, and accuracy levels exceeding 90%, showcasing that our proposed tool allows for reliable initial cataract diagnoses in patients without the need for high-cost equipment.

Keywords: Cataract · Fundus image · Web Application · Deep Learning · Azure Custom Vision

1 Introduction

Cataracts are defined as the opacity of the crystalline lens of the eye, progressively affecting vision and leading to increasing blurriness, and may even result in blindness if not treated in a timely manner [1]. The risk of developing this disease increases with age [1]. Specifically, senile cataract, the type linked to the natural aging of the lens, affects between 13% and 50% of the world's population aged 60 years or older [2]. Because cataracts worsen over time, patients who delay seeking medical care and surgery may experience more significant complications

M. Botto-Tobar et al. (Eds.): ICAT 2023, CCIS 2049, pp. 44–58, 2024.
https://doi.org/10.1007/978-3-031-58956-0_4

and have a worse prognosis [2]. The low coverage of ophthalmologists and the limited availability of specialized equipment have been shown to be contributing factors to the lack of early detection of the disease [3,4].

Deep Learning (DL) is a branch of Machine Learning [5] that incorporates computational models and algorithms mimicking the neural networks of the brain. Its objective is to provide machines with the ability to analyze, learn, and recognize text, images, and sounds in a manner similar to humans [6]. Several DL models have been developed for cataract detection based on various types of images, such as slit lamp images [7–10], optical coherence tomography images [11], and infrared camera images [12]. All reviewed studies have demonstrated successful validations, achieving accuracy metrics of up to 98.3%. However, it is crucial to note that the devices used to capture such images are not universally available in all medical centers and require trained personnel for operation. This limitation results in reduced patient access in centers where these devices are unavailable. In such circumstances, fundus images can be used, as they are easily and inexpensively obtained [13].

Fundus images are obtained through ophthalmoscopic examination [14]. They play a crucial role in the diagnosis and treatment of eye diseases by providing a detailed image of the retina, optic nerve, and blood vessels. This enables ophthalmologists to detect even the slightest alterations in the eye [15]. Various studies have been conducted based on this type of image. For instance, in [16], a DL model is proposed that classifies fundus images as normal or with cataracts, achieving an accuracy of 83.47%. In another study [17], a Convolutional Neural Network (CNN) was developed, achieving an accuracy higher than 84%. While these models demonstrated accuracy in fundus image analysis, none of them were integrated into a system for use by clinicians or patients.

To address this limitation, this article proposes the use of a web application integrated with a DL model capable of detecting the probability percentage of cataract presence in fundus images, serving as a diagnostic tool. This web application provides medical centers lacking ophthalmology expertise with the means to conduct initial cataract diagnoses. Consequently, they can promptly refer patients to a specialist. We employ Custom Vision, a DL neural network-based service in the Microsoft Azure cloud designed for content recognition in images [18,19]. It allows for the uploading and labeling of images for training and adapts to various scenarios [20]. Capable of recognizing different objects, it continuously improves with ongoing model training [19]. Our training dataset comprised 1446 fundus images of individuals over 60 years old, encompassing both healthy and cataract-afflicted eyes. The web application was developed using the JavaScript programming language, with the React library for the Frontend and the Express.js Framework for the Backend. Additionally, we integrated it with an image preprocessing function in Azure Functions and established the connection between the web application and the DL model through an endpoint provided by Azure.

With this application, our primary objective is to offer a valuable tool to physicians in medical centers lacking an ophthalmology specialist. Through the application, physicians can conduct a pre-diagnosis of patients, obtaining crucial information to refer them to medical centers with specialists. This ensures timely care for patients who previously lacked access to ophthalmology services. Furthermore, physicians will have a tool that provides valuable information for patient referral, registration, and follow-up. Thus, the application not only enhances accessibility to ophthalmologic care but also strengthens the overall medical process for the benefit of patients.

The article is organized into the following sections: First, the review of previous research on cataract detection using DL techniques is presented in the "Related Work" section. The construction of the web application, the procedure for training the DL model, and the deployment of the application are detailed in the "Method" section. The "Results and Discussion" section includes the description of the validation protocol, the experiment performed, and the discussion of the obtained results. Finally, the "Conclusions" section provides the research conclusions and suggestions for future work

2 Related Works

In this section, we will analyze solutions related to cataract detection that employ techniques similar to DL. We will also compare them to our proposal and describe how we contribute to the area of expertise.

In [21], researchers presented a method for identifying cataracts using smartphone illumination features. They utilized the Axis-Scientific 7-Part device to create a dataset simulating both healthy and diseased eyes. The study involved feature extraction from the images, employing Support Vector Machine (SVM) for cataract classification. In contrast, our approach focuses on analyzing fundus images, providing visualization of internal eye structures such as the retina, optic nerve, and blood vessels. Additionally, we leverage a Cloud solution based on Deep Learning, enabling the automatic extraction of features in our model.

In [7], a Deep Learning algorithm designed for cataract detection is presented. This algorithm analyzes short video clips of the eye, recorded using an adapter designed to simulate a slit lamp. The video capture is facilitated by the ISpector Mini device, in conjunction with a mobile application called RUIMU-APP, which uploads the image to the server for cataract detection. Building upon this approach, our work is oriented towards cataract detection employing fundus image analysis. Moreover, we will implement a web application that is compatible with a wide range of devices.

Additionally, in [8], the authors propose using various techniques to evaluate cataracts in slit-lamp images. They begin by capturing images using a smartphone, followed by localizing the nuclear region of the lens within the image using the YOLOv3 algorithm. Subsequently, they employ a combination of a DL network and an SVM classifier to grade the severity of the cataract. In contrast, our approach involves using fundus images and applying DL technology for model building, utilizing the Azure Custom Vision service.

Finally, in [16], the authors conduct the analysis of fundus images for cataract detection using a CNN. While the images analyzed are the same as in our work, the procedures differ. In that study, image preprocessing was initially performed, followed by the extraction of features from the detected regions. In our approach, we aimed to simplify the process by leveraging the Azure Custom Vision service, which automatically processes and extracts features from the image without the need for advanced technical knowledge.

3 Method

3.1 Web Application Architecture Design

We designed the physical architecture of the web application, specifying the devices and users that will interact with it (see Fig. 1). Additionally, we defined the Azure services employed for deploying the application in the cloud and integrating it with the DL model. These include Azure App Service for deployment, Azure Blob Storage for image storage, Azure Custom Vision for building the cataract detection model, Azure Database for PostgreSQL for data storage, and Azure Functions for preprocessing images before analysis by the model.

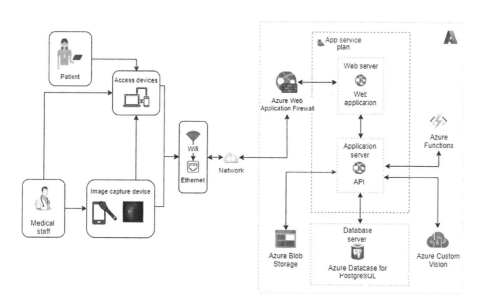

Fig. 1. Physical application architecture with Azure services, devices and users.

Similarly, we created mockups and designed the database, taking into account the necessary entities for the proper functioning of the application.

3.2 Deep Learning Model Implementation

The model creation involved following a series of steps in a flow (see Fig. 2) defined by the CRISP-DM methodology.

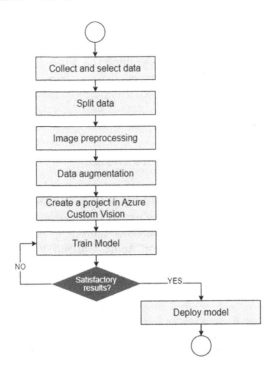

Fig. 2. Model creation flow followed in Azure Custom Vision

1. **Collect and Select Data**: Our study utilized the Ocular Disease Intelligent Recognition (ODIR) dataset, an ophthalmic database comprising 5,000 real patient eye images, including information about age, and gender, along with diagnoses provided by doctors [22]. Compiled by Shanggong Medical Technology Co., Ltd. from diverse medical centers and hospitals across China, the dataset encompasses fundus images captured using various cameras, including Canon, Zeiss, and Kowa [22].
   While the dataset encompasses various ophthalmic conditions, we selected a targeted subset to focus on identifying cataracts in individuals aged 60 and above (see Fig. 3). Data cleaning procedures were then applied, including the elimination of duplicate and blurred images. This resulted in a dataset composed of 452 images from a total of 375 individuals, with 215 females and 160 males.
2. **Split Data**: To validate the model using the "Holdout Validation" method [23], as detailed in the "Experiment Protocol" section, we divided the data into training and test sets with an 80-20 ratio. We ensured an equal number of images with cataracts and without cataracts for each ratio. In total, 362 images were assigned to the training phase, and 90 images were allocated to the validation phase.
3. **Image Preprocessing**: Previous research has demonstrated that better results are achieved in the analysis of a fundus image by working exclusively

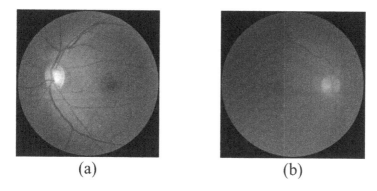

Fig. 3. Fundus images: (a) Normal, (b) Cataract.

with the green channel. This channel contains more relevant information for cataract detection compared to the red and blue channels [24,25]. By doing so, the luminance value of the image is improved, and the visible features of the retinal veins are enhanced. Our study utilizes Python with the Pillow and OpenCV libraries to process the fundus images and extract only the green channel (see Fig. 4).

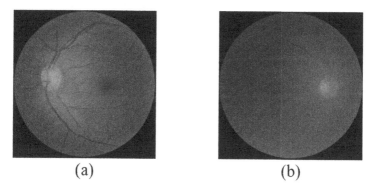

Fig. 4. Fundus images using green channel: (a) Normal, (b) Cataract. (Color figure online)

4. **Data Augmentation**: We processed the images from the training set using data augmentation techniques, including rotation, horizontal reflection, and brightness adjustment (see Fig. 5). In total, we generated an additional 1084 images, expanding the set to 540 fundus images with cataracts and 544 without cataracts. All image processing was performed using Keras.
5. **Create a project in Azure Custom Vision**: In setting up a new project on Azure Custom Vision, we chose the multiclass classification within the Classification Types, organizing images into individual categories. Subsequently, we

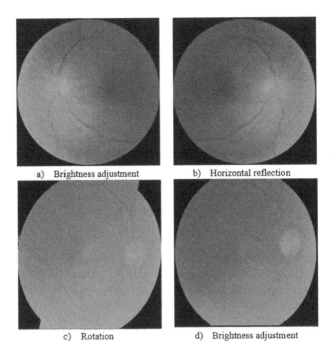

a) Brightness adjustment   b) Horizontal reflection

c) Rotation   d) Brightness adjustment

Fig. 5. Effects of variations on images

selected the General A2 configuration, one of the available domains designed to optimize the model for specific image types. This choice aimed to achieve optimized accuracy with a quicker inference time, as recommended for most datasets, and a reduced training time compared to other general domains. Within the project, we defined labels such as "Cataracts" and "Normal" to categorize the images. Subsequently, we uploaded a total of 1446 images for training, assigning each one its respective label. This process provided the necessary data for the model to learn and distinguish between the specified categories.

6. **Train Model**: The model was trained for 5 h, and its performance was evaluated using metrics provided by the service, including accuracy and recall. The results were found to be satisfactory.

7. **Deploy Model**: We published the classification model's API on the Azure portal, generating a key and endpoint for integration into the web application.

To ensure the quality of the data, we follow Microsoft's recommendations for optimal results in our model [26]. To prevent data overfitting and train the model with a diverse set of images, we incorporate a data augmentation process into our implementation flow. This process generates variations in brightness, rotation, and horizontal reflection, equipping the model to assess a wide variety of images.

Furthermore, Microsoft suggests a minimum of 50 images for each label in the Azure Custom Vision model. In our case, we have used more than 700 images for each label, surpassing the recommended minimum.

Additionally, the balanced distribution of images among tag groups enhances the model's accuracy in predicting a given tag.

3.3   Web Application Development

The web application consists of two main components, Frontend and Backend, which interact with each other through APIs. The Frontend was developed with React v18.2.0 and Node.js v16.16.0, while the Backend utilized Express.js v14.18.2, Node.js v16.17.0, and integrated with Azure Blob Storage, Azure Functions, and Azure Custom Vision services. The database connection was established with a PostgreSQL 15 database.

The web application covers functionalities such as user authentication, patient data management, analysis of fundus images, and history of patient analyses. All the functionalities of the web application cover a total of 17 User Stories. The analysis data recording screen was developed, featuring fields for entering the patient's symptom description, selecting the eye for analysis, and uploading the image to be analyzed (see Fig. 6). After the analysis, the results can be displayed on the screen (see Fig. 7). Additionally, medical personnel using the system can record their final diagnosis and indicate whether the patient requires a referral to a specialist. The source code and dataset used in this project are available in a repository[1].

3.4   Deploy

We deployed the application using the Azure components specified in the physical architecture. We utilized the same resource group where the Azure Custom Vision, Azure Functions, and Azure Blob Storage services were created.

First, we created the Azure Database for PostgreSQL instance and migrated the database data from our development environment. Next, we set up an Azure App Service instance with the Basic B1 plan (1.75 GB RAM and 1 CPU) and the Linux operating system to deploy the Backend. Finally, another instance with the Basic B1 plan and the Windows operating system was created to deploy the Frontend. The deployment of both was automated using GitHub Actions.

4   Results and Discussions

This section will present the experiments performed to validate our proposal and the results obtained from this procedure.

---

[1] https://gitfront.io/r/user-5082728/GGsekMuELVSr/cataract-project/.

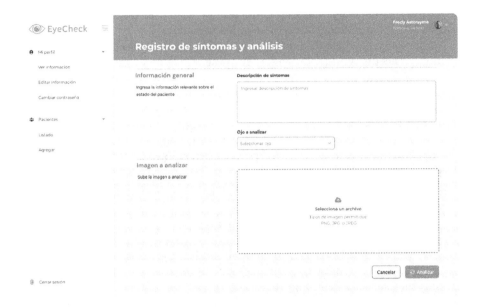

Fig. 6. Data registration form and image of the patient's fundus.

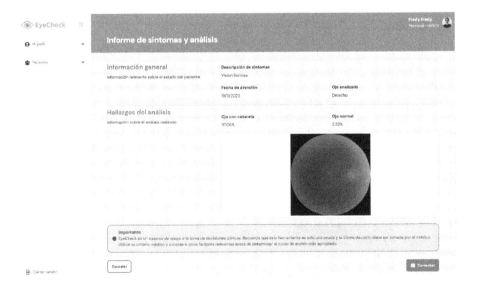

Fig. 7. Screen with cataract analysis results

4.1   Experiment Protocol

The decision to validate the model involved using the widely adopted "Holdout Validation" method [23], which divides the dataset into training and test groups. The training set is employed for model construction, while the test set assesses performance on unknown data. Notably, it's essential to avoid using test data in model training. In our case, with the Azure Custom Vision service, we split the original dataset into 80% for training and 20% for evaluating the model with unknown data.

To execute the validation, we developed the web application and used the registration and analysis results views. In the first view, patient data, such as the eye to be examined, symptoms, and the image, is registered. In the second view, the results of the analysis performed by the DL model are displayed, showing confidence percentages indicating the presence or absence of cataract signs in the image.

The images used in the validation process were the 90 previously selected (20% of the original dataset), divided into 45 fundus images with cataracts and 45 without cataracts. These images were loaded one by one into the application to verify the accuracy of the DL model, and the results were recorded in the database.

To obtain quantitative validation results, we are using the confusion matrix, a binary classification tool commonly applied in medical applications [27]. It helps define classification outcomes, such as cataract/non-cataract, providing a robust quantitative assessment.

The metrics used to evaluate the performance of the image analysis results were:

$$Sensitivity = \frac{TP}{TP + FN} \tag{1}$$

$$Precision = \frac{TP}{TP + FP} \tag{2}$$

$$Specificity = \frac{TN}{TN + FP} \tag{3}$$

$$Accuracy = \frac{TP + TN}{AllImages} \tag{4}$$

In which:

- TP, or True Positive, is the total predictions of eyes with cataracts that were classified as "Cataracts".
- FN, or False Negative, is the total predictions of eyes with cataracts that were classified as "Normal".
- FP, or False Positive, is the total predictions of healthy eyes that were classified as "Cataracts".
- TN, or True Negative, is the total predictions of healthy eyes that were classified as "Normal".
- AllImages, is the total number of images used to perform the validation.

4.2   Results

Since the dataset used already has labels defined as "Cataract" and "Normal" for each image, we could compare the real values with the results of the DL model to calculate the values of TP, TN, FP, and FN. Based on the comparison results, we obtained the confusion matrix (see Fig. 8), from which we derived TP as 41, TN as 45, FP as 0, and FN as 4.

In conclusion, the model exhibited a sensitivity of 91%, precision of 100%, specificity of 100%, and accuracy of 96%. Using the SKlearn library and the percentages obtained from image analysis during model validation, we calculated the ROC curve. The resulting AUC of 0.98 indicates that the trained model demonstrates high image classification ability, with low false positive and negative rates (see Fig. 9).

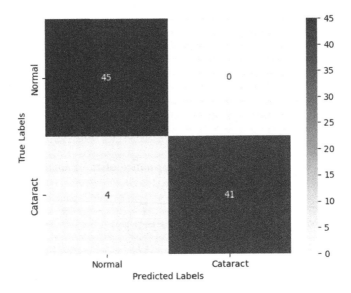

Fig. 8. Results confusion matrix

4.3   Discussions

Our results revealed promising performance in cataract detection. Precision indicates that 100% of the cases classified as positive by the model were indeed positive, meaning the diagnosis was correct. Accuracy indicates that 96% of the model's inferences were correctly classified. In the context of disease detection, sensitivity and specificity metrics are the most important. The sensitivity result showed that it can recognize 91% of the total number of positive cataract cases, allowing most patients to receive appropriate treatment in the early stages. Specificity indicates that our solution can identify 100% of negative cases out

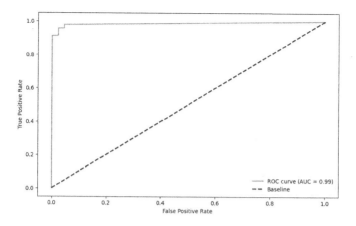

Fig. 9. ROC Curve

of the total number of real negative cases, meaning eyes without cataracts. Therefore, the application minimizes misdiagnosis and even avoids unnecessary treatment.

Due to the sensitive nature of handling personal data, which is considered private information, and the complexity associated with collecting a new dataset along with obtaining relevant permissions from patients, we decided to utilize the publicly available ODIR dataset. This dataset already contained the necessary information for the present study. In strict adherence to ethical guidelines and principles of transparency in research, the use of the ODIR dataset followed rigorous protocols for anonymization and patient privacy, removing any personally identifiable information. Efforts were also made to preserve the integrity of the data and ensure that the research contributes to the advancement of medical knowledge in an ethical and responsible manner.

4.4   Limitations

Azure Custom Vision is designed to simplify training processes, making it accessible for users with less experience in DL. While it allows customization of settings such as the number of iterations and the amount of training data, the user interface does not provide direct access to hyperparameter adjustments, such as specific learning rates, the number of layers and nodes in a neural network, and loss functions.

On the other hand, despite leveraging over 1000 images for training after applying data augmentation techniques, it is imperative to recognize the limited scale of our dataset. This limitation can impact the model's generalizability across a broader spectrum of clinical cases. Additionally, a notable limitation lies in the demographic homogeneity of our dataset, comprising solely images from patients in China, introducing potential biases.

In the implementation of our solution, operational limitations may arise. Variability in the lighting of fundus eye images, along with diversity in image quality due to camera resolution, could impact the detection task. Additionally, the need to acquire capture equipment could pose a challenge in clinical settings with very limited resources.

5 Conclusions and Future Work

5.1 Conclusions

In this study, we demonstrate the effectiveness of our solution in detecting cataract features through a classification model based on Deep Learning integrated into a web application. We utilized Azure services, which provided the necessary infrastructure, computational power, and availability for successful implementation.

Following the experiment, positive results were achieved across accuracy, precision, sensitivity, and specificity metrics. Notably, the last two metrics hold particular significance in this study as they directly influence the early detection of cataracts and ensure the accurate identification of healthy patients.

These findings establish the viability of using the web application for fundus image analysis in patients, whether with or without cataracts, thereby enabling medical personnel to make well-informed clinical decisions.

5.2 Future Work

As part of our future work, we plan to expand our fundus image dataset to include a broader range of demographic features. Additionally, we will employ advanced data augmentation techniques to enrich our model, enabling us to cover a greater number of clinical cases and thereby improving the representativeness of our solution. Furthermore, we intend to validate our model in a real clinical environment, subjecting it to inherent complexities and challenges. This validation process will be conducted in collaboration with medical professionals and ophthalmologists, allowing us to assess the usability of our application.

Financing: Universidad Peruana de Ciencias Aplicadas / UPC-EXPOST-2023-2

Acknowledgments. We extend our appreciation to the Research Department of Universidad Peruana de Ciencias Aplicadas for their support in this research project, made possible through the UPC-EXPOST-2023-2 incentive.

References

1. Organización Mundial de la Salud (WHO): Informe mundial sobre la visión (2020). https://apps.who.int/iris/bitstream/handle/10665/331423/9789240000346-spa.pdf
2. Xiang, Y., Jiang, H., Zhao, L., Liu, Q., Lin, H.: Delays in seeking medical services in elderly patients with senile cataract. Front. Psychol. **13**, 930726 (2022). https://doi.org/10.3389/fpsyg.2022.930726
3. Reis, T., Lansingh, V., Ramke, J., Silva, J.C., Resnikoff, S., Furtado, J.M.: Cataract as a cause of blindness and vision impairment in Latin America: progress made and challenges beyond 2020. Am. J. Ophthalmol. **225**, 1–10 (2021). https://doi.org/10.1016/j.ajo.2020.12.022
4. Castaneda, C., et al.: Clinical decision support systems for improving diagnostic accuracy and achieving precision medicine. J. Clin. Bioinform. **5**, 1–16 (2015). https://pubmed.ncbi.nlm.nih.gov/25834725/
5. Zhao, Q., Shang, Z.: Deep learning and its development. J. Phys: Conf. Ser. **1948**(1), 012023 (2021). https://doi.org/10.1088/1742-6596/1948/1/012023
6. Jakhar, D., Kaur, I.: Artificial intelligence, machine learning and deep learning: definitions and differences. Clin. Exp. Dermatol. **45**, 131–132 (2019). https://doi.org/10.1111/ced.14029
7. Hu, S., et al.: ACCV: automatic classification algorithm of cataract video based on deep learning. Biomed. Eng. Online **20**, 78 (2021). https://doi.org/10.1186/s12938-021-00906-3
8. Hu, S., et al.: Unified diagnosis framework for automated nuclear cataract grading based on smartphone slit-lamp images. IEEE Access **8**, 174169–174178 (2020). https://doi.org/10.1109/ACCESS.2020.3025346
9. Xu, X., Zhang, L., Li, J., Guan, y., Zhang, L.: A hybrid global-local representation CNN model for automatic cataract grading. IEEE J. Biomed. Health Inform. **24**, 556–567 (2019) https://doi.org/10.1109/JBHI.2019.2914690
10. Zhou, Y., Li, G., Li, H.: Automatic cataract classification using deep neural network with discrete state transition. IEEE Trans. Med. Imaging **39**, 436–446 (2019). https://doi.org/10.1109/TMI.2019.2928229
11. Zéboulon, P., Panthier, C., Rouger, H., Bijon, J., Ghazal, W., Gatinel, D.: Development and validation of a pixel wise deep learning model to detect cataract on swept-source optical coherence tomography images. J. Optom. **15**, S43–S49 (2022). https://doi.org/10.1016/j.optom.2022.08.003
12. Tripathi, P., et al.: MTCD: cataract detection via near infrared eye images. Comput. Vis. Image Underst. **214**(C), 103303 (2022). https://doi.org/10.1016/j.cviu.2021.103303
13. Zheng, J., Guo, L., Peng, L., Li, J., Yang, J., Liang, Q.: Fundus image based cataract classification. In: 2014 IEEE International Conference on Imaging Systems and Techniques (IST) Proceedings, pp. 90–94 (2014). https://doi.org/10.1109/IST.2014.6958452
14. Chitaranjan, M., Koushik, T.: Fundus Camera. StatPearls (2023), https://www.ncbi.nlm.nih.gov/books/NBK585111/
15. Mitra, A., Roy, S., Roy, S., Setua, S.K.: Enhancement and restoration of non-uniform illuminated fundus image of retina obtained through thin layer of cataract. Comput. Methods Programs Biomed. **156**, 169–178 (2018). https://doi.org/10.1016/j.cmpb.2018.01.001

16. Xu, X., et al.: GLA-NET: a global-local attention network for automatic cataract classification. J. Biomed. Inform. **124**, 103939 (2021). https://doi.org/10.1016/j. jbi.2021.103939

17. Wu, X., et al.: Artificial intelligence model for antiinterference cataract automatic diagnosis: a diagnostic accuracy study. Front. Cell Dev. Biol. **10**, 906042 (2022). https://doi.org/10.3389/fcell.2022.906042

18. Lema, D.G., Pedrayes, O.D., Usamentiaga, R., Garcia, D.F., Alonso, A.: Cost-performance evaluation of a recognition service of livestock activity using aerial images. Remote Sens. **13**(12), 2318 (2021). https://doi.org/10.3390/rs13122318

19. Microsoft cognitive services: Custom vision service. https://azure.microsoft.com/ es-es/updates/cognitive-services-custom-vision-service/

20. Balakreshnan, B., Richards, G., Nanda, G., Mao, H., Athinarayanan, R., Zaccaria, J.: PPE compliance detection using artificial intelligence in learning factories. Procedia Manuf. **45**, 277–282 (2020). https://doi.org/10.1016/j.promfg.2020.04.017

21. Askarian, B., Ho, P., Chong, J.: Detecting cataract using smartphones. IEEE J. Transl. Eng. Health Med. **9**, 3800110 (2021). https://doi.org/10.1109/JTEHM. 2021.3074597

22. Ocular disease recognition. https://www.kaggle.com/datasets/andrewmvd/ocular-disease-recognition-odir5k

23. Pérez-Planells, L., Delegido, J., Rivera-Caicedo, J.P., Verrelst, J.: Analysis of cross-validation methods for robust retrieval of biophysical parameters. Revista de Teledetección **44**, 55–65 (2015). https://doi.org/10.4995/RAET.2015.4153

24. Bilal, A., Mazhar, S., Imran, A., Latif, J.: A transfer learning and U-Net-based automatic detection of diabetic retinopathy from fundus images. Comput. Methods Biomech. Biomed. Eng. Imaging Vis. **10**, 663–674 (2022). https://doi.org/10.1080/ 21681163.2021.2021111

25. Pratap, T., Kokil, P.: Automatic cataract detection in fundus retinal images using singular value decomposition. In: 2019 International Conference on Wireless Communications Signal Processing and Networking (WiSPNET), pp. 373–377 (2019). https://doi.org/10.1109/WiSPNET45539.2019.9032867

26. How to improve your custom vision model. https://learn.microsoft.com/en-us/ azure/ai-services/custom-vision-service/getting-started-improving-your-classifier

27. Hicks, S., et al.: On evaluation metrics for medical applications of artificial intelligence. Sci. Rep. **12**, 5979 (2021). https://doi.org/10.1101/2021.04.07.21254975

Analyze and Implement a Reinforced AI Chatbot in Guayaquil to Improve Mental Health in Adolescents with the Use of the Neural Generative Models

Nicole Wayn-Tze Wong Delacruz and Marco Sotomayor Sanchez[✉]

Universidad Espiritu Santo, Samborondon, Ecuador
{ndelacruz,mvinicio}@uees.edu.ec

Abstract. Mental health is vital to the development of young adolescents to create strong relationships and resilience, keeping a positive influence on society. The impact of COVID-19 on mental health is anticipated to be significant to the population, especially adolescents by depriving social contact and creating mental disorders. Currently, there are countless Chatbots that give dynamic chatbot services in health. In recent years, neural networks for natural language processing (NLP) have shown to generate more responses learned by the machine. This study aims to implement and compare two Chatbot mobile applications using Neural generative with sentiment models: OpenAI GPT-3 model, and personalized chatbot based on deep Learning, Transformer BERT, and TextBlob model. The dataset for this model was generated from a database of the flow conversation from GPT-3 and the trained bot, frequently asked questions collected at the beginning and end of the term of academic. To analyze, the sentiment it trains the dataset used in the conversation which validates the prediction through a confusion matrix which resulted in test accuracy frequently correct is 70% for Transformer Bert and 68% in TextBlob. To test the usability of the chatbot and application, a survey was conducted on a group of 30 participants, using Chatbot Usability Questionnaire (CUQ) and Linkert scale, it showed that GPT-3 CUQ Mean is 77,71 higher than Deep Learning. As for the Linkert scale, it was verified that 68% of participants perceived that the chatbot was adequate to their concerns, as well that the acceptance rate was 90%.

Keywords: Chatbot · Artificial Intelligence · Sentimental Analysis · OpenAI · Transformers

1 Introduction

Mental health services are vital for children and adolescents, positively impacting well-being and introducing a revised care paradigm [12]. The 2019, COVID-19 pandemic amplified concerns about mental health, prompting technological solutions for timely support and counseling [1]. In the realm of chatbots, the Turing Test initiated AI-driven conversational development, necessitating substantial data for effective chatbot functioning [6, 21]. Over two decades, AI in healthcare faced challenges, exploring user-facing AI systems via the Turing test [16].

Advancements in neural network language models, notably the transformer architecture, replaced traditional models and birthed transformative models like BERT, GPT, and T5 [17]. BERT excels in tasks such as question answering and text generation, focusing on the encoder scheme, while GPT-3's release in 2022 showcased the power of unsupervised learning for healthcare challenges [14].

This study deploys two AI chatbots, OpenAI's GPT-3 and a personalized Deep Learning-based chatbot, for mental health improvement. Analyzing user interactions from Guayaquil residents and university students (ages 10–20) using BERT and TextBlob models, the study aims to evaluate the models' accuracy in identifying text sentiment and assess the chatbots' usability in addressing user concerns.

2   Related Work

2.1   Chatbots in Mental Health

Chatbots have evolved significantly since Turing's "imitation game" [22]. From early versions like ELIZA [7] to more advanced forms used in mental health [5], these chatbots now help express emotions, resonating with Roger's therapy concepts [11, 18]. Modern chatbots incorporate advanced NLP techniques [3], moving towards using pre-trained models like BERT and GPT-2, despite their limitations [26].

2.2   AI and Healthcare

AI's role in healthcare, especially with neural network language models, has been transformative. The transition from traditional models to advanced architectures like BERT and GPT [17] has opened new possibilities in healthcare AI. OpenAI and DeepMind are key players in this field [2, 20], with models like GPT-3 showing remarkable capabilities in text generation and analysis [20, 25].

2.3   Key Concepts

– **Neural Network** [19]: A system designed to mimic the human brain, processing data for pattern recognition and problem-solving.
– **Deep Learning** [8, 13]: A complex form of AI, where deep networks learn from data to perform tasks like image classification and language processing.
– **Transformer Language Model** [23, 24]: A modern approach in AI that significantly enhances chatbot development and NLP by adopting mechanisms like positional encoding and attention.

3   Methodology

This research uses a mixed-methods approach, leveraging Deep Learning to predict and classify user sentiments. The study involves two main components:

3.1 Chatbot Development

- **Chatbots Used:** The study incorporates two chatbots, OpenAI's GPT-3 and a personalized Deep Learning chatbot.
- **Tools:** The GPT-3 chatbot is developed using OpenAI's Davinci model, fine-tuned for specific tasks. The personalized chatbot, built using Python and NLP libraries, employs sentiment analysis with TextBlob and Transformer BERT models.
- **Application Design:** The chatbot application is implemented in Android Studios using Java, with its design prototyped in Adobe XD (Fig. 1).

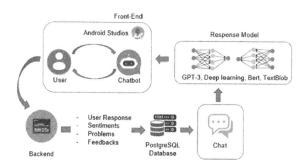

Fig. 1. System Overview

3.2 Methodological Design

- **SCRUM Methodology:** The project follows the SCRUM agile development methodology, comprising four phases: Data Collection, Preparation, Model Design, and Results Analysis (Fig. 2).

- **Data Collection:** Involves gathering data from professional therapists, individuals in Guayaquil and Samborondon, Ecuador, and university faculties.

- **Data Preparation:** To customize GPT-3's behavior and incorporate specific topics, the initial step involved fine-tuning the pre-trained model by modifying it according to our requirements. This process began with formatting the topics and defining the AI's user interactions into a.txt file with a specific structure.

[Description of the AI]
Imagine a conversation with the Friend and a AI. The AI start a conversation and ask how are things going to the Friend, be kind, friendly, considerate and give advice when the user ask for help. The Friend is a sentimental and lonely person.
<<BLOCK>>
[Topics]

- Loneliness from being single
- Being burned out from work
- Difficult family members

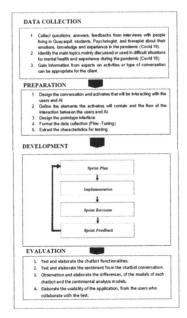

Fig. 2. Methodology design for the present study of the investigation.

- Struggling with anxiety
- Coping with depression
- Difficult people at work
- Teenaged children problems
- Mental problems
- Break up with boyfriend
- Being betrayed by friends and family
- Anger control issues
- Anxiety of being home alone
- Asking for mental health advice
- Friend talks about violent thoughts but AI discourages acting out in violence and recommends safe alternatives.

After formatting the information into a .txt file, training involves converting it into a JSON file to match OpenAI's input format. The training process utilizes GPT-3 and requires an OpenAI API key, available on the OpenAI website. Developers can follow the provided documentation to fine-tune the chatbot and personalize responses. The assigned parameters for this process are detailed below:

- Prompt
- Engine: 'text-curie-001'
- Temp: 0.7
- Top_p = 1.0
- Tokens = 1000
- Freq_pen = 0.0
- Pres_pen = 0.0
- Stop = ['<<END>>']

To obtain the API key and also reference on the Fine-tuning is based from OpenAI page [15].

Using the set parameters and descriptions for the 14 selected topics, the chatbot is generated four times. This results in a total of 56 unique conversations for each topic, showcasing how the chatbot responds to users. The saved conversations are formatted into a .json file.

The .json file is uploaded to the OpenAI website using the API key for authorization, specifying the personalized model ID as "chatbotcompanion" within the davinci model. Once submitted, OpenAI creates the model with the assigned ID, allowing its integration into our engine. The chatbot implementation then utilizes these parameters in the following format:

- Prompt
- Engine: 'davinci: ft-personal:chatbotcompanion-2022-07-19-13-20-16'
- Temp: 0.7
- Top_p = 1.0
- Tokens = 400
- Freq_pen = 0.0
- Pres_pen = 0.0
- Stop = ['<<END>>', 'AI', 'Friend']

For the Deep Learning-based chatbot, the intents, tags, patterns, and responses were formatted in a JSON file, as illustrated below:

```
{
  "intents":[{
        "tag":"greeting",
        "patterns":[
          "Hi",
          "Hey",
          "How are you",
          "How are you doing",
          "Is anyone there?",
          "What's up?",
          "Hello",
          "Good day",
          "What's popping"
  ],
  "responses":[
      "Hi there, I'm doing well! What can I do for you?",
      "Hey there, your mental health friend. How can I help you today?"],
        "context_set":""
  },
      ...
```

The formatted file is trained using Python 3.10.4 with libraries like nltk, Numpy, Tensorflow, Flask, and tflearn. Neurons are configured with a softmax activation function, involving six output neurons with associated probabilities, trained over 1000 epochs and a batch size of 8 for two hidden layers.

- **Model Training:** The GPT-3 model is fine-tuned with formatted topics and user interactions. The Deep Learning-based chatbot's training involves Python libraries and an analysis of test metrics (Table 1).

Table 1. Matric Value of generating the model.

Epoch	Train Loss	Accuracy	Time
400	0.14413	0.9599	0.062s
500	0.18598	0.9383	0.062s
600	0.14356	0.9577	0.062s
700	0.12844	0.9656	0.031s
800	0.09319	0.9647	0.031s
900	1.25993	0.8614	0.047s
1000	0.17790	0.9298	0.047s

Note. Result of the testing has a training loss of 0.17 and accuracy is 0.92.

4 Implementation

The implementation process follows the four stages of the methodological design:

Phase 1 - Data Collection: Data is collected via Zoom meetings, and a Google survey distributed through social media.

Phase 2 - Preparation: The chatbot's conversation design and activities are guided by psychological recommendations from Sharmilla Persaud and Jane Persaud MS, and the mobile application prototype is created (Fig. 3).

Fig. 3. Principal page and the Main Menu page elaborated in Adobe XD.

Phase 3 - Development: The screens are integrated on OpenAI GPT-3 and a Python-trained bot into Android Studios (Fig. 4). TextBlob for sentiment analysis was implemented, measuring polarity from 1 to −1. User testing captured conversations in a compressed PostgreSQL dataset (.csv) with user and AI responses and sentiments (Positive, Negative, Neutral). Navigation and front-end were completed. Feedback from users in Samborondon and Guayaquil was incorporated, leading to design improvements. Information from user conversations will be analyzed using TextBlob and Transformer BERT sentimental models in Google Colab for efficiency and effectiveness (Fig. 5).

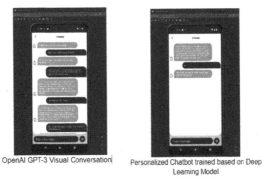

OpenAI GPT-3 Visual Conversation | Personalized Chatbot trained based on Deep Learning Model

Fig. 4. Development of the chatbots and test in console to visualization for Front-end.

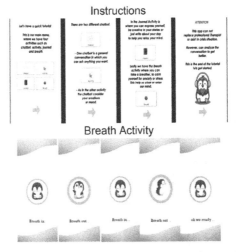

Fig. 5. Screens added that have been indicated for instructions and Breath Activity.

After testing the chatbot, we gather 809 chat datasets and convert the database to a .csv file. Using Google Colab, we train sentiment analysis models, Transformer Bert, and TextBlob. For Transformer BERT, we follow Jacob Devlin's practices at Google [4], adapting the model to our chatbot's conversation database. The process involves the following libraries:

- Numpy version: 1.21.6
- Pandas version: 1.3.5
- Torch version: 1.12.0+cu113
- Transformers version: 4.21.0

Using an NVIDIA-SMI processor GPU for faster Google Colab execution, Data Preprocessing for BERT demands specific steps:

- Add special tokens for sentence separation and classification.
- Enforce constant sequence length (introduce padding).

– Create an array of 0 s (pad token) and 1 s (real token) as an attention mask.

Leveraging the Transformers library, we utilize the 'bert-base-cased' pretrained model and tokenizer for BERT. Special tokens like [SEP] for sentence ending, [CLS] for classification start, and [PAD] for padding are incorporated. BERT recognizes tokens from the training set, with [UNK] representing unknown tokens. This approach determines token quantity in each sequence from the dataset, allowing us to choose an appropriate sequence length based on the conversation database with users and AI, aligning with BERT's fixed-length sequence requirement (Fig. 6).

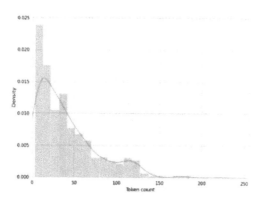

Fig. 6. Distribution of the token length of each conversation of the chatbot and user.

Opting for a maximum length of 160, as most conversations contain fewer than 128 tokens, our BERT sentimental classification training employs the following hyperparameters with the Adam model version:

– Batch size: 16, 32
– Learning rate (Adam): 5e−5, 3e−5, 2e−5
– Number of epochs: Ignoring the recommended number, focusing on the rest.

The best model is saved based on the highest validation accuracy, observed on the 5th epoch, achieving an accuracy of 0.72 (Table 2).

Achieving a 70% accuracy in test results, the training CPU time for users is 2 min and 4 s, for the system is 1 min and 3 s, totaling 3 min and 8 s of wait. The wall time is 3 min and 15 s. The TextBlob model, utilizing TensorFlow, Pandas, NLTK, and Scikit-learn on the same database as BERT, labels sentiments as Positive, Neutral, and Negative during chatbot conversations.These sentiments are replaced with polarity values of 1, 0, and − 1, respectively. Initially, sentiments are dropped, focusing on the content of user replies to the first 5 rows (Fig. 7).

Applying polarity measures to each text, categorizing them as greater than 0, equal to 0, or less than 0 (Fig. 8).

With this we convert these numbers to sentiments dividing it to Negative, Neutral and Positive (Fig. 9).

Table 2. Matric Value generated by the model.

Epoch	Train loss	Accuracy	Value loss	Accuracy
1	1 0398	0 4876	1 0164	0 5
2	0 8099	0 6085	0 8399	0 55
3	0 5862	0 7101	0 9104	0 55
4	0 3627	0.8461	1.0852	0 65
5	0 1289	0.9258	1.2832	0.72
6	0 0985	0 9725	1 6637	0 7
7	0 0574	0 9862	2 0206	0 7
8	0 0274	0 9903	2 1144	0 7
9	0 0270	0 9903	2 1801	0 7
10	0 0208	0 9931	2 2007	0 7

Note. The result of the testing of the highest validation accuracy is in the 5 Epoch of 0.72.

	content
0	im fine thank you and you?
1	Hey!
2	thanks
3	why?
4	how are you?

Fig. 7. First 5 rows of the Dataset from the Chatbot.

Fig. 8. Polarity of each text from the User.

After defining each context with sentiment, the model was trained on user conversation content and sentiments in the database. The test accuracy, based on a 20% test size and a seed of 42, was 68.57%.

	content	polarity	sentiment
0	im fine thank you and you?	0.416667	Positive
1	Hey!	0.000000	Neutral
2	thanks	0.200000	Positive
3	why?	0.000000	Neutral
4	how are you?	0.000000	Neutral

Fig. 9. Applying Sentiments to Polarity.

Phase 4 - Sprint 4: Final adjustments are made to enhance user interactions with the chatbot.

5 Evaluation

5.1 Model Validation

- **Method:** Sentiment models (Transformer BERT and TextBlob) were evaluated using a confusion matrix for accuracy in sentiment prediction [9].
- **Results:** TextBlob showed 72% precision in identifying positive sentiments, while Transformer BERT had 85% precision for positive sentiments (Figs. 10 and 11). BERT was more effective in sentiment analysis, with higher positive polarity (0.87) and overall test accuracy of 70% compared to TextBlob's 68% (Fig. 12).

	precision	recall	f1-score	support
Negative	0.12	0.05	0.07	21
Neutral	0.71	0.44	0.55	27
Positive	0.72	0.90	0.80	92
accuracy			0.69	140
macro avg	0.52	0.46	0.47	140
weighted avg	0.63	0.69	0.64	140

Fig. 10. TextBlob classification report.

	precision	recall	f1-score	support
negative	0.50	0.14	0.22	7
neutral	0.58	0.73	0.65	15
positive	0.85	0.89	0.87	19
accuracy			0.71	41
macro avg	0.64	0.59	0.58	41
weighted avg	0.69	0.71	0.68	41

Fig. 11. Transformer BERT classification report.

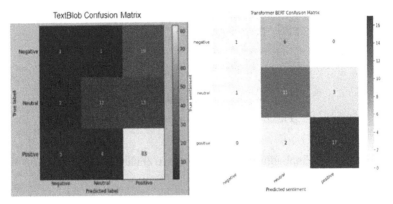

Fig. 12. TextBlob and Transformer Confusion Matrix

5.2 Chatbot Usability Measurement

To evaluate our models there are three separate sections in which evaluate the usability for the OpenAI GPT-3, personalized trained based Deep learning chatbot and the last questionnaire is the use of the application flow. The following questionnaire was used. For the chatbot questionnaire of usability for personalized trained based Deep Learning OpenAI GPT-3:

1. The chatbot personality was realistic and engaging.
2. The chatbot seemed too robotic.
3. The chatbot was welcoming during the initial setup.
4. The chatbot seemed very unfriendly.
5. The chatbot explained its purpose well.
6. The chatbot gave no indication as to its purpose.
7. The chatbot was easy to navigate.
8. It would be easy to get confused when using the chatbot.
9. The chatbot understood me well.
10. It was repeating the same answer/questions.
11. The chatbot was very easy to use.
12. The Chatbot failed to recognize a lot of my responses/questions.
13. The chatbot helped me through the process.
14. The chatbot was very complex.
15. The chatbot was useful and helpful.
16. Chatbot responses were irrelevant.

5.3 Usability Study Results (According to CUQ)

- **Tool:** Chatbot-specific Usability Questionnaire (CUQ) based on a 16-question format [10]. Usage method in which the odd number questions are positive responses and the even number questions are negative responses the qualification for each response is based on an agreement of the question such as: 1 (Strongly Disagree), 2 (Disagree), 3 (Neutral), 4 (Agree), 5 (Strongly Agree). With this information obtained from each response on both chatbot demonstrated in Table 3 and 4.

Table 3. Survey result of measuring the Open AI GPT-3 chatbot usability.

	CUQ Score		CUQ Score		CUQ Score
P1	65,63	P11	90,63	P21	87,50
P2	64,06	P12	71,88	P22	59,38
P3	79,69	P13	75,00	P23	75,00
P4	78,13	P14	71,88	P24	95,31
P5	62,50	P15	85,94	P25	90,63
P6	79,69	P16	57,81	P26	78,13
P7	90,63	P17	73,44	P27	76,56
P8	70,31	P18	82,21	P28	93,75
P9	64,06	P19	78,13	P29	73,44
P10	89,06	P20	81,25	P30	84,38

Note. The survey was conducted with 30 people who live in Samborondon, Guayaquil, and students from the university campus.

Table 4. Survey result of measuring the personalized pretrained chatbot based on Deep Learning usability.

	CUQ Score		CUQ Score		CUQ Score
P1	32,81	P11	37,5	P21	10,94
P2	35,94	P12	21,88	P22	32,81
P3	45,31	P13	28,13	P23	28,13
P4	39,06	P14	37,5	P24	29,69
P5	32,81	P15	39,06	P25	7,81
P6	39,06	P16	35,94	P26	23,44
P7	45,31	P17	17,19	P27	1,56
P8	37,5	P18	21,88	P28	20,31
P9	35,94	P19	17,19	P29	12,5
P10	14,06	P20	26,56	P30	10,94

Note. The survey was conducted with 30 people who live in Samborondon, Guayaquil, and students from the university campus.

Analyzing responses from 30 participants in Samborondon, Guayaquil, and university students, the CUQ Score was calculated using the following steps:

1. Calculate the sum of all the odd number questions.
2. Calculate the sum of all the even number questions.
3. Subtract 8 from step 2.
4. Subtract the total number of step 3 from 40.
5. Add steps 3 and 4 giving you the total out of 64.
6. Lastly convert step 5 to a score out of 100.

As an example we will take the first participant in OpenAI GPT-3 dataset:

1. Add all the odd number (Positive) questions:
   $5 + 4 + 4 + 3 + 4 + 4 + 2 + 4 = 30$
2. Add all the even number (Negative) questions:
   $2 + 3 + 1 + 2 + 4 + 3 + 3 + 2 = 20$
3. Subtract 8 from step 1:
   $30 - 8 = 22$

4. Subtract step 2 from 40:
   $40 - 20 = 20$
5. Add step 3 and 4:
   $22 + 20 = 42$ (out of 64)
6. Convert step 5 to a score out of 100:
   $(42/64) * 100 = 65, 63\%$
   CUQ Score $= 65, 63\%$

For all 30 participants, the CUQ Scores were calculated, demonstrating a preference for OpenAI GPT-3 over the personalized chatbot based on Deep Learning, with OpenAI GPT-3 being more successful.

– **Results:** CUQ scores indicated a preference for OpenAI GPT-3 over the personalized Deep Learning chatbot, with GPT-3 scoring higher on positive aspects like realistic personality (4.53 vs. 2.13) and welcoming setup (4.3 vs. 2.7) (Figs. 13 and 14). GPT-3's average CUQ score was higher (77.71 vs. 27.29) (Table 5).

Fig. 13. Average ranking for the positive aspects of OpenAI GPT-3 and personalized chatbot based on Deep Learning.

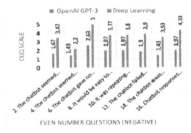

Fig. 14. Average ranking for the negative aspects of OpenAI GPT-3 and the personalized chatbot based on Deep Learning usability.

5.4 Mobile Application Usability

– **Method:** Likert scale questionnaire assessing various aspects of the mobile application's usability.

Table 5. CUQ Calculation results of the Survey

Chatbot	CUQ Mean	CUQ Median	Highest Score	Lowest Score
OpenAl GPT-3	77,71	78,13	95,31	57,81
Deep Learning	27,29	28,91	45,31	1,56

Note. Chatbot Usability Questionnaire (CUQ) Scores for study participants (n = 30).

– **Questions Asked for the Usability of the Mobile Application:**
1. How helpful and friendly the service is?
2. Did it help you with your concerns or problems?
3. Speed of Service.
4. Was the language familiar?
5. How smooth the conversation went?
6. The overall quality of the service.
7. How much would you recommend it?

Table 6. Survey Results for measuring the mobile application usability.

	Total		Total		Total
P1	21	P11	22	P21	26
P2	21	P12	26	P22	21
P3	22	P13	28	P23	21
P4	21	P14	21	P24	32
P5	19	P15	21	P25	28
P6	20	P16	21	P26	28
P7	25	P17	22	P27	25
P8	21	P18	21	P28	28
P9	24	P19	26	P29	25
P10	23	P20	23	P30	35

Note. The survey was conducted with 30 people who live in Samborondon, Guayaquil and students from the university campus.

Analyzing Table 6, participants scored a maximum of 35 points (7 items multiplied by 5). Ranges include 0–12 (dissatisfaction), 13–24 (recognizing goodness with room for improvement), and 25–35 (satisfaction with room for enhancement). Participants scored within 13 to 24, indicating recognition of the chatbot's potential usability. The average score per subject is calculated by dividing the total score by the number of items. For example, a subject scoring 21 out of 35, divided by 7 items, yields an average of 3, suggesting a favorable scenario.

– **Results:** Participants gave scores indicating recognition of the chatbot's potential usability, with an average score of 3.41 out of 5, suggesting a favorable scenario (Fig. 15). Overall satisfaction average was 3.41 (Fig. 16).

Fig. 15. Average of Satisfaction of the Survey of the Chatbot usability.

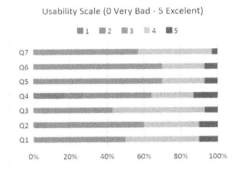

Fig. 16. Linkert Graph of chatbot Usability

6   Conclusions, Limitations, and Future Work

This study implements a reinforced AI Chatbot for mental health, comparing OpenAI GPT-3 with a personalized Deep Learning model. The Deep Learning model achieves a loss of 0.17 and accuracy of 0.92, indicating acceptable language prediction. Transformer BERT and TextBlob correctly identify emotions, with BERT having higher precision (0.85 vs. 0.80). Usability evaluation using CUQ favors GPT-3 (mean 77.71) over the personalized chatbot (mean 27.29). Application usability scores 3.41/5, suggesting participants are not entirely satisfied. However, 90% approve of the application's potential mental health impact. Limitations include GPT-3's English-only support, API costs, and challenges in real-time response accuracy. Future research should focus on refining GPT-3's capabilities for specific user situations and exploring concurrent use of GPT-3 and Transformer BERT.

References

1. Abd-Alrazaq, A.A., Alajlani, M., Ali, N., Denecke, K., Bewick, B.M., Househ, M.: Perceptions and opinions of patients about mental health chatbots: scoping review. JMIR Publ. **23**(1), e17828 (2021). https://doi.org/10.2196/17828
2. Brockman, G.: Microsoft Invest in and Partners with OpenAI to Support us Building Beneficial AI. OpenAI, 22 July 2019. https://openai.com/blog/microsoft/
3. Chen, T., Xu, R., He, Y., Wang, X.: Improving sentiment analysis via sentence type classification using BiLSTM-CRF and CNN, 221–230 (2017). https://doi.org/10.1016/j.eswa.2016.10.065
4. Devlin, J., Chang, M.-W., Lee, K., Toutanova, K.: BERT: Pre-training of Deep Bidirectional Transformers for Language Understanding. Cornell University, pp. 1–16 (2019). https://arxiv.org/pdf/1810.04805.pdf

5. Hawton, K.D., Saunders, K.E., O'Connor, R.: Self-harm and suicide in adolescents. Lancet **379**(9834), 2373–2382 (2012). https://doi.org/10.1016/SO140-6736(12)60322-5
6. Hutapea, A.: Chatbot: Architecture, Design & Development. Academia Accelerating the world's research, pp. 1–46 (2017). https://d1wqtxts1xzle7.cloudfront.net/57035006/CHA TBOT_thesis_final-with-cover-page-v2.pdf?Expires=1659211295&Signature=amkLr8qfq 5FTBy4vFhvIZoHXIvidiOXYYhtVsMHyN6F3RjamW1k1x9a5n~NTqU-4zAB8qTJjdYX MsSsXWiQDc9GkFNMF6mJ8kDVMcZVxHGS3pX74kuEHDQzB9AzeLJeCrOIIfBi
7. K.M., C.: Artificial Paranoia: a computer program for the study of natural language communication between man and machine. Commun. ACM, 36–45 (1975). Artificial Intelligence Laboratory
8. Kriegeskorte, N., Golan, T.: Neural network models and deep learning. Curr. Biol. Mag. **29** (2019). https://reader.elsevier.com/reader/sd/pii/S0960982219302040?token=B299B4 B1DCF55E7FB3646AC97D10763E253DF446465CABD6D69176C1BB930244CD0DD 3F418CD13CA57D3C712779A834D&originRegion=us-east-1&originCreation=202208 01180444
9. Krstinic, D., Braovic, M., Seric, L., Stulic, D.B.: Multi-label classifier performance evaluation with confusion matrix. Faculty of Electrical Engineering, Mechanical Engineering and Naval Architecture, pp. 1–14 (2020). file:///C:/Users/SMARTPC/Downloads/1069692.csit100801.pdf
10. Larbi, D., Denecke, K., Gabarron, E.: Usability testing of a social media chatbot for increasing physical activity behavior. J. Pers. Med., 1–10 (2022). https://doi.org/10.3390/jpm12050828
11. Liu, Y., Liu, M., Wang, X., Wang, L., Li , J.: PAL: A Chatterbot System for Answering Domain-specific Questions. Harbin Institute of Technology, pp. 67–72 (2013). https://aclant hology.org/P13-4012.pdf
12. Farmer, E.M., Burns, B.J., Phillips, S.D., Angold, A., Costello, E.J.: Pathways into and through mental health services for children and adolescents. Psychiatr. Serv., 60–66 (2003). https://doi.org/10.1176/appi.ps.54.1.60
13. Micheli, A., Schleif, F., Tiño, P.: Novel approaches in machine learning and computational intelligence. Neurocomputing **112**, 1–3 (2013)
14. Nath, S., Marie, A., Ellershaw, S., Korot, E., Kaene, P.A.: New meaning for NLP: the trials and tribulations of natural language processing with GPT-3 in ophthalmology. BMJ J. **106**(7), 1 (2022). https://doi.org/10.1136/bjophthalmol-2022-321141
15. OpenAI.: OpenAI. Obtenido de Build next-gen apps with OpenAI's powerful models (2015–2022). https://openai.com/api/
16. Powell, J.: Trust me, i'm a chatbot: how artificial intelligence in health care fails the turing test. JMIR Publ. Adv. Digit. Health Open Sci. **21**(10), 1–4 (2019). https://doi.org/10.2196/16222
17. Ravichandiran,S.: Getting Started with Google BERT: Build and Train State-of-the-Art Natural Models Using BERT. Packt Publishing Ltd., United Kingdom (2021). https://books.google.es/books?hl=es&lr=&id=CvsWEAAAQBAJ&oi=fnd&pg=PP1&dq=when+transf ormer+and+bert+started&ots=3GjLu1mf7-&sig=25w1qC8zB7HD_Yi98ASDA5gExKw# v=onepage&q=when%20transformer%20and%20bert%20started&f=false
18. Rogers, C.R.: On becoming a person: A therapist's view of psychotherapy. Houghton Mifflin Company, Boston (1995). https://books.google.es/books?hl=es&lr=&id=0yHBXX hJbKQC&oi=fnd&pg=PR9&dq=On+becoming+a+person:+A+therapist%27s+view+of+ psychotherapy&ots=7u-Ss9GykZ&sig=RGUNb_OzHX12OWuGMRhQAyvEM3Q#v= onepage&q=On%20becoming%20a%20person%3A%20A%20therapist's%20view%20o f%20p
19. Rohil, H.: ResearchGate. Retrieved from License Plate Recognition System using Back Propagation Neural Network, August 2014. https://www.researchgate.net/figure/Block-Diagram-of-Artificial-Neural-Network_fig3_272863336

20. Scott, K.: Microsoft teams up with OpenAI to exclusively license GPT-3 language model, 22 September 2020. Official Microsoft Blog. https://blogs.microsoft.com/blog/2020/09/22/microsoft-teams-up-with-openai-to-exclusively-license-gpt-3-language-model/
21. Setiaji, B., Wibowo, F.W.: Chatbot using a knowledge in database: human-to-machine conversation modeling. In: 2016 7th International Conference on Intelligent Systems, Modelling and Simulation (ISMS), pp. 72–77 (2016). https://doi.org/10.1109/ISMS.2016.53
22. Turing, A., Haugeland, J.: Computing machinery and intelligence. In: Shieber, S.M. (ed.) The Turing Test: Verbal Behavior as the Hallmark of Intelligence, pp. 29–56. 2004 Massachusetts Institute of Technology, Cambridge (1950). https://books.google.es/books?hl=es&lr=&id=CEMYUU_HFMAC&oi=fnd&pg=PA67&dq=turing+1950+computing+machinery+and+intelligence&ots=dQijOW10cA&sig=GUOR45Qdbxf5BRq8-Ho9g0Qrmkw#v=onepage&q=turing%201950%20computing%20machinery%20and%20intelligence&f=false
23. Vaswani, A., et al.: Attention is all you need. In: 31st Conference on Neural Information Processing Systems, pp. 1–15 (2017). https://arxiv.org/pdf/1706.03762.pdf
24. Vaswani, A., et al.: Attention is all you need. Cornell University, pp. 1–15 (2017). https://arxiv.org/pdf/1706.03762v5.pdf
25. Wiggers, K.: OpenAI's massive GPT-3 model is impressive, nit size isn't everything. VentureBeat (2020)
26. Zhang, J., Oh, Y.J., Lange, P., Yu, Z., Fukuoka, Y.: Artificial intelligence chatbot behavior change model for designing artificial intelligence chatbots to promote physical activity and a healthy diet: viewpoint. JMIR Publ. **22**(9), 1–33 (2020)

Detection of Ovarian Cancer Using Improved Deep Learning Model

Mohammed Ahmed Mustafa[1]($\boxtimes$), Zainab Failh Allami[2], Mohammed Yousif Arabi[3], Maki Mahdi Abdulhasan[4], Ghadir Kamil Ghadir[5], and Hayder Musaad Al-Tmimi[6]

[1] Department of Medical Laboratory Technology, University of Imam Jaafar AL-Sadiq, Baghdad, Iraq
Mohammed.ahmed.mustafa@sadiq.edu.iq
[2] Al-Manara College For Medical Sciences, Maysan, Iraq
[3] College of Computer, National University of Science and Technology, Dhi Qar, Iraq
[4] Department of Medical Laboratories Technology, AL-Nisour University College, Baghdad, Iraq
[5] College of Pharmacy, Al-Farahidi University, Baghdad, Iraq
[6] College of Health Medical Techniques, Al-Bayan University, Baghdad, Iraq

Abstract. Ovarian cancer (OC), the most common kind, accounts for more than half of all cases of gynecological cancer in women. The classification of OC might result in several distinct diagnoses (Serous, Mucinous, Endometrioid, Clear Cell). Pathologists use computer-aided diagnosis to assist them make accurate diagnoses. Deep convolutional neural networks (DCNNs) that have previously been trained can recognize, forecast, and classify the different kinds of ovarian cancer. An improved VGG-16 algorithmic structure contains thirteen convolution layers, three of which are linked. In addition, there are five maximum pooling layers and one softmax layer. After capturing 500 images, the model was only recognized with a 50% accuracy rate after training (100 from each class). Using a variety of image processing techniques, we were able to produce a total of 24742 more images from the initial dataset of 500 shots. Only after training on a much bigger dataset did the model's accuracy increase from 50 to 84%. For the first time, VGG16 histopathological scans are being utilized to diagnose and forecast cancer ovarian tissue.

Keywords: Computer-Aided Design · Deep learning · Histopathological Image Classification · Ovarian cancer · VGG16

1 Introduction

The most common kind of gynecological cancer, ovarian cancer is commonly referred to as "ovarian cancer". Ovarian cancer is classified into four subtypes: mucous, endometrioid/clear cell, mucinous, and serous. The most common kind of ovarian cancer is serious. Only pathologists are qualified to distinguish between the four forms of cancer show hematologicalgical slides. Pathologists are the only medical specialists who can tell the difference in this way [1–3]. When a huge number of images must be reviewed and identified, the possibility of human error increases. Automated diagnosis, or CAD, was utilised in a variety of tests to increase pathologists' accuracy while reducing the amount of manual labour they had to undertake. The use of frameworks like CAD allows for more exact measurements, while prior information plays a less important role in the analysis. Much of our recent success in CAD innovation may be attributed to technological advancements. A rising number of studies [4, 5] have used advanced medical imaging technologies such as computer-aided design. Chang et al. developed this method for analysing liver cancer based on multiphase CT images that highlight tumour characteristics. CAD to discriminate between benign and malignant thyroid tumours [6], a decision assistance system for cone beam computer tomography to aid in the early diagnosis of keratocystic and dental periapical cysts. This approach's purpose is to aid in the identification of these disorders. The purpose of creating this framework was to make it easier to recognise various ailments [7]. CAD systems, also known as "second opinions," are a type of medical diagnostic software designed to provide an unbiased "second opinion" during the identification and diagnosis of health issues. In addition to aiding in diagnosis and treatment, CAD technology may be used to "review" patient data. This can be achieved by employing a distinct method of data analysis. This is made feasible by the utilisation of various technological applications. The data visualisation tools provide these options. CAD solutions can cut down on the time spent figuring out what a picture means while making the diagnostic process more accurate. A system for analysing breast cell histopathology images that uses a programmatically quantified support vector machine. This method was used to analyse images [8]. Researchers employed computer vision and machine learning techniques like pattern recognition and image processing to detect lung nodules. The approach described in follows many of the same concepts. The CAD system uses fuzzy systems and evolutionary algorithms [9], in research that combined arterial spin labelling and diffusion tensor imaging, support vector machines [10, 11]. Because of the findings of this evaluation, the participants in the research were separated into two distinct groups: those with Alzheimer's disease and those with frontotemporal dementia. A unique method of testing to detect whether a person has a brain condition. This method is routinely used to identify the source of a neurological condition. According to recent evaluation results, ML is widely employed in CAD because it was first utilised in biological image processing, it is possible to connect it to the concept of deep learning. You may begin right here, at the beginning. Deep learning, as opposed to task-specific algorithms, encompasses a broader range of approaches. These strategies enable the development of competence in data representation.

Deep learning algorithms such as DBNs and CNNs use raw pixel data in its unprocessed condition as input. Classic image processing systems are built around models that have been trained on object segmentation characteristics, for a more basic and appetising depiction of the original, an image might be broken into pieces. This can make navigating the image simpler. Segmenting is a technique for finding and separating specific traits and limitations within an image (such as lines, curves, etc.). This fundamental approach combines expanding regions, spreading regions, and merging regions to discover neighbouring pixels within an image. Following that, models of these features are trained to recognise them in others. Deep learning algorithms such as DBNs and CNNs use raw pixel data in its unprocessed form as input. It is faster and easier to understand because the process of computing features and segmenting objects is no longer necessary. Deep learning, a fast-expanding topic, has subsequently drawn academics from a variety of domains, including biomedical imaging [12, 13]. DCNN initiation features may be utilised to segment, categorise, and display tissue histology pictures. A computerised system for diagnosing lung tumours using Deep Convolutional Neural Networks [14]. Microscopy was utilised to examine these images of lung tumours, produced with the same procedure [15]. DCNNs as they are more officially termed, have been shown by Gao and colleagues to be capable of independently detecting pictures of cells collected from human epithelial-2. In practise, the structure proved to be exact as well as adaptable.

A convolutional neural network to diagnose the kind of lung cancer present in pulmonic nodules, the purpose of this technique was to provide computer-aided decision assistance. A variety of organisations are now attempting to use CNNs in clinical imaging, with varying degrees of success. According to our findings, VGGNet has never been used to classify ovarian tumours. Wu M's pre-trained AlexNet improved from 78% to 84% after training. As the focus of our work, we employed DCNN to classify a range of ovarian cancer subtypes using histology images, both with and without augmentation. The outcomes of this study can help clinical pathologists and technologists decide whether to undertake a biopsy on a suspected tumour. AlexNet was used to build and train Deep Convolutional Neural Networks (DCNNs) that might be used to automatically detect the subtype of ovarian cancer seen in cytological pictures. The deep convolutional neural network includes seven layers in total, with five of them being convolutional layers, three being max pooling levels, and two being complete reconnect layers (DCNN). The model was then trained using two distinct sets of input data: (1) raw data from the original photographs; and (2) iterations of the same images that had been rotated and enhanced. The testing results reveal that the classification model's accuracy rose from 72.76% to 78.20% as the picture quality utilised as training data improved. The 10-fold cross-validation method was used to show that this claim is true.

The following is a list of each author's different contributions: In the first phase, one data set is analysed, the default class count for the pre-trained model was 1,000, but this was lowered to 5 to represent the scope's various subtypes. Using this method, it was feasible to reduce the node count of the pre-trained architecture from 4096 to 128. In data categorization models, network topologies such as AlexNet, Google, and VGGNet are employed. These structural characteristics can help differentiate malignant tissue from surrounding benign tissue on histology slides. The healthy and malignant tissue were close together. Because of their high degree of flexibility, multi-layer artificial neural networks are prone to overfitting the training data, which is problematic when the training dataset is small. This is especially true if only a small quantity of training data was used. This issue is more likely when the quantity of the training dataset is limited. Our primary framework was built on top of pre-trained convolutional neural networks. The ImageNet dataset was used to produce the weights for these networks, which were then used to train the models. This was done to prevent the possibility of overfitting, and it worked! Frameworks that have been trained on millions of images have been shown to extract essential visual information from images. These frameworks have been shown to be suitable for the purpose. There must be more allusions to this. Some of these parts, like edges, circles, and object bulbs, may be the building blocks for more difficult tasks involving picture recognition. According to our review of relevant published material, ovarian cancer has not been classified using VGGNet. This was discovered following an extensive assessment of the existing literature. Several papers have recently emphasised VGGNet's potential utility in cancer prediction. One of these early research projects inspired the idea for our original product.

2 Material and Method

2.1 Dataset

The Cancer Genome Atlas Ovarian Cancer Collection (TCGA-OV) is utilised in this study [16]. Owing to the hospital's small patient population, collecting histology slides of the carcinoma subtype OC was difficult due to the absence of other types of cancer. Experimental pathologists gathered the patients' tissue and treated it so that it could be examined on slides. They prepared and coloured the cell samples using equipment and materials from their own laboratory. The images were captured on film with a Leica ICC50, a smaller version of the company's famed camera. This 5-megapixel camera can send video to desktop PCs as well as mobile devices. The examination of the Cancer Genome Atlas-Ovarian Cancer database yielded pictures of carcinomas related to certain clinical circumstances. Figure 1 illustrates this concept by using a real-world event. "Total Community Genome Analysis" is the acronym for the joint initiative formed by several different organisations. Only a few additional organisations, most of which are tiny, have agreed to participate in this endeavour. After successfully logging in, anyone may access the whole repository and participate in the debate. The pictures were saved in JPG format to keep their original resolution of 220 pixels across and 220 pixels high. As a result, each pixel's size was enlarged from twice to three times its former value. The OC with malignant tumours collection contains non-carcinoma images of normal tissues and non-tumor glandular tissues for each of the four different subtypes. This website has more than simply cancer images; it also contains a variety of other information. The goal of this dataset is to use histological pictures of distinct carcinoma and non-carcinoma subtypes to automatically categorise people who have been diagnosed with oral cancer.

2.2 Data Augmentation

The lack of readily available training materials is a significant barrier in medical imaging. Using data augmentation, any missing data from the time of data collection will be added to this dataset, allowing it to be fully utilised. It has a significant impact on the total quantity of information in the dataset [17, 18]. The images were blown up, twisted, and improved in such a way that the lecture could continue while the alterations were made to the images. A total of 29,187 images were taken when the modifications were completed. Figure 2 depicts a variety of ways that may be utilised to increase the quality of training data. If the rows and columns of each pixel are flipped, it is feasible to flip in both the horizontal and vertical directions.

Starting at zero degrees, the pictures were rotated about their axis of rotation from 0 to 3600°. Table 1 offers a summary of some of the available parameter possibilities. It is

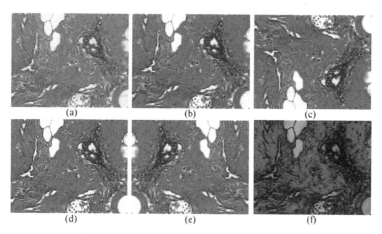

Fig. 1. (a–f) Image Augmentation Techniques

critical to modify the brightness levels in the images to optimise the document validation process [19–21]. This is one of the reasons behind the current scenario. If you zoom in or out using a method called interpolation, you can get a better grasp of the model. These augmentation techniques aim to reduce instances of overfitting and underfitting in deep neural networks to improve their generalizability. The modules offered by Python make it easier to implement these tactics.

Table 1. Data Augmentations and augmentation Values.

Image Parameters	Augmentation Values
Rescaling	100, 200 and 400%
Zooming	0.25, 0.50, 0.75
Rotation	30, 45, 60, 90
Shifting	3
Flipping	Horizontal and Vertical

Table 2 shows how many images were captured prior to and following the rise in the number of shots in each category. This comparison is performed for each of the many types of images.

2.3   The Improved VGG-16 Model

It is critical to be aware of the wide range of levels of complexity in a computer system, in general, CNNs are structured around these layers, with each having a distinct role. The word "filtering" is frequently used to describe this sort of function. Stacking these layers in a certain order during the last decade resulted in the development of several CNN

Table 2. A different number of images are available for every type of ovarian cancer.

Type of Ovarian Cancer	Original Images	Augmented Images
Serous	286	6751
Mucinous	210	6334
Endometrioid	72	5464
Clear Cell	82	5000
Non-Cancerous	96	5638
Total	746	29,187

layouts, each with its own distinct appearance. This approach allows for the collection of data on a wide variety of scales. An example this is done without altering the overall quality of the image in any way. Stretching out the convolution kernel allows you to increase the size of a convolution field without introducing extra model parameters. To do this, we'll use a method called convolution kernel dilation. As the convolutions become wider, the receptive field grows, but the spatial resolution stays constant. It is not necessary to add any extra layers to prevent gridding in pre-existing neural networks with dilated convolutional layers [16]. Dilated spatial convolution units can be utilised to apply the maximum and stochastic pooling algorithms to pictures that provide considerable difficulty at the same time. Figure 2 depicts this. It's available here. To reduce the size of the feature map, use the max pooling approach. Because the pooling zone's activation is decided at random, stochastic pooling takes this activity into account [17]. Based on the current value of this variable, pooling zones are enabled. The maximum pooling approach selects the feature that occurs the most frequently in the final, filtered form of the feature map. This happens at several points throughout the pooling process. Following that, the max-pooling layer would provide a feature map that highlights the most important parts of the previous feature map. A Softmax layer can be added to a neural network before the layer that outputs the results of the network's calculations. The output layer and the softmax layer must have the same number of nodes. It is much easier to determine the pool's average and maximum size when using stochastic pooling, which is a big advantage of the approach. If you have all the required attributes, a higher value can be averaged down to a lower number until you achieve your goal average value. There is no limit to the number of times this can be repeated until the average is attained. It will continue even after the average has been determined.

The practise of max pooling, which assures that the maximum possible value is retained, exacerbates the problem. A probability map must be created for each block entry that will be used in the pooling process. This must be completed before the programme can begin. To do this, the stochastic pooling technique is employed, as discussed further below. If your random variable has an influence on your discrete probability distribution, your discrete probability distribution may assist in keeping your random variable in equilibrium. Batch normalisation and dropouts should be utilised to avoid overfitting. The application of this product is simple and quick. Because there are no constraints on how it may be utilised, everyone can put it to good use however they see fit. Finally,

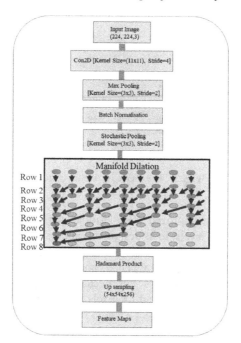

Fig. 2. The Improved Model

"dilation" is used to expand the size of an object while retaining the same processing and memory requirements as before. A second Hadamard step of processing is then applied to both the batch-normalized characteristics and the input image. To begin, the aim is to collect features of the same size, which may be accomplished by upsampling. More research on these characteristics is recommended to better understand the differences between benign and malignant cancer cells.

To retrieve the features, multiply the feature map by the images and gives to the VGG model for further processing. The combination of the global average pool and the maximum pool yields aggregate characteristics. These improve the most important information while lowering the quantity of superfluous stuff. They can forecast cancer cells better because they have a better idea of where they are. AlexNet and other DCNNs were first defined in a blueprint published in 2012. There were six stages in all, including a softmax layer [22–24]. There were two levels of normalisation and three maximum pooling levels to choose from. It is possible to save up to 60 million unique configurations at the same time. a large amount of information. The Visual Geometry Group at Oxford University has since launched the VGG-16 network shown in Fig. 3 to replace AlexNet. As a result, the group at issue no longer has any control over what happens next. AlexNet was conceived by a group of Oxford University academics. They created it for the 2014 ImageNet Challenge to increase their chances of winning the localization and classification project. VGG's Karen Simonyan and Andrew Zisserman created it for that purpose. When compared to prior designs, the VGG-16 has a higher level of complexity and more layers than any of the others.

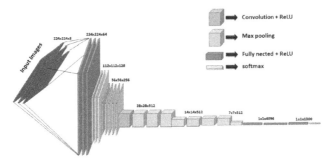

Fig. 3. The VGG 16 Architecture

Because each level in the improved VGG-16 model performs a separate function, the model has a total of sixteen levels. In its design, this approach employs thirteen layers of convolutional filters. An image with a surface area of 224 square inches on each side and a height of three inches may have an influence on the design of the improved VGG-16. The image has been pre-trained for this shot. Because each layer contains 64 filters, the image in Fig. 3 is 224 pixels down and 64 pixels tall. This is since each layer has 64 filters. Each of these levels is made up of a single kernel and is organised in a three-by-three grid. Because the window size is two by two and the stride is two, the volume may be decreased to 112 by 112 by 64. It is feasible to achieve this aim by reducing both the game window and the game stride. The final image has 112 pixels in width, 112 pixels in height, and 128 pixels in depth. 128 filters and two more convolutions are used to achieve this aim. There are now just 56 by 56 by 128 units of volume remaining after reaching the layer with the maximum feasible pooling potential. Following that are three further convolution layers, each with 256 filter units to bring out even more information in the image. The completed picture has a dimension of 28 by 28 pixels and is made up of 256 individual pixels. The presence of a max-pool layer in the centre provides a simple distinction between the two higher-level stacks. The output on the screen is the result of processing each of these stacks with 512 filters and three convolution layers. After the last pooling layer is completed, the flattened images of a $7 \times 7 \times 512$ volume are delivered to the FC layer to be processed. As a result of this, the FC layer is free to continue its task.

The pictures are flattened such that they are uniform in appearance on the FC layer, which has 4096 channels and a dropout of 0.5. The Softmax will be the very final layer to be put together. The remaining blocks, as shown in Fig. 3, were trained using a modified version of the improved VGG-16 model. The dropout value in this model has been drastically lowered, dropping from 0.5 to 0.2, a significant reduction. This is the current condition of the fundamental building component, which is frozen. There were 4096 nodes in the fully connected layers of the pre-trained architecture; however, in the present design, only 128 nodes are in use since some nodes have been eliminated. This is since certain nodes were redundant. The number of classes contained in the pre-trained model is set to 1000 by default. In addition to the pre-existing category of non-cancerous disorders, this has been expanded to include five new subcategories. As a result, we should not be surprised if the overall number of categories we wish to construct corresponds to the number of subtypes we end up with. All training, validation, and testing datasets were obtained from a single original dataset [25]. Each component was given its own name, and a count of the training and validation losses is conducted at the end of each session. This total includes not only the early-stopping condition, but also the accuracy of the training and validation methods. An iterative technique can be considered successful if the validation loss is less than a preset threshold.

3   Results and Discussion

Before delving into the DCNN model's performance measures and the opportunities that may be generated by modifying its hyper parameters, we'll discuss the project's general backdrop.

3.1 Implementation

The Google Collaboratory, which has a 1.569 GHz Nvidia T4 GPU and 16 GB of GPU RAM, was used for all testing in this study. Python frameworks like TensorFlow and Keras are used for testing and training of pre-trained and created VGGNet models. These frameworks are used to test and train models. Cloud computing has made it much easier to locate GPUs.

3.2 Evaluation Metrics

In this section, we'll go through the most crucial performance indicators to monitor while working on your project. Measures such as the F1 score, and the model accuracy statistic may be useful. These performance criteria are developed using a matrix described with a focus on four major features. Some of the performance indicators used to measure staff efficiency and productivity include FP, TP, TN, and FN. There is no reason to be concerned about any of this. The abbreviation "FP" may be used to describe a false positive (FN). False positives are represented by the letters FP for benign lesions, whereas false negatives are represented by the letters TP for malignant tumours. The initials FN and TN have been assigned to malignant pictures to indicate that they belong to a distinct malignancy subtype. Examining instances where the outcome can be any two or more classes is one technique to assess the performance of deep learning systems. Let's get right to it: there's a lot of territory to cover in this discussion.

1. Accuracy: One method for determining forecast accuracy is the proportion of correct predictions to the total number of forecasts. This may be expressed mathematically using the following formula:

$$\text{Accuracy} = \frac{TP}{TP + FP + FN} \tag{1}$$

2. Recall: This conclusion is drawn from the precision with which positive classifications are predicted and the frequency with which such predictions are correct.

$$\text{Recall} = \frac{TP}{TP + FN} \tag{2}$$

3. Precision: The fraction of predicted events that were confirmed to have occurred.

$$\text{Precision} = \frac{TP}{TP + FP} \tag{3}$$

4. F1-Score: This result was derived by dividing the recall/accuracy ratio by two and then adding the product to the original number.

$$\text{F1-Score} = 2 * \frac{\text{Recall} * \text{Precision}}{\text{Recall} + \text{Precision}} \tag{4}$$

3.3 Hyper Parameter Tuning

Neural networks may form connections between inputs and outputs via a process known as self-organization, which reduces the need for external supervision. The model may have been trained using data that was not included in the testing dataset, which increases the chance of sampling noise. Because of this overfitting, there was cause for concern about the deep learning model's capacity to give reliable future estimates. We accomplished this because modifying the hyperparameters of the DCNN model was required to get the best possible degree of performance. We were able to collect correct measurements for each of our hyperparameters by following the steps outlined in this section. We made the thrilling discovery that the solution to our classification problem was a cross-entropy-based loss function. We found ourselves in this scenario when we realised it worked. To further optimise our system, we ran twenty iterations of stochastic gradient descent, often known as SGD. Before any additional training may begin, the validation accuracy must fall below a particular level. This maximum number is determined prior to the start of training. The validity of the validation is documented and evaluated after each epoch, and checks are also made to verify whether it has been lost. By preserving just, the model with the highest degree of accuracy and the least amount of loss, the danger of overfitting is reduced.

Several alternative learning rates were tested during deployment. Batch sizes of 32 and 64 were used to reduce the generalisation gap between training and validation loss by 0.001 and 0.0001, respectively. The 0.3 dropout helps to reduce both the amount of overfitting during training and overall overtraining. The withdrawal was beneficial to both parties involved in the circumstance. Ovarian cancer is a broad term that refers to a variety of tumours that share many clinical, histological, and molecular features. A few distinct traits separate ovarian carcinomas from other tumour forms. Ovarian carcinomas are certainly neoplasms when these criteria are present. This aspect must be carefully considered in the research of ovarian cancer. Despite this, a clearer classification based on clinicopathological, and molecular markers has been developed. Currently, pathologists mostly examine the appearance of the tumour to determine which group the sickness falls into. The clinical appearance, tumour growth, and molecular genetic mutations separate type I and type II ovarian carcinomas.

3.4 Results

During the current round of this debate, we will go through our results and observations. According to Fig. 4, we can see the outcomes of comparing the training set to the validation set's accuracy as well as the loss per epoch for comparison. As a result, they can both exist at two separate places in space and time, making it possible for both to live at the same time. The graphs in A and B may be easily comprehended due to the evident association between the accuracy decline during training and subsequent improvement during validation. Figure 4 clearly demonstrates this. Premature halting began in this manner in the 11th century. Our model's training accuracy climbed to 84.64% because of the extra dataset, and its training loss decreased to 0.021%. Even if only half of the errors were correctly anticipated, the model could be trained. For example, in the basic dataset, for example, the model lost only 0.0855 points. When trained with the enriched dataset, model 2 has an accuracy of 84.64%, whereas model 1 has a 50% accuracy when validated without any further augmentation. A graph displaying the accuracy of the validation data is shown above the one showing the accuracy of the training data in Graph C. Based on this statistical data, we may infer that model 2 is both the most accurate and the most generalizable. As seen in Table 3 the types of ovarian cancers, Type 1 Clear Cell, Type 2 Endometrioi, Type 3Mucinous, Type 4 Non – Cancerous and Type 5 Serous including additional information resulted in more accurate data classification [26, 27]. To determine classification accuracy, utilise the confusion matrix and the equations presented in the section on assessment metrics.

As indicated in Table 3, the inclusion of new data into our collection directly contributed to a 34-percentage point increase in overall classification accuracy. The supplemented dataset's accuracy rate was much greater than the baseline dataset's accuracy rate, which was just 50% right. The inclusion of aesthetic enhancements and tighter zooming is most likely explained by advancements in generalizability made possible by these changes. Even though both models are based on the same underlying architecture, they each use their own unique method of data collection to arrive at their findings. Underfitting is a major contributor to the problem, and as a result, the dataset contains much too few observations to accurately describe the scenario. It's likely that numerous separate factors all worked together to decide its development at the same time. It is feasible to conclude from this that the DCNN architecture may be improved by using proper picture augmentation parameters, as proven in this study. The approaches indicated in the section on assessment metrics were used to construct a wide range of performance indicators, which were then examined in the section that followed. Table 4 shows the graphical representation of the many performance indicators that were discovered. This is seen in the diagram below. Students' performance ratings in each model 2 class and subclass have been greater than or equal to 70% of the total points available. Applying the criteria, which are all equally important, is one technique to assess a model's validity and efficacy. If you follow these guidelines, you will be able to create the most beautiful model that is even somewhat believable.

This early ending structure allowed the model to be saved at the perfect time since it could be saved at epoch 11, when its performance was at its pinnacle. This was possible because of the early termination provision. If the training dataset differs from the new dataset, we may make predictions based on our best model and the new dataset. It was compared to the preceding dataset, which served as a reference point. Figure 5 demonstrates a way of predicting and categorising a wide range of probable events.

88   M. A. Mustafa et al.

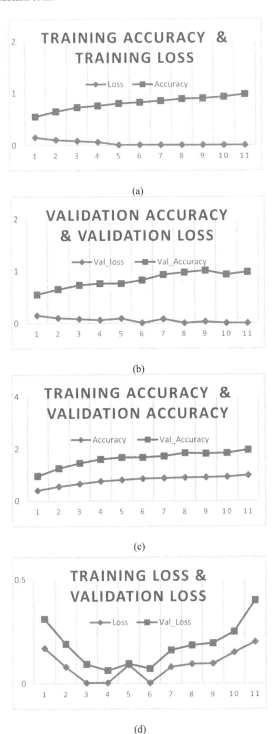

(a)

(b)

(c)

(d)

Fig. 4. (a–d) A comparison of the accuracy and loss in the training dataset and the validation dataset, on an epoch-by-epoch basis

Table 3. Comparative accuracy of the Model 1 and Model 2 classifiers

Ovarian Cancer Types	Classification Accuracy	
	Original Dataset	Augmented Dataset
Type 1	51.66%	83.95%
Type 2	65.45%	95.72%
Type 3	63.21%	84%
Type 4	59.13%	91%
Type 5	61.23%	90%

Table 4. Performance Evaluation Using Proposed Model

Dataset Type	Sub-Types	Precision	Recall	F1-Score	Accuracy
Dataset	Clear Cell	0.43	0.60	0.68	50%
	Endometrioid	0.55	0.63	0.74	
	Mucinous	0.50	0.45	0.67	
	Non-Cancerous	0.64	0.48	0.51	
	Serous	0.55	0.52	0.71	
Augmented Dataset	Clear Cell	0.80	0.88	0.94	84.64%
	Endometrioid	0.95	0.90	0.89	
	Mucinous	0.80	0.73	0.87	
	Non-Cancerous	0.94	0.66	0.85	
	Serous	0.63	0.84	0.83	

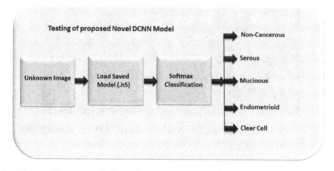

Fig. 5. The prediction and classification process using Improved VGG-16 model

We discovered that many images were wrongly classified due to the model's poor learning from a very small dataset of 24,742 enhanced images. This was owing to the small size of the dataset. This was due, in part, to the model being presented in this manner during prior education. Figure 6, 7 and 8 depicts the decisive findings, which are in conformity with our hypothesis.

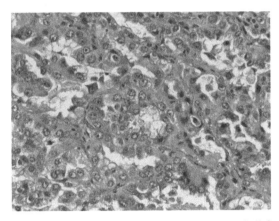

Fig. 6. Representation Of H&E Staining of Ovarian Clear Cell Carcinoma

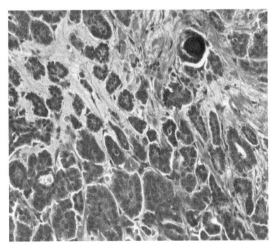

Fig. 7. The image on the right illustrates the typical pattern of H&E staining that is seen in cases of low-grade serous ovarian cancer. Ovarian cancer or ovarian cancer

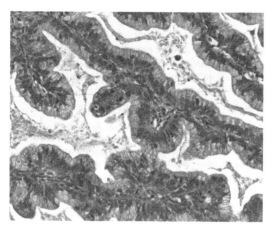

Fig. 8. This is a typical example of H&E staining used to diagnose mucinous ovarian cancer

4   Conclusion

To achieve the study's objectives, an ovarian cancer subtype classification based on improved VGG-16 was used. In the past, there has never been an attempt to categorize items using this novel technique. To help in the investigation, histopathological pictures were evaluated. When more images were provided, the accuracy of the categorization increased from a respectable 50% to an incredible 84.6%. When this research is published in a public forum and made available to the public, a pathologist will be able to properly categorise OC and its subtypes. In the next step of our research, pathologists will be able to submit images of their patients, and our researchers will be able to use these images to make diagnoses. The DCNN may be fed a variety of different pre-trained networks. This allows the DCNN's basic architecture to be fine-tuned. Certain networks are better fitted than others to handle the traffic that they encounter. A closer examination of the accuracy of various techniques will indicate how accurate they are. As a result, we'll be able to examine the accuracy of our forecasts and classifications in more depth. The two-step screening technique has achieved appropriate specificity and a distinct stage shift in early-stage ovarian cancer but not with acceptable sensitivity. This is since the procedure has two phases. This is the case when new and cutting-edge technological breakthroughs are required to give suitable sensitivity. More research is needed in both the imaging area and the field of serum biomarkers.

References

1. Labidi-Galy, S.I., Treilleux, I., Goddard-Leon, S., et al.: Plasmacytoid dendritic cells infiltrating ovarian cancer are associated with poor prognosis. Oncoimmunology 1(3), 380–382 (2012)
2. Tanaka, Y.O., et al.: Differentiation of epithelial ovarian cancer subtypes by use of imaging and clinical data: a detailed analysis. Cancer Imaging **16**, 3 (2016)

3. Nair, R., Bhagat, A.: An introduction to clustering algorithms in big data. In: Encyclopedia of Information Science and Technology, 5th edn., pp. 559–576 (2021). https://doi.org/10.4018/978-1-7998-3479-3.ch040. Accessed 14 June 2022

4. Chang, C.-C., Chen, H.-H., Chang, Y.-C., et al.: Computer-aided diagnosis of liver tumors on computed tomography images. Comput. Methods Programs Biomed. **145**, 45–51 (2017)

5. Ahmad, I., Serbaya, S.H., Rizwan, A., Mehmood, M.S.: Spectroscopic analysis for harnessing the quality and potential of gemstones for small and medium-sized enterprises (SMEs). J. Spectrosc. **2021** (2021)

6. Almarzouki, H.Z., Alsulami, H., Rizwan, A., Basingab, M.S., Bukhari, H., Shabaz, M.: An internet of medical things-based model for real-time monitoring and averting stroke sensors. J. Healthc. Eng. (2021)

7. Alnuaim, A.A., et al.: Human-computer interaction for recognizing speech emotions using multilayer perceptron classifier. J. Healthc. Eng. **2022**, 12 p. (2022). Article no. 6005446. https://doi.org/10.1155/2022/6005446

8. Sathya, M., et al.: A novel, efficient, and secure anomaly detection technique using DWU-ODBN for IoT-enabled multimedia communication systems. Wirel. Commun. Mob. Comput. **2021**, 12 p. (2021). Article no. 4989410. https://doi.org/10.1155/2021/4989410

9. Alnuaim, A.A., et al.: Human-computer interaction with detection of speaker emotions using convolution neural networks. Comput. Intell. Neurosci. **2022**, 16 p. (2022). Article no. 7463091. https://doi.org/10.1155/2022/7463091

10. Alnuaim, A.A., et al.: Speaker gender recognition based on deep neural networks and ResNet50. Wirel. Commun. Mob. Comput. **2022**, 13 p. (2022). Article no. 4444388. https://doi.org/10.1155/2022/4444388

11. Nair, R., Bhagat, A.: An application of big data analytics in road transportation. In: Advances in Systems Analysis, Software Engineering, and High Performance Computing, pp. 39–54 (2018). https://doi.org/10.4018/978-1-5225-3870-7.ch003. Accessed 14 June 2022

12. Nair, R., et al.: Blockchain-based decentralized cloud solutions for data transfer. Comput. Intell. Neurosci. **2022**, 1–12 (2022). https://doi.org/10.1155/2022/8209854. Accessed 14 June 2022

13. Xu, Y., Jia, Z., Wang, L.-B.., et al.: Large scale tissue histopathology image classification, segmentation, and visualization via deep convolutional activation features. BMC Bioinform. **18**(1) (2017)

14. Teramoto, A., Tsukamoto, T., Kiriyama, Y., et al.: Automated classification of lung cancer types from cytological images using deep convolutional neural networks. Biomed. Res. Int. (2017)

15. Gao, Z ., Wang, L., Zhou, L., et al.: HEp-2 cell image classification with deep convolutional neural networks. IEEE J. Biomed. Health Inform. **21**(2), 416–428 (2017)

16. The Cancer Genome Atlas Ovarian Cancer Collection (TCGA-OV) - The Cancer Imaging Archive (TCIA) Public Access - Cancer Imaging Archive Wiki. Wiki.cancerimagingarchive.net (2022). https://wiki.cancerimagingarchive.net/pages/viewpage.action?pageId=7569497. Accessed 03 Aug 2022

17. Kashyap, R.: Breast cancer histopathological image classification using stochastic dilated residual ghost model. Int. J. Inf. Retr. Res. **12**(1), 1–24 (2022). https://doi.org/10.4018/ijirr.289655. Accessed 3 Aug 2022

18. Pang, S., Yu, Z., Orgun, M.A.: A novel end-to-end classifier using domain transferred deep convolutional neural networks for biomedical images. Comput. Methods Programs Biomed. **140**, 283–293 (2017)

19. Kashyap, R.: Evolution of histopathological breast cancer images classification using stochasticdilated residual ghost model. Turk. J. Electr. Eng. Comput. Scie. **29**(8) (2021). Article no. 12. https://doi.org/10.3906/elk-2104-40

20. Sharma, H., et al.: Deep convolutional neural networks for automatic classification of gastric carcinoma using whole slide images in digital histopathology. Comput. Med. Imaging Graph. (2017)
21. Kashyap, R.: Dilated residual grooming kernel model for breast cancer detection. Pattern Recognit. Lett. **159**, 157–164 (2022). https://doi.org/10.1016/j.patrec.2022.04.037. Accessed 17 July 2022
22. Kashyap, R.: Machine learning for Internet of Things. In: Research Anthology on Artificial Intelligence Applications in Security, pp. 976–1002 (2021). https://doi.org/10.4018/978-1-7998-7705-9.ch046. Accessed 18 Apr 2022
23. Krizhevsky, A., Sutskever, I., Hinton, G.E.: ImageNet classification with deep convolutional neural network. In: Advances in Neural Information Processing Systems, NIPS, vol. 25, pp. 1106–1114 (2012)
24. Hinton, G.E., et al.: Improving neural networks by preventing coadaptation of feature detectors. arXiv:1207.0580 (2012)
25. Nair, R., Gupta, S., Soni, M., Kumar Shukla, P., Dhiman, G.: An approach to minimize the energy consumption during blockchain transaction. Mater. Today Proc. (2020). https://doi.org/10.1016/j.matpr.2020.10.361. Accessed 14 June 2022
26. Schwartz, D., et al.: Ovarian cancer detection using optical coherence tomography and convolutional neural networks. Neural Comput. Appl. **34**(11), 8977–8987 (2022)
27. Ahamad, M.M., et al.: Early-stage detection of ovarian cancer based on clinical data using machine learning approaches. J. Pers. Med. **12**(8), 1211 (2022)

Navigating the Chatbot Terrain: AI-Driven Conversational Interfaces

Siddharth Jain[1], Ghanshyam Prasad Dubey[1(✉)], Devendra Kumar Mishra[1], Tanushka Pandey[1], Ayush Giri[1], and Rajit Nair[2]

[1] Department of CSE, Amity School of Engineering and Technology, Amity University, Gwalior, Madhya Pradesh, India
ghanshyam_dubey2@yahoo.com, dkmishra@gwa.amity.edu
[2] VIT Bhopal University, Bhopal, India

Abstract. The Artificial Intelligence (AI) chatbots have emerged as transformative tools across various fields, catalyzing advancements in customer service, healthcare, education, and more. Their versatile nature allows them to engage with users, providing solutions and information while streamlining processes. In customer service, AI chatbots enhance interactions, offering prompt responses and personalized assistance. In healthcare, they facilitate preliminary diagnosis and appointment scheduling, augmenting medical services. Education witnesses their role in interactive learning, delivering knowledge through dynamic conversations. The evolution of AI chatbots in diverse fields showcases their potential to revolutionize how humans and technology interact, intertwining complexity with conciseness, and variability with cohesion, propelling us into an era of enhanced connectivity. This paper provides an insight into what a chatbot is and the types of chatbots. This paper also proposes a classification based on the current trends and uses of chatbots in different fields.

Keywords: Artificial Intelligence · Chatbots · Evolution of chatbots · Chatbot system process

1 Introduction

In our everyday lives, technology is like a big puzzle piece. It fits into so many different parts of the world, shaping how user live. Think about it: from the way user connect with others to how user work, technology is all around globe. And lately, something really interesting has been happening – they are seeing the rise of Artificial Intelligence (AI). This is like a new player on the stage, trying to act just like the brains do [1]. Imagine AI as a mirror for minds. It's trying its best to be as smart. And guess what? It's getting pretty close. To make this connection even stronger, AI has given birth to chatbots. These are like digital friends that talk to user, making user feel like having a real conversation. But here's the twist – they're not human, they're made of code and circuits [2, 3].

The Chatbots acts as a middleman in a conversation between users and the machines. They're like the translators of the digital world [4]. But these translators aren't just

M. Botto-Tobar et al. (Eds.): ICAT 2023, CCIS 2049, pp. 94–106, 2024.
https://doi.org/10.1007/978-3-031-58956-0_7

repeating words – they're using fancy math and rules to make sure the conversation flows smoothly [5]. This digital friend is getting really popular, and there's a good reason why. Behind the scenes, there are super smart technologies working together to make chatbots awesome. In this paper there are artificial intelligence, which is like the brainpower, machine learning that helps them learn from us, and cool tech like neural networks and natural language processing that lets them understand how user talk [6, 7]. There are a lot of chatbots like this. They're like a big family of virtual helpers. Think of IBM Watson, Clever Bot, and ELIZA – they're like the rock stars of the chatbot world. Each of them brings something special to the table, making conversations with machines more exciting than ever before [8]. It's not just about talking; it's about the art of conversation. Back in the day, talking to machines felt stiff and awkward. But times have changed, and now it's like having a chat with a friend. It's like the machines have learned the dance of human conversation, moving smoothly from topic to topic [9]. This Paper explore AI chatbots – what makes them tick, how they're built, and how they've transformed the way user talk to technology [10, 11].

2   Evolution of Chatbots

Long ago, when computers were just starting out, people began to think about making machines that could talk like humans. Two important things to remember here: "perplexity," which is about how complex the talking is, and "burstiness," which means mixing different kinds of talking [12].

Early Beginnings (1950s-1960s): Imagine a time when computers were new. A smart person named Alan Turing had an idea in the 1950s. Alan Turing made something called the "Turing Test". It was like a puzzle to see if a machine could talk so smartly that user couldn't tell it apart from a person. This was the first step toward making chatbots [13].

ELIZA (1960s): Next, in the 1960s, a clever person named Joseph Weizenbaum created something called ELIZA. It was like a simple chatbot that could talk back when a user typed things. ELIZA acted like a friendly therapist and had basic conversations. It was like practicing talking with a machine [13].

Scripted Chatbots (1980s-1990s): As time went on, chatbots got better but were still a bit basic. They followed specific rules like a script in a play. Using some certain words, chatbots would respond with pre-written lines. These chatbots were used mostly for simple tasks, like helping customers [12].

ALICE (1995): Then, in 1995, a smart person named Dr. Richard Wallace created ALICE. This chatbot was more advanced and used a special language to understand and talk. It was like teaching a machine to understand us better. ALICE became popular, and other clever people could build on it [12].

Rise of Machine Learning (2000s): In the 2000s, things got even more interesting. Chatbots started using something called machine learning, which helped them talk more naturally. It was like they were learning to talk like us by looking at lots of examples. Google and other cool tech helped chatbots understand our words better [12].

Siri and Voice Assistants (2010s): Around 2011, Apple introduced Siri. This was a game-changer. Siri could understand when user spoke and answer the questions. It was like having a chat with a smart friend through the devices. Other companies started making similar voice assistants too [12, 13].

Deep Learning and Neural Networks (2010s-Present): Then, really smart people came up with new ways for chatbots to learn. They used something called deep learning, which made chatbots talk almost like humans. These chatbots can understand what user say and give really good answers. They're like super chatty buddies [13].

Integration in Various Industries (Present): Now, chatbots are everywhere! They help user shop, get medical info, and learn new things. Companies use chatbots to make their services better. It's like having a helper that never takes a break [12]. Ongoing Research and Ethical Considerations (Present and Future): People are still making chatbots even better. They're learning new tricks to understand user even more. But, as users get smarter with chatbots, user also need to think about how to use them right. Be careful and think about things like privacy and fairness [12, 13].

3   Chatbot System Process

Step 1: Getting Ready to Chat: First step requires a computer to chat with the chatbot. It's like having a special place to talk. Imagine this place as the chatbot's home, and this acts a computer key to open the door [14].

Step 2: Talking to the Chatbot: While opening the chatbots home, there's a special screen that pops up –it's the chatbot screen. On this screen, there's a space where user can type words. It's like talking to the chatbot by typing on a special keyboard just for it [14].

Step 3: Breaking Down Words: While typing a whole sentence, the chatbot takes that sentence and breaks it into smaller parts, like taking apart a puzzle. These smaller parts are like building blocks made of words [14].

Step 4: Finding the Important Bits: Now, these word blocks are special because they hold important pieces of information. They're like little gold nuggets hidden inside the puzzle pieces. The chatbot looks at these word blocks and figures out what they're all about. It's like discovering the treasures hidden in a story [14].

Step 5: Putting the Puzzle Together: With all these treasures gathered, the chatbot starts putting them together like a puzzle. It's like taking the slices of cake and arranging them back into a delicious dessert. This arrangement helps the chatbot understand what it's saying and how it should respond. It's like the chatbot's way of having a conversation [14].

Step 6: The Chatbot's Magic Touch: Finally, the chatbot does its magic! It takes the arrangement of treasures – those word blocks – and matches them with special patterns it knows. Think of these patterns like maps that lead the chatbot to the right answers. When the chatbot finds the right map, it knows exactly what to say to the user. It's like a storyteller who always knows the perfect story for every moment [14]. It's like using words to create a beautiful picture. Start by getting the computer ready and entering the chatbot's world. Then, user can have a chat on the special screen. The words get broken down into blocks, and the chatbot finds the hidden gems in them. These gems are then pieced together using special patterns, and voila – the chatbot's response pops up, like the finishing touch to a fantastic painting.

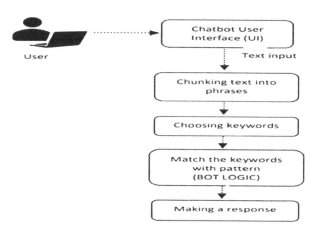

Fig. 1. System Process of Chatbot [14].

Figure 1 represents common steps of chatbot system process. These are the common steps taken to generate response through chatbot mechanism.

3.1 Chatbot Architecture

RabbitMQ is a software tool that helps manage messages. It follows a standard called AMQP and focuses on dealing with messages [15] (Fig. 2). Messenger is a tool like Facebook or Telegram. It's what people use to talk with each other. Messenger Server is like the brain of the messenger. It handles the messages going back and forth between the messenger and the chat-bot platform. Kubernetes service API is like a guide for messages. It helps decide where messages should go and groups them together for better handling [15]. Kubernetes is like a manager for special software boxes. It takes care of putting the chat bot, Worker, and Gateway code into separate boxes. It creates more boxes without making things messy. Worker is a busy bee. It takes messages from users and puts them in a special line for processing. Gateway is another bee, but it helps messages leave the chat-bot platform and go to users.

Data storage is like a digital storage room. It keeps all the chats and media files used by chat bots in one place [15]. Backend Dashboard is like a control center. It's where the chat-bot platform's administrators can manage things behind the scenes. Frontend Dashboard is the website part of the control center. It's where administrators can manage things visually. NLU Engine is like a language expert. It listens to what users say and turns it into something the chat bot can understand. It's super smart and can figure out

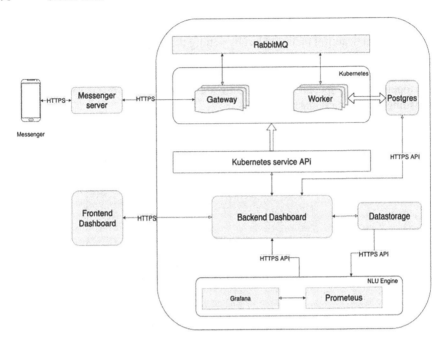

Fig. 2. Architecture of Chatbot [15].

what users want to do [15]. Postgres is a computer system that keeps track of lots of information, like a digital filing cabinet.

3.2 Types of Chatbots

In the past, before all the high-tech stuff user have now, people used to do a lot of things by hand in various industries. But things have changed a lot with all the amazing technology user have today. One exciting development is the creation of chatbots, which are like virtual assistants that can help user out, especially when user need help with things like talking to customers. However, not all chatbots are the same. They come in various Flavors, kind of like different types of ice cream.

Menu/Button-Based Chatbots: Think about those chatbots that have seen with buttons and menus. These are the most common and perhaps the simplest types. It's almost like a story where user get to choose what happens next. Press buttons or pick from menus, and the chatbot gives answers based on the choice. It's like making an adventure. But here's the thing, these chatbots can be a bit slow at times, and they might not always give the exact [16].

Keyword Recognition-Based Chatbots: Then there's another kind of chatbot that's a bit different. These ones listen carefully to the words user say and try to understand what it mean by focusing on certain important words. Imagine talking to a friend, and they pay attention to the specific words using to figure out what user is saying. These chatbots work a bit like that. They have a list of special words they're on the lookout for, and when they hear those words, they know what to say back. But there's a challenge – if some words sound similar, these chatbots might get a little confused [16].

Contextual Chatbots: Now, let's talk about the super smart chatbots. These ones are like the brain of the chatbot world. They use some really clever technology like learning from their past experiences and understanding the way people talk. Imagine if a chatbot could about feeling just by the voice or the words. That's what these chatbots do! They're like virtual mind-readers. For example, think about a food delivery app that remembers the ordered before and then suggests things based on that. These chatbots learn and get better over time as they talk to more and more people. It's almost like they're becoming expert conversationalists [16]. So, different types of chatbots, each with their own special skills, all using cool technology to chat with user in different ways.

3.3 Applications of Chatbots

Chatbots might seem like they're just good for simple stuff, but hold on – they're actually way more interesting than that! There's this thing called Artificial Intelligence that makes chatbots pretty cool. Over the past few years, these chatty bots have been catching everyone's attention because businesses are finding all sorts of clever ways to use them. It's like discovering a new superhero power! Now, let's talk about two important ideas when it comes to writing: "perplexity" and "burstiness." Imagine perplexity like a puzzle level. High perplexity means the puzzle is really challenging, and low perplexity means it's easy to solve. Burstiness, on the other hand, is like a roller coaster of sentences – some are short and sweet, while others are long and full of twists. Okay, back to chatbots! They've become like helpful buddies that are available 24/7, making life smoother for customers. But here's the secret sauce: they're not just for answering questions. Nope, they're doing much more. They're like those super organized friends who help businesses with their tasks. Imagine a chatbot wearing a superhero cape, tackling challenges like a pro. Starting off, chatbots found their groove in customer service, giving people quick answers. But guess what? They've gone beyond that! They're not just answering questions; they're also part of the business dream team. They're like sidekicks to sales and marketing, making sure everyone gets the right info at the right time. Think of them as tour guides through the world of products and services.

The Humorist Chatbot System: Imagine having a chatbot that's all about making people laugh. It's like having a joke-telling friend! This funny bot collects loads of hilarious stories and jokes. And it's smart too – it knows which ones will tickle the funny bone most. Not only that, but it's got a trick up its sleeve – it can understand jokes tell it and respond with funny pictures and words. It's like having a personal comedy show on demand! [16].

The Dorothy Network Management Chatbot: Businesses need a digital organizer too, and that's where Dorothy comes in. Dorothy is like a digital superhero guarding the network. Using some fancy tech called ALICE, always watching over the digital world, making sure it's safe and sound. Imagine her as a friendly digital security guard, making sure no sneaky problems get in [16].

The Adaptive Modular Architecture Based Chatbot: Think about a chatbot that's super flexible and smart, like a ninja of conversations. This chatbot isn't just about memorizing stuff – it's got pieces of information that it uses like building blocks. When it talks it picks the right blocks to create the perfect conversation. It's like chatting with a buddy who knows a lot about a lot of things. It's really good at keeping things flowing smoothly [16].

The Web-Based Voice Chatbot: Last but not least, picture a chatbot that's all about talking and listening. It's like having a digital friend who understands voice. These Chatbots are like that, but they live on the internet. They're learning as they go, so they're getting better at chatting with users every day. They can understand what users say or type, making them super language-savvy. It's like having a conversation with a buddy, like typing or talking [16].

3.4   Challenges in Chatbot Development

Navigating context and unraveling queries with multiple interpretations can pose a challenge, particularly in conversations spanning multiple exchanges. Slang and Abbreviations: Chatbots must decipher slang, informal expressions, and shortened forms that users might utilize during conversations. Polysemy is managing words carrying multiple meanings based on context presents a hurdle for achieving accurate comprehension [17]. Juggling Multiple Tasks is navigating through conversations that encompass various subjects or duties presents a test for chatbots. Intricate Inquiries are offering proficient responses to intricate or technical inquiries necessitate a profound grasp of the subject matter. Dealing with Multiple Users Simultaneously: Ensuring steady performance and consistent responses when many people are using the system at once can pose a difficulty. Allocation of Resources: Effectively handling the distribution of computational resources to host and operate chatbots can present a challenge [17].

Adapting to Shifting Patterns in Chatbots need to stay in sync with evolving linguistic trends and remain well-informed about novel terms, expressions, and ideas. Navigating Modifications is assimilating alterations in user conduct and an expectation necessitates constant vigilance and enhancements. Spotting Emotions is the task of recognizing user emotions and delivering responses that show understanding is tough but essential for making communication truly effective [17].

3.5   Techniques to Improve Responses

Some of the techniques that are used to improve the response of chatbots are:

- It Employ a wide array of representative training data to mitigate biases and ensure a comprehensive grasp of language nuances and context.
- Tailor the chatbot's pre-existing model using domain-specific data, enhancing its pertinence and accuracy for the particular application.
- Integrate techniques for managing conversation context to uphold awareness of past dialogues, leading to more coherent and pertinent replies.

- Elevate the chatbot's ability to discern user intentions accurately, thus enabling appropriate and fitting responses.
- Elevate the chatbot's capacity to detect user emotions and sentiments, empowering it to offer empathetic and contextually fitting answers.
- Implement a mechanism to gather user feedback, facilitating the collection of data on response quality and its utilization in the chatbot's ongoing improvement.
- Construct a dynamic response system that generates answers based on user inputs, ensuring the availability of current and pertinent information.
- Incorporate diversity into responses to prevent monotonous answers, thereby crafting a more captivating and natural conversational ambiance.
- Enhance the chatbot's prowess in managing multi-turn dialogues by referencing prior messages and context, fostering a seamless and authentic user experience.
- Continuously accumulate user feedback and inputs to iteratively boost the chatbot's replies and identify zones necessitating improvement.

4 Chatbot in Different Fields

4.1 Healthcare

Patient Assistance and Engagement: Appointment Scheduling: Chatbots can help patients schedule appointments, reducing administrative burden and offering 24/7 availability. Medication Reminders: Chatbots can remind patients to take their medications on time, improving adherence to treatment plans. Follow-up Care: After treatments or surgeries, chatbots can provide follow-up care instructions and answer patient questions [18].

Medical Information and Education: Symptom Checker: Chatbots can assist patients in understanding their symptoms and provide initial guidance on whether to seek medical attention. Health Information: Chatbots can deliver accurate information about medical conditions, treatments, and preventive measures. Healthy Lifestyle Advice: Chatbots can offer personalized advice for maintaining a healthy lifestyle, including diet, exercise, and stress management.

Mental Health Support: Emotional Support: Chatbots can engage in conversations to provide emotional support and coping strategies for individuals dealing with stress, anxiety, or depression. Crisis Intervention: Chatbots can identify signs of distress and connect users to human professionals in urgent situations.

Telemedicine and Remote Monitoring: Remote Consultations: Chatbots can facilitate preliminary assessments and help patients articulate their concerns before telemedicine appointments with doctors. Remote Monitoring: Chatbots can collect and analyze patient data, such as vitals, and alert healthcare providers to any concerning changes [18].

Clinical Decision Support: Diagnostic Assistance: Chatbots can aid clinicians in diagnosing patients by processing symptoms, medical history, and test results. Treatment Recommendations: Chatbots can provide evidence-based treatment recommendations and drug information to assist doctors.

4.2 E-Commerce

- *Nonstop Availability:* AI chatbots are available around the clock to provide customer support, addressing questions and concerns at any hour [19].
- *Answering Pre-Purchase Questions:* Chatbots assist customers in obtaining information about products, comparing options, and making well-informed buying choices.
- *Offering Product Recommendations:* AI chatbots help to evaluate customer preferences, buying history, and browsing behavior to present individualized product suggestions.
- *Reconnecting with Customers:* Chatbots are capable of sending reminders to customers who left their shopping carts behind, urging them to finalize their purchases.
- *Assisted Shopping:* Chatbots can escort customers through the shopping procedure, helping them discover items that match their requirements.
- *Guiding on Size and Fit:* Fashion and clothing retailers employ chatbots to guide customers in selecting the right size based on measurements.
- *Guidance with Orders:* Chatbots aid customers in placing orders, picking shipping preferences, and completing payments.
- *Inquiries about Payments:* Chatbots supply information about accepted payment methods, currency conversion, and transaction safety.
- *Collecting Feedback:* Chatbots are equipped to gather customer opinions and conduct surveys to assess satisfaction levels and pinpoint areas for enhancement [20].
- *Notifications about Promotions:* Chatbots apprise customers of ongoing sales, discounts, and special promotions [19].

4.3 Education

- *Adaptive Learning:* AI-powered chatbots have the capability to adjust educational materials and pacing according to the unique needs and abilities of each student [21].
- *Tailored Content:* Chatbots provide individualized study resources, quizzes, and exercises tailored to the specific learning preferences of students.
- *Addressing Queries:* Chatbots are handled students' inquiries concerning with course content, assignments, and due dates.
- *Tutoring:* Chatbots provide immediate explanations and guidance on intricate concepts [21].
- *Language Practice:* Chatbots extend opportunities to language learners for practicing speaking, listening, and writing in a foreign language.
- *Creating Study Timetables:* Chatbots assist students in forming and managing study schedules, sending reminders and aiding in time management.
- *Revision Aid:* Chatbots present revision strategies, review hints, and practice quizzes to bolster exam preparation efforts.
- *Instant Feedback:* Chatbots furnish instantaneous feedback on assignments and quizzes, enabling students to learn from their errors.
- *Assistance with Grading:* Chatbots lend a hand in automated grading and assessment processes for assignments and exams [21].
- *Insight into Courses:* Chatbots offer insights into course contents, syllabi, prerequisites, and learning objectives.

- *Enrolment Guidance:* Chatbots lead students through the steps of course registration and enrolment.
- *Career Path Consultation:* Chatbots guide students in exploring potential career trajectories, essential skills, and prevailing industry trends.
- *Crafting Resumes:* Chatbots provide assistance to students in formulating impactful resumes and persuasive cover letters.
- *Registration and Enrolment:* Chatbots aid students in navigating the intricacies of enrollment procedures, course selection, and class timetable management.
- *Fee Payment Information:* Chatbots supply details concerning tuition fees, due dates, and methods of payment.
- *Campus Navigation:* Chatbots serve as virtual guides, imparting directions, building locations, and other pertinent campus information to both new and visiting students.
- *Event Notifications:* Chatbots keep students informed about upcoming campus events, seminars, workshops, and extracurricular undertakings.

4.4 Social Media Management

- *Instant Replies:* Chatbots offer immediate answers to customer inquiries, comments, and messages on social media platforms [22].
- *Resolving Issues:* Chatbots help solve customer worries, fix problems, and pass complex questions to human agents.
- *Automated Publishing:* Chatbots schedule and release social media posts, letting businesses keep a steady posting rhythm.
- *Idea Suggestions:* Chatbots propose content concepts and subjects based on current trends and what the audience likes.
- *Feeling Analysis:* Chatbots study user remarks and mentions to measure public feelings and spot positive or negative feedback. Tracking Mentions: Chatbots keep an eye on brand mentions and important keywords across social media platforms.
- *Performance Metrics:* Chatbots provide real-time statistics and insights on social media engagement, reach, and audience demographics. Making Reports: Chatbots generate summaries of social media performance during specific time periods.
- *Competitions and Prizes:* Chatbots manage interactive contests, giveaways, and promotions to involve users and raise brand recognition.
- *Questionnaires and Surveys:* Chatbots create interactive quizzes and surveys to motivate user involvement and gather insights [22].
- *Finding Products:* Chatbots aid users in discovering products, responding to product inquiries, and suggesting purchasing options.
- *Tracking Orders:* Chatbots assist customers in tracking orders, checking order status, and addressing order-related questions.
- *Language Variety:* Chatbots communicate with users in various languages, making social media interactions more comprehensive and reachable.
- *Urgent Notifications:* Chatbots can distribute important updates and safety information during crises or emergencies.
- *Ad Campaign Control:* Chatbots aid in initiating and managing social media ad campaigns, enhancing budget usage and targeting [22].

5 Future Trends in AI Chatbots

Engaging in Complex Conversations and Contextual Comprehension: AI chatbots are likely to enhance their capacity for participating in more intricate and natural discussions, grasping context, subtleties, and even emotions. This might involve incorporating sentiment analysis and emotion detection to tailor responses accordingly.

Multilingual and Interlingual Proficiency: Future chatbots could become more skilled at managing multiple languages, potentially even within the same conversation. This would facilitate smooth communication across language barriers [23].

Customization and User Profiling: Chatbots might become more proficient at gleaning insights from users' previous interactions to personalize responses and suggestions. This would require comprehending user preferences and adjusting the conversation accordingly. Integration with Internet of Things (IoT) Devices: Chatbots may progressively integrate with Internet of Things (IoT) devices, empowering users to manage smart homes, appliances, and other connected gadgets through natural language interactions. Voice and Visual Engagement: AI chatbots might expand their horizons beyond text- based communication to encompass voice and visual interactions. This could entail comprehending spoken language, recognizing images, and even interpreting gestures. Domain Expertise and Specialization: Instead of being universally applicable, chatbots could become more specialized within specific industries or domains. For example, there might be AI chatbots tailored for healthcare, finance, customer service, and other sectors.

Ethical and Responsible AI: Given mounting concerns about bias and ethical quandaries in AI, there will likely be a focus on developing chatbots that engage in equitable, transparent, and respectful interactions while avoiding misinformation and harmful content. Hybrid Human-AI Interaction: Future chatbots could be designed to smoothly transfer conversations between humans and AI, recognizing situations that necessitate human intervention and ensuring a seamless transition. Ongoing Learning and Adjustment: AI chatbots might continue to learn and adapt from real-time data and user interactions, enhancing their abilities over time without the need for manual updates. Integration with Virtual and Augmented Reality: As virtual and augmented reality technologies progress, chatbots could be seamlessly incorporated, experience within immersive spaces. Enhanced Incorporation into Business Procedures: In the realm of business, chatbots could play an expanded role in automating routine tasks, assisting in customer support, sales, and other operational functions. Emphasis on Data Privacy and Security: With the escalation of data privacy apprehensions, AI chatbots might be designed with more robust data protection measures, guaranteeing that user data is managed securely and transparently [23].

6 Conclusion

AI chatbots bring together technology and communication, serving various purposes across different fields. Their structure, types, pros, cons, and future directions all point to their significant potential. AI chatbots structure is based on language processing and machine learning, allowing them to understand and reply to human language well. Depending on complexity, chatbots can be simple, pattern-based, or creative, each with strengths and limits. Simple chatbots work well for structured tasks and common questions, making them fit for customer support. Pattern-based ones use recognized responses and are adaptable, useful as virtual assistants. Creative chatbots, driven by deep learning, create human-like replies, suitable for complex, changing discussions. AI chatbots have many advantages. They work all the time, giving quick responses and reducing human work. They offer consistent quality, personal interactions, and scalability. Also, chatbots gather and analyze data, leading to insights and better choices. Still, chatbots have drawbacks. They might struggle with complex or unclear questions and lack emotional understanding. They can raise privacy worries with sensitive data and show bias if not trained well. Costs for advanced chatbots, in terms of maintenance and development, can be high. AI chatbots have many uses. In customer service, they make problem-solving faster. In healthcare, they help assess symptoms and set appointments. E-commerce relies on them for advice and support. Education uses them as tutors, and finance for management and advice. They also find roles in healthcare, education, social media, e-commerce, and more. Looking forward, AI chatbots have a bright future. They will grow more advanced, handling complex tasks and emotionally rich talks. Chatbots will use text, voice, and visuals together. As ethics and privacy concerns increase, chatbots will follow stricter rules and be more open about their actions.

References

1. Khan, R., Das, A.: Introduction to chatbots. Build better chatbots: a complete guide to getting started with chatbots, pp. 1–11 (2018)
2. Følstad, A., Brandtzæg. P.B.: Chatbots and the new world of HCI. Interactions **24**(4), 38–42 (2017). ACM.org
3. Schlesinger, A., O'Hara, K.P., Taylor, A.S.: Let's talk about race: Identity, chatbots, and AI. In: Proceedings of the 2018 CHI Conference on Human Factors in Computing Systems, CHI 2018, pp. 1–14 (2018)
4. Dale, R.: The return of the chatbots. Nat. Lang. Eng. **22**(5), 811–817 (2016)
5. Turing, A.M.: Computing machinery and intelligence. Mind **49**, 433–460 (1950)
6. Brandtzaeg, P.B., Følstad, A.: Why people use chatbots. In: Kompatsiaris, I., et al. (eds.) INSCI 2017. LNCS, vol. 10673, pp. 377–392. Springer, Cham (2017). https://doi.org/10.1007/978-3-319-70284-1_30
7. Hoy, M.B.: Alexa, Siri, Cortana, and More: an introduction to voice assistants. Med. Ref. Serv. Q. **37**(1), 81–88 (2018)
8. Pinola, M.: History of voice recognition: from Audrey to Siri. ITBusiness.ca (2011). https://www.itbusiness.ca/news/history-of-voice-recognitionfrom-audrey-to-siri/15008
9. Saba, M.: A brief history of voice recognition technology. Call Analytics, Call Intelligence, Call Recording (2021)
10. Athota, L., Shukla, V.K., Pandey, N., Rana, A.: Chatbot for healthcare system using artificial intelligence. In: 2020 8th IEEE, International Conference on Reliability, Infocom Technologies and Optimization (Trends and Future Directions) (ICRITO), pp. 619–622 (2020)
11. Cui, L., Huang, S., Wei, F., Tan, C., Duan, C., Zhou, M.: SuperAgent: a customer service chatbot for e-commerce websites. In: Proceedings of ACL 2017, System Demonstrations, pp. 97–102 (2017)
12. Clarizia, F., Colace, F., Lombardi, M., Pascale, F., Santaniello, D.: Chatbot: an education support system for student. In: Castiglione, A., Pop, F., Ficco, M., Palmieri, F. (eds.) CSS 2018. LNCS, vol. 11161, pp. 291–302. Springer, Cham (2018). https://doi.org/10.1007/978-3-030-01689-0_23

13. Xu, A., Liu, Z., Guo, Y., Sinha, V., Akkiraju, R.: A new chatbot for customer service on social media. In: Proceedings of the 2017 CHI Conference on Human Factors in Computing Systems, pp. 3506–3510 (2017)
14. Paliwal, S., Bharti, V., Mishra, A.K.: AI chatbots: transforming the digital world. In: Balas, V., Kumar, R., Srivastava, R. (eds.) Recent Trends and Advances in Artificial Intelligence and Internet of Things. ISRL, vol. 172, pp. 455–482. Springer, Cham (2020). https://doi.org/10.1007/978-3-030-32644-9_34
15. https://www.callrail.com/blog/history-voice-recognition/. Accessed 13 Aug 2023
16. Sim, H.: Voice assistants: this is what the future of technology looks like. Forbes. https://www.forbes.com/sites/herbertrsim/2017/11/01/voiceassistants-this-is-what-the-future-of-technology-lookslike/#389fc513523a
17. Adamopoulou, E., Moussiades, L.: Chatbots: history, technology, and applications. Mach. Learn. Appl. **2**, 100006 (2020). ISSN 2666-8270
18. Zemčík, M.T.: A brief history of chatbots. DEStech Trans. Comput. Sci. Eng. **10** (2019)
19. Ahmad, N.A., Che, M.H., Zainal, A., Abd Rauf, M.F., Adnan, Z.: Review of chatbots design techniques. Int. J. Comput. Appl. **181**(8), 7–10 (2018)
20. Mishra, D.K., Upadhyay, A.K., Sharma, S.: Role of big data analytics in manufacturing of intelligent robot. Mater. Today Proc. **47**, 6636–6638 (2021)
21. Tebenkov, E., Prokhorov, I.: Machine learning algorithms for teaching AI chat bots. Procedia Comput. Sci. **190**, 735–744 (2021)
22. Gupta, A., Hathwar, D., Vijayakumar, A.: Introduction to AI chatbots. Int. J. Eng. Res. Technol. **9**(7), 255–258 (2020)
23. Abdellatif, A., Costa, D., Badran, K., Abdalkareem, R., Shihab, E.: Challenges in chatbot development: a study of stack overflow posts. In: Proceedings of the 17th International Conference on Mining Software Repositories, pp. 174–185 (2020)

Intelligent Virtual Assistant for Elevators Powered by Facial Recognition and Voice Commands

Bryan Yupangui Carrillo🅾 and William Montalvo(✉)🅾

Universidad Politécnica Salesiana, UPS, 170146 Quito, Ecuador
byupangui@est.ups.edu.ec, wmontalvo@ups.edu.ec

Abstract. Intelligent assistants are currently categorized as computer programs combined with Artificial Intelligence that interact with the user by voice, messages or images. Thanks to technological advances, intelligent assistants have become widely used in home automation, aiming to automate security, welfare and comfort. This project aims to provide automation for elevators improving the user experience with better security, offering information and user comfort. For this purpose, the application integrates technological tools of facial recognition as part of security and voice activation to command the actuators. Furthermore, the development of the application is oriented to help the multiple users of elevators, especially the group of users with some physical or visual impairment, since it allows the users to mention the floor to which they are going and additionally get a brief overview of what is on that floor, reducing mobility within the elevator, and the search for buttons for the operation of the elevator. The research focused on bibliographic studies on the development of virtual assistants, facial recognition and voice command using free software tools such as Python with its wide range of libraries, and hardware such as PCs, Arduino or Raspberry, depending on the resources needed for the App developed. In the end, a series of tests and satisfactory results with the intelligent virtual assistant are presented to reach the objectives of this study.

Keywords: Artificial Intelligence · Intelligent Assistant · Facial Recognition · Voice Commands · Embedded System

1 Introduction

Nowadays, technology is integrated into several areas of home automation, where tools such as machine vision and voice interaction collaborate to allow the implementation of applications to control electrical and electronic devices. Currently, intelligent systems help users with particular skills in their day-to-day activities, where their main functions range from managing a home, monitoring systems, and actuators with new technologies such as IoT to drive devices through voice commands [1].

Virtual assistants are in great demand because they can receive and send information in different forms, such as voice, and also work at the database level in real time, which is reliable for any work environment or application [2].

Facial or face recognition is a computer vision technology designed to identify an individual through images, videos or any audiovisual element of his face for better safety of an application, service or system [3].

It can be cited as an example of user-machine interaction in voice-controlled electric chairs where the device has a built-in voice recognition system. The process goes through several steps to improve the decision-making of the actuator. First, the process begins with the user's voice signal, then goes through a parameterizer where the voice signal is treated; then, its result goes to a recognizer, which is the algorithm that consists of language models and acoustic models; finally, the sequence of words spoken by the user is taken into account [4].

The application development is oriented to assist the multiple users of elevators, especially those with physical disabilities since this group is growing in the population [5].

According to the United Nations National Council, about 10% of the world's population, or 650 million people, live with a disability. This figure is increasing due to population growth, medical advances and aging, according to the World Health Organization (WHO) [6].

The prototype detailed in this work consists of two parts, the first is the development of a virtual assistant that includes facial recognition tools, where its algorithm will be developed using the cascade classifier method based on Haar functions, guaranteeing thus fast image processing and effective recognition. It will also have a voice command activation, which will use the Python libraries (Speech Recognition and gTTS). Both algorithms will be put in different circumstances and environments for training. The second stage is the design of a control board, said board will be in charge of activating the system actuators, for the coupling between the application and the actuators an Arduino will be used, which sends an analog signal of 0–10 [V] and a timed digital signal to the frequency converter, which will be responsible for activating and varying the motor speed. For visualization, a graphical interface is developed to monitor the behavior of the system.

In comparison with [12], whose work developed a Virtual Assistant for people with physical disabilities, using voice commands to activate actuators with the help of Alexa technology, this being a useful and highly reliable tool for recognition. Voice commands, however, said device has little flexibility to customize some functions that the person with disabilities needs, it also requires a constant Internet connection with good bandwidth, limiting voice recognition actions, at the moment the The virtual assistant developed in this work does not need an internet connection, thus providing its reliability in case of losing connection to the world.

With all these tools, the elevator begins to have artificial intelligence since it is capable of having interactions with the user since when reaching the destination or required floor it provides information about what is in the indicated area. Additionally, with this you can reduce costs, spaces and resources for the automation of elevators without the need to use PLC's or other control devices as was done in the past, in addition, this system provides different users with better security, obtaining information and comfort.

2 Methodology

2.1 System Architecture

Figure 1 presents the elements and devices that make up the virtual assistant and the control board. As a first instance, the virtual assistant will manage the facial and voice recognition algorithms and send the commands through the serial port to activate the Arduino. This device will send a timed digital signal and an analog signal to the inverter to drive the final actuator.

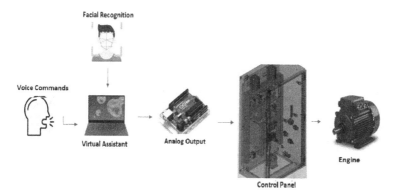

Fig. 1. Virtual assistant architecture.

2.2 Assistant Design

The study proposes a practical approach for developing an intelligent assistant. For this purpose, facial recognition tools are used as a security algorithm and voice activation to execute the tasks of the embedded system. Additionally, a graphical interface was developed for the observation and analysis of the system.

As shown in Fig. 2, several free technological tools were used to develop the assistant, such as Visual Studio Code, Python, Open CV, gTTS. However, for facial recognition, it is necessary to perform previous training on the user's images to compare with the database and allow access to the other options of the application.

The application was developed in the Visual Studio Code environment using libraries, functions and scripts.

2.3 Facial Recognition Algorithm

Figure 3 shows the process of performing face detection, which starts in Step 1 for the data collection, and then recognizing it through cascade classifiers based on Haar functions, which performs a machine learning approach where the function is trained from positive and negative images. In this process, the more images obtained, the faster the detection will be [7].

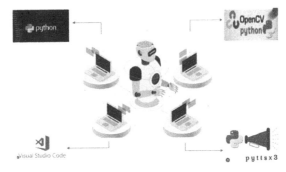

Fig. 2. App Development Diagram.

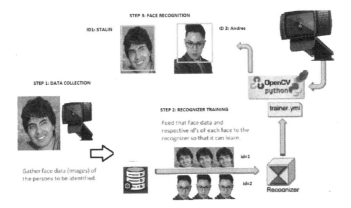

Fig. 3. Face recognition process.

Good results have been obtained with the cascade method since it effectively detects the trained face previously stored in the database. If several postures or examples of how the user will appear are presented in training, the algorithm will have a higher percentage of similarity for the respective recognition, as shown in Fig. 4.

Fig. 4. (a) Face capture, (b) Face recognition.

The results such as: numbers of images obtained for the set, training times, number of failures, configured users are reflected in Table 4.

2.4 Voice Command Algorithm

Python libraries were used to perform the voice actuation: SpeechRecognition for voice recognition (with support for various engines and APIs online and offline) and gTTS. Several parameters had to be considered, such as the noise in the environment, the way words are pronounced, and the volume of the pronunciation, since all this would help the understanding of the virtual assistant. For all this, a database with pre-established words was used for later comparison and command triggering. The commands configured in the virtual assistant are shown in Table 5 as well as the successful and unsuccessful attempts. Six pronunciation tests of the commands were carried out with noise in the environment.

When performing speech recognition, the most difficult thing is performingast and concise reliable search [8, 9].

2.5 Embedded System

The main elements of the embedded system are the virtual assistant located in a computer with the ability to perform facial recognition and voice command acquisition, as shown in Fig. 5.

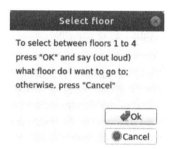

Fig. 5. Virtual assistant.

Mentioning the commands from floor 1 to floor 4 gives the power-on instruction to the control board for the subsequent start of the elevator.

Figure 6 shows the Altivar 71 board that contains the frequency inverter with its respective power distributions in alternating and continuous voltage as 220 [Vac], 120 [Vac], and 24 [Vdc] for starting the 1.5 [HP] motor.

The programmable card will receive the voice commands provided by the virtual assistant through serial communication.

The card will send a PWM signal to the frequency inverter Altivar 71; then a digital signal of 24 [v] is sent for the timed start of the inverter by programming a scaling from 0 [v] to 10 [v] to deliver an analog signal that will be responsible for performing the speed control in the inverter in the same way, as shown in Fig. 7.

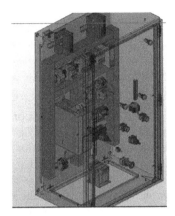

Fig. 6. Altivar board 71.

Fig. 7. Programmable card.

As shown in Fig. 8, the Altivar 71 Variable Frequency Drive was installed with the connections to start the motor. In the same way, a soft start can be performed by the parameters set by the user thanks to the SoMove desktop application, in addition to configuring several parameters for diagnosing the motor status, such as acceleration and deceleration ramps and communication protocols [10].

Finally, in Fig. 9, the graphic interface is shown, which shows the behavior of the frequency inverter and also the established parameters of the motor. For this purpose, a graphic interface development software was used, which has several tools for its development and is also capable of acquiring data and visualization of images [11].

A Modbus RTU to Modbus protocol converter was used for communication between the graphic interface and the frequency inverter.

2.6 Actuator Parameterization and Connectivity

To determine the configuration parameters of the variable of *frequency drive*, the nameplate data of the motor to be started was observed, as described below in Table 1.

A protocol converter was used to communicate between the frequency inverter and the graphic display since the frequency inverter communicates via Modbus RTU and the display via Modbus TCP/IP. As seen in Fig. 10.

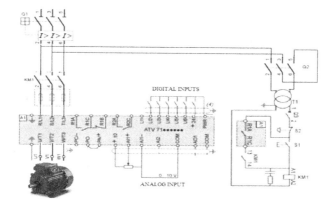

Fig. 8. Force diagram of the Motor-Variator system.

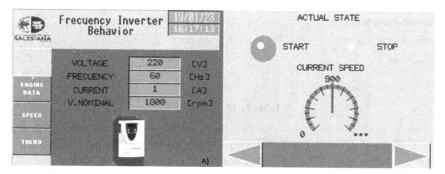

Fig. 9. Graphical interface.

Table 1. List of parameters.

Table of Parameters		Value	Units
# of Parameter	Description		
1	Motor frequency	60	Hz
2	Power rating	3.00	HP
3	Rated voltage	230	V
4	Rated current	1.5	A
5	Nominal speed	1800	Rpm

The same parameters must be configured in the frequency inverter for successful connectivity, as described in Table 2.

To check the communication between devices, the IP addresses of the devices must be clear, so Table 3 was established with the addresses of the devices.

Communication between devices was successful, as shown in Fig. 11.

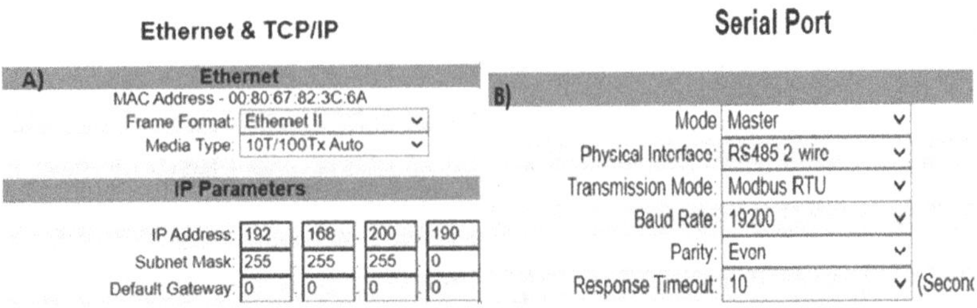

Ethernet & TCP/IP   **Serial Port**

Fig. 10. Converter configuration.

Table 2. Serial Configuration.

Serial parameters	
Modbus address	1
Transmission Speed	19200 [Bd]
Modbus format	8 par 1
Waiting time	10.0 [Sec]

Table 3. IP Addresses.

Description	IP address	Mask
Protocol converter	192.168.200.190	255.255.255.0
Graphic Display	192.168.200.75	255.255.255.0
Computer	192.168.200.98	255.255.255.0

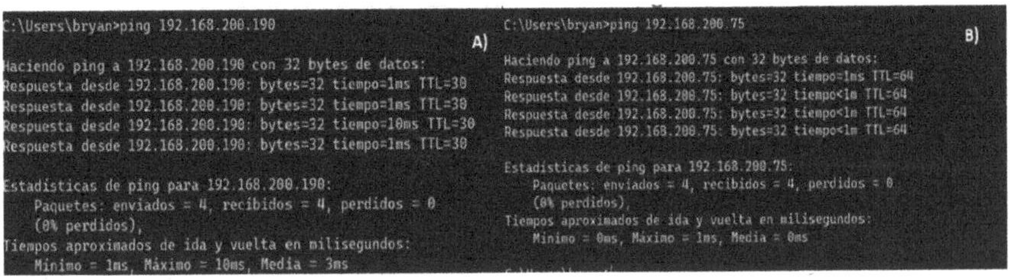

Fig. 11. Ping to devices.

3   Results

For the recognition algorithm, tests were performed using cascade classifiers based on Haar functions, using the Python OpenCv library, 40 images belonging to two people were captured, the detection time of the images and the training time of each of the users were measured, and the results are shown in Table 4.

Table 4. Facial Recognition Tests.

	User 1	User 2
No of Images	40	40
No of Detections	40	37
Faults	0	3
Detection time	500.25 [ms]	700.48 [ms]
Training time	10 [Sec]	12 [Seg]

Figure 12 shows the results obtained using a confusion matrix for the two established users.

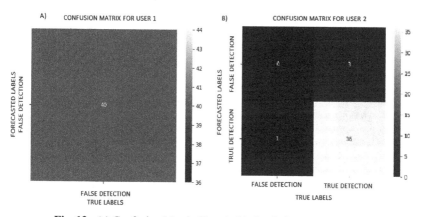

Fig. 12. (a) Confusion Matrix User 1, (b) Confusion Matrix User 2

Forty image samples were taken since, with this number, the training and recognition are fast and reliable because the space where the tests were performed is controlled with the same lighting and position. However, the number of samples can be increased for better training because the processing time for training is increased.

LBPH is one of the best and fastest in detection since it labels the pixels of an image using the threshold of the neighborhood of each pixel and considers the result as a binary number, however, this method presents new features when changing the lighting. of the environment, confusing the algorithm since it performs its calculation pixel by pixel, however the algorithm presented by the cascade method appears to be more robust when subjected to changes in the environment since it performs the comparison between quadrants of the image obtained with a set of pixels and no longer pixel by pixel, thus avoiding confusion in decision-making.

In the voice command algorithm, tests were performed with the Python SpeechRecognition library for voice recognition and gTTS for the interaction between the assistant and the user, and the following results were obtained as shown in Table 5 (representing green as accepted command and red as a rejected command) with their respective confusion matrix shown in Fig. 13. These tests were performed with noise in the environment.

Table 5. Command test results.

COMMAND	NOISE						ACHIEVEMENTS (%)
FLOOR 1							83.33%
FLOOR 2							66.66%
FLOOR 3							83.33%
FLOOR 4							100%

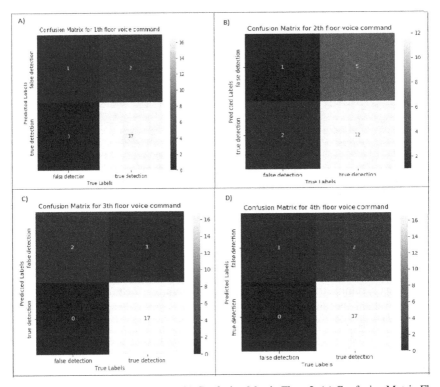

Fig. 13. (a) Confusion Matrix Floor 1, (b) Confusion Matrix Floor 2, (c) Confusion Matrix Floor 3, (d) Confusion Matrix Floor (4).

Using the Python gTTS library you can improve interaction with the user and you can also vary the voices between male and female. Additionally, you can also configure the language in which you want the virtual assistant to speak, thus giving a great variety of configurations compared to other voice systems.

Mentioning the established commands, the control card activates a timed digital input for the automatic drive of the motor and also delivers an analog signal scaled from

0 [v] to 10 [v] for the speed variation between the different floors. The results are shown in Table 6.

Table 6. Drive tests

Floors	Output voltage 0[v] to 10[v]	Actuation time
1	3.20 [v]	10 [Sec]
2	5.57[v]	20 [Sec]
3	7.5[v]	40 [Sec]
4	9.3[v]	60 [Sec]

Using SoMove software, the voltage, amperage and frequency of the drive were probed.

Figure 14 shows the 10 [Sec] of activation, and the voltage is also shown in red, the frequency in green and the current in blue.

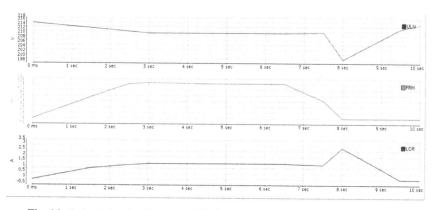

Fig. 14. Drive behavior: Command, Floor 1, Mains voltage, Frequency, Current.

Figure 15 shows the behavior of the inverter by mentioning the voice command Floor 2, which lasts 20 [Sec], where the first graph shows the voltage, the second the frequency, and finally the current.

The drive's behavior is shown in Fig. 16, mentioning the voice command Floor 3 which lasts 40 [Sec], where it first graphs the voltage, then the frequency, and finally the current.

Figure 17 shows the drive's behavior by mentioning the voice command Floor 4, which lasts 60 [Sec], where it first plots the voltage, then the frequency, and finally the current.

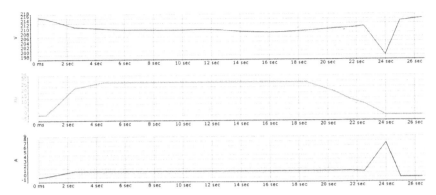

Fig. 15. Drive behavior: Command Floor 2, Mains Voltage, Frequency, Current

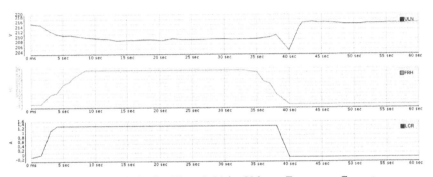

Fig. 16. Drive behavior: Floor 3, Mains Voltage, Frequency, Current

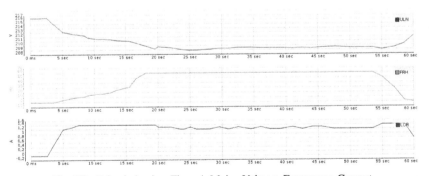

Fig. 17. Drive behavior: Floor 4, Mains Voltage, Frequency, Current

4   Discussion

According to the author in [12], voice commands help people with physical disabilities to activate actuators that perform specific functions with the help of Alexa technology, being this a helpful tool and good reliability for the recognition of voice commands; however, this device has little flexibility to customize some functions needed by the person with disabilities, it also needs a constant internet connection and good bandwidth, limiting the actions of voice recognition. The study conducted by [13] mentions that the LBPH method for face recognition is one of the best and fastest in detection since it labels the pixels of an image through the threshold of the neighborhood of each pixel and considers the result as a binary number. However, this method presents novelties when changing the environment's illumination, confusing the algorithm since it performs its calculation pixel by pixel.

This work presents the union of the two technologies for creating a virtual assistant using Python libraries such as SpeechRecognition and gTTS to distinguish and execute voice commands without needing an Internet connection. It is also reliable for an environment with noise and is also flexible with the needs presented by the user as the change of language, words, and others. Furthermore, as a facial recognition method, cascade classifiers based on Haar functions were used to improve the tolerance to light and environment changes, thus presenting greater reliability.

5 Conclusions

In the development of the face recognition algorithm, the cascade method was used, which works with automatic learning and the function is trained from many positive and negative images, thus improving tolerance to changes in environment and light for faster processing and recognition.

The algorithm for voice commands that was implemented was SpeechRecognition and gTTS, which converts the voice to text for understanding the virtual assistant and also changes the text to voice using Python libraries, thus giving an artificial intelligence interaction between the virtual assistant and the user. This algorithm must be trained with the existing noise in the environment to reduce the error rate and give better reliability to the system.

The Virtual Assistant is more efficient when running on a Linux operating system since certain functions for facial recognition and voice commands are executed in less time in this environment, thus improving its performance.

The system developed in this study has scalability characteristics thanks to the microcontrollers' ability to acquire data from other devices because they have digital and analog inputs. In addition, the programming code was written in Python, which facilitates the implementation of actuators that can add robustness to the algorithm.

The development of an intelligent virtual assistant for elevators and elevators driven by facial recognition and voice actuation obtained favorable results, given that the behavior of the drive is reliable, with which it can be concluded that it is optimal for implementation in an elevator.

References

1. Méndez, M.: Automatización y control de residencias, utilizando tecnologías de información y sistemas expertos (2018). https://biblioteca-farmacia.usac.edu.gt/Tesis/MAIES271.pdf
2. Santos, R.: Desarrollo de un asistente virtual turístico para la ciudad de Madrid (2018). https://eprints.ucm.es/id/eprint/48836/

3. Espinoza, D., Jorquera, P.: Reconocimiento Facial (2015). http://opac.pucv.cl/pucv_txt/txt-1000/UCD1453_01.pdf
4. Jiménez, R.: Desarrollo de un sistema mecatrónico para controlar una silla de ruedas motorizada mediante diversos dispositivos por enlace inalámbrico (2017). https://hdl.handle.net/20.500.12371/558
5. Consejo Nacional para la Igualdad de Discapacidades, "Estadísticas de Discapacidad.," https://www.consejodiscapacidades.gob.ec/estadisticas-de-discapacidad/. Accessed 17 Nov 2022
6. Crespo, B., Baquero, Y., Gaibor, E.: Módulo sobre atención inclusiva para personas con discapacidad (2022). chrome-extension://efaidnbmnnnibpcajpcglclefindmkaj/. https://www.cepam.org.ec/wp-content/uploads/2022/09/Modulo-1-Servidores-Publicos-FINAL-1.pdf
7. Costa, D.: Análisis de un sistema de reconocimiento facial a partir de una base de datos realizado mediante python (2020). http://hdl.handle.net/2117/331277
8. Rodríguez, P.: Micrófono inteligente para smartphone con reconocimiento de voz y cloud-computing (2019). chorome-extension://efaidnbmnnnibpcajpcglclefindmkaj/. https://oa.upm.es/63429/1/TFG_PABLO_RODRIGUEZ_LOPEZ.pdf
9. Krbec, P.: Modelado de lenguaje para reconocimiento de voz de checo (2005). https://is.cuni.cz/webapps/zzp/detail/43987/?lang=en
10. Altivar 71. Accessed 15 Jan 2023. www.schneider-electric.com
11. Electric, S.: Vijeo Designer - Tutorial - 03/2014 (2014). Accessed 15 Jan 2023. www.schneider-electric.com
12. Palacios, J., Bosquez, V., Palacios, A.: Integración de un asistente virtual en ambientes de vida asistida por computador para personas con discapacidad física. Rev. Investig. Talent. **7**(1), 48–61 (2020)
13. Verdeguer, D., Campos, N.: Diseño e implementación de un sistema de identificación de personas para la seguridad de los accesos a condominios, basado en el algoritmo de reconocimiento facial lbph (2022). https://doi.org/10.18687/LACCEI2021.1.1.213

Otsu Segmentation and Deep Learning Models for the Detection of Melanoma

Mohammed Ahmed Mustafa[1], Zainab Failh Allami[2], Mohammed Yousif Arabi[3],
Maki Mahdi Abdulhasan[4], Ghadir Kamil Ghadir[5(✉)], and Hayder Musaad Al-Tmimi[6]

[1] Department of Medical Laboratory Technology, University of Imam Jaafar AL-Sadiq,
Baghdad, Iraq
[2] Al-Manara College for Medical Sciences, Maysan, Iraq
[3] College of Computer, National University of Science and Technology, Dhi Qar, Iraq
[4] Department of Medical Laboratories Technology, AL-Nisour University College, Baghdad,
Iraq
[5] College of Pharmacy, Al-Farahidi University, Baghdad, Iraq
zaidkhalid92@yahoo.com
[6] College of Health Medical Techniques, Al-Bayan University, Baghdad, Iraq

Abstract. It is now easier than ever to "mine" photographs for information and discovers new points of view using techniques. Medical workers now have access to images that can assist them in more swiftly and efficiently diagnosing and treating a broader range of diseases. Dermatologists are working with deep neural networks to discriminate between photographs of healthy skin and those of patients with skin cancer. We have focused our efforts on two important areas of study to gain a better understanding of melanoma. Examining this issue as early in the process as feasible is crucial. Even small changes in dataset properties can have a significant impact on classifier performance. In this part, we'll discuss the challenges that arise when attempting to adapt what we've learned in one environment to another. We believe that repeated training and testing cycles are essential for developing reliable prediction models. Furthermore, a system that is more adaptable and sensitive to changes in training datasets is urgently required. As a result of this, hybrid architecture for service delivery that integrates both clinical and dermoscopic images has been suggested. This approach may be used in a variety of ways, including cloud computing, fog computing, and edge computing. This architecture must be able to analyze large amounts of data while simultaneously speeding up the process of constantly improving its knowledge. In this example, one computer and many distribution mechanisms are employed, demonstrating that the output is obtained in far less time than would be the case with a centralized system. This is in comparison to the guarantees provided by a centralized plan.

Keywords: Alexnet · Augmented Data · Classification · Convolutional Neural Networks · Data Augmentation · Deep Learning · Dermatology · Diagnosis · Distributed Computing · Google Inceptionv3 · Googlenet

1 Introduction

Melanoma originates in the epidermal cells known as melanocytes to create melanin, the pigment that gives the skin its colour. Melanoma begins to develop and spread to the skin's surface in these cells. If you have melanoma, you may have cells in your body that can give birth to more melanoma cells. This is because it is the type of skin cancer that happens most commonly. Since 1980, there has been a steady increase in the number of people diagnosed with melanoma [1]. Despite this, the probability of acquiring a melanoma diagnosis increases with age. Between 2007 and 2016, the mortality rate for individuals over the age of 50 increased by an average of 2.2% each year, while the death rate for people under the age of 50 decreased by an average of 1.2% per year. Furthermore, it is expected that these totals will rise in the next few years. The implications of these discoveries are equally applicable to men and women. As the scientific community is aware, early melanoma detection still requires improvement [2]. A physician must be able to distinguish between the many different types of lesions that may appear on a patient's skin to successfully diagnose their skin illness. In the most severe cases, a biopsy is the only way to be certain of a diagnosis. Early diagnosis of melanoma has become a growing issue in recent years, particularly for people who are predisposed to the illness. As a result, a larger percentage of patients have had their illnesses satisfactorily addressed. In most cases, a dermatologist's initial visual examination is the best technique to identify melanoma [3]. Dermoscopy, which employs polarised light, is a preferred method for this evaluation. Innovative diagnostic systems have the potential to change people's perceptions of medicine, and technology plays an important role in determining the best ways to treat patients [4]. There are a few crucial factors to consider. Answers to clinical concerns are inextricably tied to medical research and attending physician ability. Only by combining the efforts of professionals in the medical and technological fields can the end product's quality be ensured.

A newer generation of computer software, such as those developed in the last few years, can assist physicians in determining if a skin irregularity has the potential to develop into melanoma. There have been a few recommendations for a computer-aided system in dermatology [5]. Despite forecasts that artificial intelligence (AI) could soon overtake doctors, many concerns remain unresolved. Some of the computer vision algorithms employed in this application are border identification, symmetry and asymmetry analysis, colour analysis, and dimension detection [5]. Electronic health records (EHRs) can also be utilised to improve the accuracy of some prediction algorithms. Melanoma can only be identified correctly if a range of imaging modalities are utilised, each with its own set of obstacles. As a result, lesions may have uneven borders, images may have noise and artefacts owing to insufficient illumination, the contrast may be low, and images may have low contrast [6, 7].

To make things easier for you, we've summarised the development process for these systems below. As a first step, gather or construct an image library of images of both skin malignancies and healthy skin. While the second option may not have as much data available owing to dermoscopy requirements, the third option has more data and is less difficult to obtain. Dermoscopy is required to capture dermoscopic images. The characteristics of the images are then extracted using various computer vision and image processing techniques [8, 9]. Transfer learning shortens training time by using previously learned networks. This is possible due to the use of pre-trained networks and the reduction of training durations. If we choose, we may focus on the classification system's most superficial tiers in this situation. This transfer presupposes that the source and destination datasets are both in the same feature space and are distributed in the same way for machine learning [10–12].

2 Background and Related Works

In recent years, it has become more important for dermatologists to have rapid and easy access to technology that aids in the detection of melanomas. Melanomas may now be diagnosed and categorised more precisely, even in their early stages, thanks to advances in diagnostic technology. Support vector machines [10, 11], logistic regression [12], and Bayesian classifiers [13–15] are examples of decision trees that may be found in many classification models. Convolutional neural networks, often known as CNNs, are widely used in the field of image-based algorithms for disease detection [14]. Their importance has been proved beyond any reasonable question since their discovery in the field of melanocytic lesion detection and classification [15, 16]. In addition, the numerals and [17] are mentioned in the discussion. Convolutional neural networks have been tested and evaluated by dermatologists and have a proven convolutional neural network. The study's goal was to determine which subjects were better than others at detecting skin lesions. Dermatologists were classified as novices, proficients, or experts based on their level of experience in the use of dermoscopy. Dermatologists were provided access to a one-of-a-kind database with information on each of the categories. Beginner groups (level I) were shown dermoscopic images, whilst competent and expert groups (level II) were given written information. Many medical specialists believe that getting a correct diagnosis and developing a treatment strategy for the tumour, which might be prema-lignant, benign, or even malignant, is the single most important step that can be taken at this point. The accuracy percentage of dermatologists who just looked at the first level of data was 776%, which was higher than the total accuracy rate of 83.8%. As a result of including secondary data in the inquiry, both our sensitivity (90.6%) and specificity (95.7%) increased (82.4%). Recent advances in machine learning and deep learning may provide some light on why there has been such a spike in studies into melanomas in recent years. In the last several years, neural networks have had a signif-icant impact on the amount of accuracy with which we can identify melanomas. The researchers used an eight-layer convolutional neural network named AlexNet in their investigation [18, 19]. The max-pooling layers appeared after the first five convolutional layers, and the levels that followed were all highly connected to one another. Previous research has established the effectiveness of a non-saturated activation function known as ReLU; this function was used in the experiment that we conducted. To evaluate the network's authenticity, data from MED-NODE, Derm (IS-Quest), and ISIC were utilised as input parameters. This evaluation was conducted alongside transfer learning and the data augmentation technique. The examination results were as follows: 96.86%, 97.70%, and 95.91%, respectively. The authors were able to achieve their goal owing to the use of transfer learning and the incorporation of extra data. Convolutions, average pooling, maximum pooling, and contacts are some of the building blocks used in the development of GoogleNet [20] and other deep convolutional neural networks. Another critical part is gathering as much information as possible [21–23]. The groundbreaking project known as Inception, which began operations in 2015 and was defined as a system capable of doing calculations despite having limited access to a computer's resources, served as the motivation for the creation of this new network. We are expanding on the prior network's basis with the construction of this new network. Even while decentralising processing capacity for machine learning and deep learning approaches might theoretically accelerate problem identification, the organization's foundations continue to be a source of problems [27].

3 Methodology

Both constraints were investigated in two separate studies to determine how they affect classifiers and AI-based detection systems. Our analysis did not concentrate on feature extraction because there has been a lot of research on this topic. There are several instances, including segmentation and boundary analysis. As a result, as preprocessing approaches, we employ Otsu segmentation and Gaussian filtering. This technique, which focused on activities that required a considerable amount of computer processing power, was utilised to detect melanoma in clinical research. In the preprocessing step, artefacts were removed, clinical characteristics were retrieved for diagnosis in accordance with dermatological standards, and the overall quality of the image was enhanced. The schedule for the project's progress is as follows: The treatment method is highly reliant on the segmentation of malignant tumours. While designing your project, keep the following factors in mind, the cloud layer can handle huge calculations since it acts as both a computing platform and a data repository. A cloud-based system must get new instructions from fresh images. Validation and testing may also be carried out via cloud-based services. When a new classifier is created, the cloud layer oversees disseminating it to the rest of the system. Cloud-based computers analyse and filter data from the edge layer before transmitting it to the cloud through the fog layer. A new layer named Layer 1 has been placed on top of the Edge layer. You can use these approaches if you have enough computational power. To handle devices with less computational power, the fog layer may apply similar tactics as the edge layer. Edge Devices on the Internet of Things refer to all the intelligent devices that comprise the architecture's edge layer. The data is now processed further in the Edge Device, and the process continues. To analyse the photos, the Edge loads the most recent version of the image classifier [28–30]. All reference labels will be the same throughout the procedure, regardless of whether the marginal distribution alters between the source and destination domains. When you apply the Otsu method to segment your data, you may see that the variation in each class is reduced [31].

Figure 1 depicts an example of Otsu output, the collection includes 170 images (100 benign and 70 malignant), and data augmentation was utilised to produce additional variations by modifying the photographs [32]. The changes that are now being considered for deployment are the outcome of an extensive examination. When the distributed method is not employed, retraining classifiers takes longer. These investigations were carried out to determine how long it takes. The training procedure is depicted in Fig. 4.

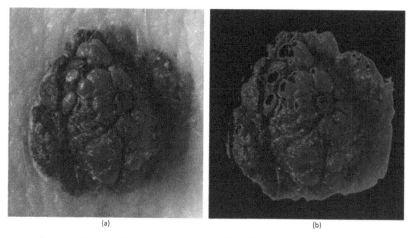

(a)   (b)

Fig. 1. The Otsu Segmentation Method Has Been Used for This Image

It's right here for you to look at. A single Intel Scientific Workstation with a total of 16 computing nodes, 16 gigabytes of RAM, and a single GeForce GTX980 graphics processing unit (GPU) was employed in this configuration. The blueprints for Google InceptionV3, GoogleNet, and AlexNet, for example, may be made available to the public. These networks had previously been taught to recognise a broad variety of image kinds. We employed these networks to attain the high levels of accuracy mentioned above. The number of classes in the final layer has decreased from 1,000 to just two. To proceed to the next level, you must first remove the soft and classification layers from the basic network. As a result, we were able to do this, and the dataset has been separated into three sections: training, validation, and testing (as seen in the table below) (ratio: 0.2). When the randomization option was enabled, we used the splitEachLabel approach. Following cycles, the training set was made up of a random selection of half of the photographs without melanoma and half of the photographs with melanoma. This collection was built from the initial batch of images. When the test set and validation set were compared, it was discovered that the ratios used in each set were different. A Gaussian filter was implemented prior to each training session to reduce network noise. Imgafilt and the dynamic sigma value were the two approaches employed for this project. A and B are two examples of varying-sigmoidal filters that employ Gaussian models, as shown in Fig. 2. (b). During training, we did 100 iterations with varying sigma values (Fig. 3).

Stochastic gradient descent with momentum was used in the training circumstances, which included 30 epochs, an initial learning rate for N of 104, and a total of 30 iterations. These were the only two possibilities that could be chosen from. A single workstation oversaw completing all 8400 training steps, each of which included 30 training epochs. According to the opinions of many, the model's median estimate is almost never as accurate as the model's best prediction. On the other hand, we saw the identical behaviour described for the ISIC 2019 challenge, which was rather discouraging.

In the second test, we assessed how well the design performed by evaluating its performance and determining how well it functioned. This gave us an indication of

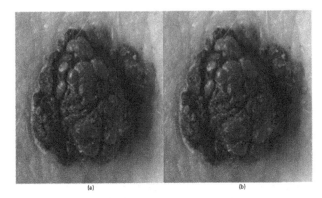

Fig. 2. (a) Normal Image (b) filter with the sigma $= 1$

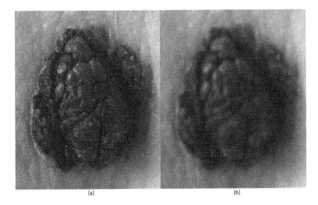

Fig. 3. (a) Normal Image (b) filter with sigma $= 7$

how well it worked. A distributed cooperative system is required for the deployment of a reliable and effective melanoma classifier that is resistant to transfer learning. On purpose, we design the architecture in this way so that it may be automatically retrained and deployed shown in Fig. 4. When dispersed components work together, their duties are completed more efficiently.

Additionally, the user gets access to all previously stored photographs. Furthermore, it is the job of this layer to upload the images to the cloud. The scientists who classify melanoma have been given a simple task: labelling newly gathered photos. The third layer of our model, termed "the cloud," was employed to create an architecture for both initial and follow-up training (see Fig. 5). We were able to distribute each iteration among many instances thanks to the GRIMD architecture. GRIMD instances were originally made accessible through Amazon Web Services (AWS). There must be a shift in the method of training, retraining, and validation. Testing and performance comparisons must be relocated as well. Fog will not be updated with a new model unless it has been demonstrated to be more accurate than the existing one. When new models are created on top of old models, they are deemed ready for release. Layer Agents, a rudimentary

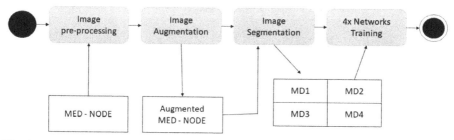

Fig. 4. The Step-By-Step Approach of The First Experiment Was Followed Identically for the Ongoing Retraining

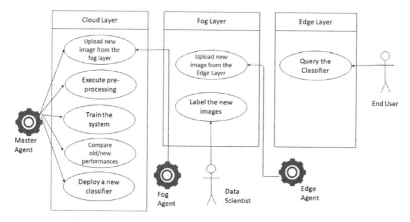

Fig. 5. A three-story building was simulated using a set-up

implementation of CROND, are now in charge of maintaining layer synchronisation. We separated the cloud layer from the rest of the system to make things obvious. Agents were instructed that a new trainer classifier would only be deployed to the fog layer if it had a higher median accuracy than the one that was already there. As a result, separating the classifier's training and execution stages enables prediction generation. This layer also houses the web server and stores the stored models. The Fog layer communicates with each end user via an application.

4 Results

The root-mean-squared error (RMSE) statistic was used to examine how well three distinct networks performed in terms of overall performance. There is a large disparity between the actual and anticipated values of the data, as seen in the first equation.

$$RMSE = \sqrt{\frac{1}{n} \sum_{i=1}^{n} (y_i - \hat{y}_i)^2} \tag{1}$$

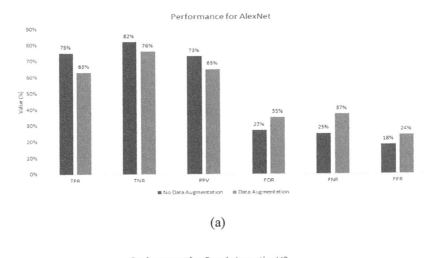

(a)

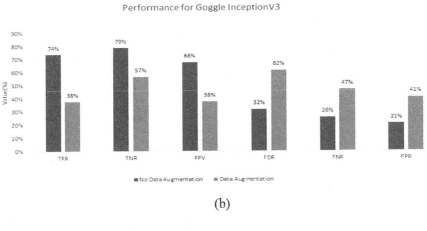

(b)

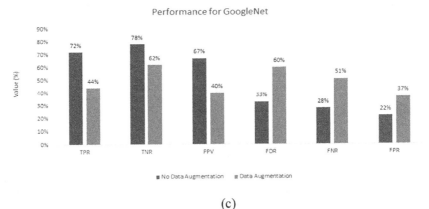

(c)

Fig. 6. Effectiveness of each network by employing Otsu segmentation (a) AlexNet (b) InceptionV3 (c) GoogleNet

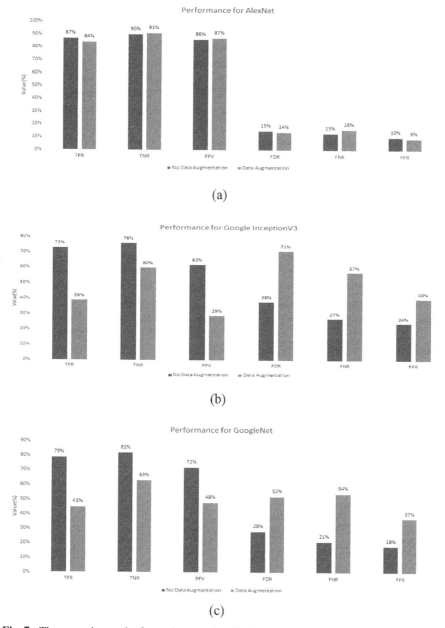

Fig. 7. These are the results for each network utilised, except for Otsu's networks, which were split into two independent networks performance without Otsu segmentation (a) AlexNet (b) InceptionV3 (c) GoogleNet

How many observations are there in total in the dataset? When used in the context of an input, yi signifies the value of the dataset. However, when used in the context of an output, yi denotes the prediction made by the network. To find the number of observations in a collection, use the symbol "n," which stands for the total number of observations contained in that collection. This is accomplished by multiplying the symbol "n" by "1". To achieve this purpose, you must conduct the necessary computations. Figures 6a–6c and Figs. 7a–6c from Otsu segmentation showed that the second group had much higher levels of sensitivity, accuracy, and the ability to tell the difference between real negatives and real positives, as well as a lower rate of false-positives. Furthermore, the latter group experienced many fewer false positives. As a result, the second group had a significantly lower percentage of false positives. As a result, the number of participants in Group 1 who had false positives was much reduced. Furthermore, it was demonstrated that the rate of false positives was significantly higher.

True positives, true negatives, and false positives are abbreviated as "TP," "TN," and "FP," respectively. However, the letters TP and FN stand for true positives and false negatives, respectively, in abbreviated. Positivity errors and inaccuracies. The terms "TP," "TN," and "FP" will be examined in further depth in the next parts of this article. The standard deviation was determined using the approach indicated in Eq. 8 to examine how much the accuracy metrics differed on average, and the results were then compared. Tables 1 and 2 exhibit the results of our investigation, respectively. In this work, both Otsu segmentation and non-Otsu segmentation studies were carried out. These networks are being brought to the reader's attention since they have the highest mean standard deviation and maximum ACC values. A standard deviation is a phrase that is used in addition to the numbers presented. The AlexNet network can be improved or split in any way to provide the greatest possible average ACC output. It makes no difference whether it is segmented or not.

Table 1. Otsu Segmentation Is Used in the Results of Tests on A Medicine-Node Database

With Otsu Segmentation					
Network	Augmented Data	Accuracy 1	Accuracy 2	Accuracy Average	ACC (sd)
Alex network	None	0.65	0.94	0.78	0.06
	Yes	0.44	0.91	0.68	0.08
Google InceptionV3	None	0.56	0.94	0.76	0.07
	Yes	0.32	0.74	0.53	0.09
GoogleNet	None	0.6	0.91	0.75	0.07
	Yes	0.32	0.74	0.55	0.09

A study of how well the networks performed was done for each dataset. The most accurate network, according to Table 3, is GoogleNet, which has a forecast accuracy loss of 19.60%. As a result, it appears that the performance of the ISIC 2018 champions in the ISIC 2019 challenge has dropped by up to 28%.

Table 2. Results without Data Augmentation

Network	Augmented Data	Accuracy 1	Accuracy 2	Accuracy Average	ACC (Sd)
AlexNet	None	0.68	1	0.89	0.05
	Yes	0.76	0.97	0.87	0.05
Google InceptionV3	None	0.56	0.94	0.74	0.07
	Yes	0.32	0.71	0.55	0.07
GoogleNet	None	0.65	0.94	0.8	0.06
	Yes	0.3	0.74	0.55	0.09

Table 3. MD1 to MD4 and Mean Drop Comparison of the Methods

Network	Measure	1	2	3	4	Mean Drop
Alex Network	Best Case	97	91	97	89	−21.95
	Average Case	81	72	81	73	
InceptionV3	Best Case	89	90	91	91	−20.96
	Average Case	81	84	82	84	
	Drop	−19.11	−18.37	−19.1	20.27	
GoogleNet	Best Case	94	93	91	89	−19.6
	Average Case	81	77	75	74	
	Drop	−16.04	−20.77	−21.33	20.27	

In one case, laboratory work is necessary to update datasets as well as to carry out training, validation, and deployment. In the other case, a distributed architecture is provided, which expedites network training.

5   Conclusion

The findings of this study raise the possibility that transfer learning, an increasingly popular method, may be less successful than previously thought. According to the results of the first experiment, even small changes to the primary training data had a significant influence on the classifier's performance. The findings provided here are consistent with those published earlier. Throughout the years, AlexNet has been shown to be the most dependable network in terms of transfer learning. Even though no data from the CNN networks used in this study was divided or altered in any manner, the researchers were able to obtain a higher average ACC. Because there are so many distinct training cycles, it is often required to complete additional training to maintain one's expert categorization abilities at their peak performance. As a result of this data, we concluded that the second experiment should be carried out. It is recommended that images be uploaded to a centralised data server or a cloud storage service to get better control over the administration of the photographic collection. Decentralizing these sorts of systems provides a variety of advantages, two of which are reduced computing time and, as a result, increased capacity. According to the findings of our experiment, CNN networks performed better when there was no segmentation in place. According to the findings of this study, those who engage in physical activity daily should pay particular attention to the skin around lesions. It may be good to repeat the same experiment, but this time focus on contrasting the various preprocessing options available. Despite our best efforts, we were unable to provide an accurate forecast on the least amount of training required to achieve an acceptable degree of robustness. Make the most of the practise time provided to you by conducting further study on the subject. The goal of this experiment is to see if working in a scattered environment results in a decreased overall amount of time spent travelling.

References

1. Esteva, A., et al.: Dermatologist-level classification of skin cancer with deep neural networks. Nature **542**(7639), 115–118 (2017)
2. Abbasi, N.R., et al.: Early diagnosis of cutaneous melanoma: revisiting the ABCD criteria. JAMA Dermatol. **292**(22), 2771–2776 (2004)
3. Nair, R., et al.: Blockchain-based decentralized cloud solutions for data transfer. Comput. Intell. Neurosci. **2022**, 1–12 (2022). https://doi.org/10.1155/2022/8209854
4. Pareek, P.K., et al.: IntOPMICM: intelligent medical image size reduction model. J. Healthc. Eng. **2022**, 11 p. (2022). Article no. 5171016. https://doi.org/10.1155/2022/5171016
5. Goyal, M., Knackstedt, T., Yan, S., Hassanpour, S.: Artificial intelligence-based image classification methods for diagnosis of skin cancer: challenges and opportunities. Comput. Biol. Med. **127** (2020). Article no. 104065. https://www.sciencedirect.com/science/article/pii/S00 10482520303966
6. Shah, V., Autee, P., Sonawane, P.: Detection of melanoma from skin lesion images using deep learning techniques. In: Proceedings of the International Conference on Data Science and Engineering 2020, pp. 1–8 (2020)
7. Adegun, A., Viriri, S.: Deep learning techniques for skin lesion analysis and melanoma cancer detection: a survey of state-of-the-art. Artif. Intell. Rev. **54**(2), 811–841 (2021)
8. Garey, M., Johnson, D., Witsenhausen, H.: The complexity of the generalized Lloyd-Max problem (corresp.). IEEE Trans. Inf. Theory **28**(2), 255–256 (1982)
9. Kashyap, R.: Big data and high-performance analyses and processes. In: Research Anthology on Big Data Analytics, Architectures, and Applications, pp. 262–293 (2022). https://doi.org/10.4018/978-1-6684-3662-2.ch013
10. Zhou, Y., Song, Z.: Binary decision trees for melanoma diagnosis. In: Proceedings of the International Workshop on Multiple Classifier Systems 2013, pp. 374–385 (2013)
11. Kashyap, R.: Dilated residual grooming kernel model for breast cancer detection. Pattern Recognit. Lett. **159**, 157–164 (2022). https://doi.org/10.1016/j.patrec.2022.04.037
12. Kashyap, R.: Machine learning for Internet of Things. In: Research Anthology on Artificial Intelligence Applications in Security, pp. 976–1002 (2021). https://doi.org/10.4018/978-1-7998-7705-9.ch046
13. Nair, R., Gupta, S., Soni, M., Kumar Shukla, P., Dhiman, G.: An approach to minimize the energy consumption during blockchain transaction. Mater. Today Proc. (2020). https://doi.org/10.1016/j.matpr.2020.10.361

14. Nair, R., Bhagat, A.: An application of big data analytics in road transportation. In: Advances in Systems Analysis, Software Engineering, and High Performance Computing, pp. 39–54 (2018). https://doi.org/10.4018/978-1-5225-3870-7.ch003

15. Naseri, M., et al.: A new cryptography algorithm for quantum images. Optik **171**, 947–959 (2018)

16. Mustafa, M.A., Meri, M.A., Ibrahim, M.D., Al-Hakeem, A.H.: Procalcitonin and NLR Measurements in COVID-19 Patients. Lat. Am. J. Pharm. **42**(Spec. Issue), 220–223 (2023)

17. Mustafa, M.A., Mustafa, H.A., Ahmed, M.T., Meri, M.A.: Virulence factors of proteus mirabilis isolated from urinary tract infection patients. Lat. Am. J. Pharm., **42**(Spec. Issue), 418–421 (2023)

18. Mustafa, M.A., et al.: Adsorption behavior of Rh-doped graphdiyne monolayer towards various gases: a quantum mechanical analysis. Inorg. Chem. Commun. **111928** (2024). https://doi.org/10.1016/j.inoche.2023.111928

19. Hosny, K.M., Kassem, M.A., Foaud, M.M.: Classification of skin lesions using transfer learning and augmentation with Alex-Net. PLoS ONE **14**(5), e0217293 (2019)

20. Szegedy, C., et al.: Going deeper with convolutions. In: Proceedings of the IEEE Conference on Computer Vision and Pattern Recognition, pp. 1–9 (2015)

21. Ahmad, I., Serbaya, S.H., Rizwan, A., Mehmood, M.S.: Spectroscopic analysis for harnessing the quality and potential of gemstones for small and medium-sized enterprises (SMEs). J. Spectrosc. **2021** (2021)

22. Almarzouki, H.Z., Alsulami, H., Rizwan, A., Basingab, M.S., Bukhari, H., Shabaz, M.: An internet of medical things-based model for real-time monitoring and averting stroke. J. Healthc. Eng. **2021** (2021)

23. Alnuaim, A.A., et al.: Human-computer interaction for recognizing speech emotions using multilayer perceptron classifier. J. Healthc. Eng. **2022**, 12 p. (2022). Article no. 6005446. https://doi.org/10.1155/2022/6005446

24. Sathya, M., et al.: A novel, efficient, and secure anomaly detection technique using DWU-ODBN for IoT-enabled multimedia communication systems. Wirel. Commun. Mob. Comput. **2021**, 12 p. (2021). Article no. 4989410. https://doi.org/10.1155/2021/4989410

25. Alnuaim, A.A., et al.: Human-computer interaction with detection of speaker emotions using convolution neural networks. Comput. Intell. Neurosci. **2022**, 16 p. (2022). Article ID 7463091. https://doi.org/10.1155/2022/7463091

26. Alnuaim, A.A., et al.: Speaker gender recognition based on deep neural networks and ResNet50. Wirel. Commun. Mob. Comput. **2022**, 13 p. (2022). Article no. 4444388. https://doi.org/10.1155/2022/4444388

27. Celebi, M.E., et al.: A methodological approach to the classification of dermoscopy images. Comput. Med. Imag. Graph. **31**(6), 362–373 (2007)

28. Sreelatha, T., Subramanyam, M.V., Prasad, M.G.: Shape and color feature based melanoma diagnosis using dermoscopic images. J. Ambient Intell. Humaniz. Comput., 1–10 (2020)

29. Nair, R., Bhagat, A.: An introduction to clustering algorithms in big data. In: Encyclopedia of Information Science and Technology, 5th edn., pp. 559–576 (2021). https://doi.org/10.4018/978-1-7998-3479-3.ch040

30. Lee, T., Ng, V., Gallagher, R., Coldman, A., McLean, D.: Dullrazor: a software approach to hair removal from images. Comput. Biol. Med. **27**(6), 533–543 (1997)

31. Otsu, N.: A threshold selection method from gray-level histograms. IEEE Trans. Syst, Man Cybern. **9**(1), 62–66 (1979)

32. Shorten, C., Khoshgoftaar, T.M.: A survey on image data augmentation for deep learning. J. Big Data **6**(1), 1–48 (2019)

Hybrid Residual Network and XGBoost Method for the Accurate Diagnosis of Lung Cancer

Mohammed Ahmed Mustafa[1]([✉]), Abual-hassan Adel[2], Maki Mahdi Abdulhasan[3], Zainab Alassedi[4], Ghadir Kamil Ghadir[5], and Hayder Musaad Al-Tmimi[6]

[1] Department of Medical Laboratory Technology, University of Imam Jaafar AL-Sadiq, Baghdad, Iraq
Mohammed.ahmed.mustafa@sadiq.edu.iq
[2] Al-Manara College for Medical Sciences, Maysan, Iraq
[3] Department of Medical Laboratories Technology, AL-Nisour University College, Baghdad, Iraq
[4] College of Computer, National University of Science and Technology, Dhi Qar, Iraq
[5] College of Pharmacy, Al-Farahidi University, Baghdad, Iraq
[6] College of Health Medical Techniques, Al-Bayan University, Baghdad, Iraq

Abstract. Lung cancer mortality is increasing in this country due to a variety of factors, including the country's increasing industrialization, the buildup of hazardous substances in the environment, and an ageing population. Computed Tomography (CT) scans are routinely used on patients as part of the diagnostic procedure to achieve a conclusive diagnosis of lung cancer. Because of the way X-rays are absorbed by biological tissues, CT scans may detect even the most deeply hidden structures. Pulmonary nodules are lumps or bumps in the lungs that are signs of disease. Because each type of nodule can take many different shapes, the chance of getting cancer varies a lot. In some cases, computer vision models can now help clinicians identify a wide range of medical disorders; in some cases, these models have been found to be more accurate than actual doctors. Deep learning advancements in recent years have made this possible. The disease diagnosis carries a great deal of significance and value for the field due to the numerous opportunities provided by modern technology. This is because the application's primary function is to serve as a diagnostic tool for a variety of illnesses. Our goals were to improve the accuracy of diagnostic tests and to find diseases earlier. We discovered that the model could detect lung cancer earlier than other approaches already in use. The suggested model includes the following elements: Identifying pulmonary nodules, discussing false positives, and discussing diagnostic uncertainty the number of lung nodules will be reduced by removing "false nodules" and classifying lung nodules as benign or malignant. Throughout human history, new network architectures and loss functions have been developed and implemented. Furthermore, the recommended deep learning mode could be improved, resulting in improved lung nodule identification accuracy. Experiments have shown that the proposed method greatly improves the ratio of accuracy to precision when evaluating the disease being studied.

Keywords: Deep Learning · Lung Cancer · Computed Tomography · computer-aided design · Disease Detection · Residual Network

M. Botto-Tobar et al. (Eds.): ICAT 2023, CCIS 2049, pp. 134–148, 2024.
https://doi.org/10.1007/978-3-031-58956-0_10

1   Introduction

The prevalence of lung cancer and the mortality rates associated with the disease are directly related to rising levels of air pollution. The National Cancer Institute in the United States estimates that 1.4 million Americans are diagnosed with lung cancer each year [1]. Every year, some form of judicial system investigates more than 60% of all cases filed anywhere in the world. Only 15% of infants survive to their fifth birthday, indicating a high infant mortality rate. This is a sizable percentage. The significance of performing lung cancer screenings at an early stage to halt disease progression has received a lot of attention in recent years. This is because studies have shown that early detection improves lung cancer survival rates. The blood flow within the brain was examined using this device. This tool was used to help with the dissection of the human brain. Since then, there has been a significant advancement in the usage of CT technologies in the field. Computed tomography, usually known as CT scans, is the most common type of medical imaging and is frequently used to detect lung abnormalities. Biopsies, which take samples of tissue from patients, are the best way to find out if someone has a disease like lung cancer. A bronchoscope is put into the patient's lungs through the mouth or nose, directed down the trachea (windpipe), and then into the area of the lungs where the suspicious lesion is located to take a biopsy sample. CT scans' high-density resolution allows for the creation of contrasted pictures even in places with incredibly minute density fluctuations, such as soft tissues in humans. This is possible because CT images have high-density resolution. This is due to CT's capacity to give separate pictures of components with even minor changes in density. Despite this, the volume of medical imaging data is growing at an alarmingly rapid rate. This is because imaging technology is constantly improving, and as a result, there has been an increase in demand from clinical settings. This has occurred due to a corresponding increase in clinical demand, which is the cause of it. The rapid development of CT technology, particularly high-resolution CT, has been one of the major factors contributing to the acceleration of this trend. According to reports, imaging data, which accounts for 90% of total data held by hospitals, is growing at a rate of 30% per year. Medical knowledge is advancing while this expansion is taking place. Even if medical technology advances, this trend is likely to continue. During this time, the number of medical professionals with training in imaging diagnostics has increased, albeit only by about 4% [2]. To obtain a complete view of the lung, it is common practice to acquire 150 to 300 images during a lung CT scan. The ongoing challenge of executing diagnostic procedures puts radiologists' mental and physical endurance under strain. This demonstrates that the amount of time spent reading through a scan sequence is directly proportional to the interpretation's suffering. Who or what must be held responsible? After looking at CT scans for a long time, a person's eyes tend to get tired, which can lead to missed diagnoses and wrong image interpretation.

According to research undertaken by a team at the prestigious Johns Hopkins University in the United States, while evaluating chest discomfort with a chest CT, a single imaging specialist has a chance of missing the shadow of clinically important lung nodules by up to 30%. As a result, medical personnel must rely on computers to interpret and diagnose patients. This change will result in a speedier and more precise diagnostic process right away. Rapid advances in computer technology and software, as well as advances in deep learning-related technologies, have enabled computer-aided diagnosis (CAD) to make significant strides in recent years. As a result, CAD technology has gradually but steadily demonstrated its practical value in the diagnosis process [3, 4]. The "second reader" capability of the CAD software is increasingly being implemented throughout the hospital. By executing an abstract simulation of the neuron network seen in the human brain, a mathematical model known as an artificial neural network was established. CT scans detect lung cancer more accurately than standard chest x-rays. Deep learning technology has some advantages over older methods like chance and statistics when it comes to segmenting, classifying, and detecting images. Excellence follows the most stringent criterion. Medical imaging is another field that extensively relies on neural network technology, particularly for medical diagnostics [3, 4]. Because of its adaptability, effectiveness, and low learning curve, deep learning technology has gained popularity as a means of medical therapy in recent years. These characteristics have contributed to the popularity of this therapy option. We created a cutting-edge medical detection algorithm to aid medical practitioners in their efforts to precisely identify prevalent diseases and anatomical features. As a result, medical specialists may now be able to make more accurate diagnoses than ever before. We discovered that the model could detect lung cancer earlier than other approaches already in use. The proposed paradigm consists of three components: Examples of (i) discovering lung nodules, (ii) obtaining a false-positive result, (iii) the detection of potentially cancerous lung nodules to reduce the number of people who undergo unnecessary biopsies It is critical to determine whether lung nodules are cancerous or benign to reduce the overall prevalence of this condition. Throughout history, numerous distinct network architectures and loss functions have been developed. The Nodule-Net detection network structure can be used to supplement the recommended deep learning-based mode for locating lung nodules. This network structure, which combines RPN and U-Net, is one of the options. This structure was created by combining U-Net and RPN. The remaining information will be organized according to the timeline displayed below. In the next section, we'll take a quick look at some of the past work that has been done on this subject, with a focus on the most important points. Deep learning could be used to find signs of lung cancer in pictures, for example.

2   Related Work

Medical imaging is one of the fields where CAD has seen increased use in recent years, and new CAD technologies are produced every year. Concurrently, a never-ending stream of cutting-edge imaging tools is being developed with the goal of detecting lung cancer. The acronym CAD, which stands for computer-aided design, was proposed for the first time in 1985. A CAD system was created after a significant amount of time was spent on research and new technology development. Using this software to eliminate the need for manual labour in the drafting process could significantly increase overall productivity. This is a well-known fact. The application of this technology can aid in the documentation of design processes as well as the acquisition of technical skills. A lot of architects, engineers, and artists use computer-aided design tools every day. The app is used by these professionals to make models in two and three dimensions. AutoCAD and Auto-CAD LT are well-known pieces of software. "Computer-aided design and drawing," or

CAD, is a common term. This app cuts down on physical work, which makes drawing faster and easier. This plan helps make papers with goals and basic skills. Two- and three-dimensional computer-aided design (CAD) software is used by both engineers and artists. CAD refers to the use of computers in the design process, AutoCAD and Auto-CAD LT are two excellent examples of programmes that meet this criterion. Autodesk provides both programmes. Given that AutoCAD was the first programme of its kind, it is not surprising that it is used by millions of people worldwide. It is suitable for a wide range of activities, including the construction of models, electrical schematics, two- and three-dimensional detailed drawings, and architectural floor plans. The CAD application used in the treatment of lung cancer focuses on both the detection and diagnosis of lung cancer as primary areas of focus. The first method is typically used by radiologists to detect lung cancer symptoms, while the second method is typically used by pathologists to identify cancerous tissue [5, 6]. Several papers have been produced and published on the topic of segmenting the lungs into discrete sections, with CT scans and chest radiography serving as the primary diagnostic techniques. As a result, intelligent CAD systems are now better able to adapt to a wide range of dynamic settings. The incorporation of artificial neural network technology into systems such as M5LCAD and MOT M5Lv1 has significantly improved performance. Recent advancements in the relevant field have directly contributed to this possibility. This is the immediate result of the events; this technology has an 80% diagnostic accuracy rate and a 95% detection accuracy rate. Both rates are significantly higher than the national average. It would not have taken much effort to determine the two different success rates [7–9]. This technology can detect and locate nodules with a minimum diameter of three millimeters. Evaluation of LUNA16 [10] for "Lung Nodule Detection" and "False Positive Reduction". The evaluation was performed to detect lung nodules. In terms of ranking, Jianpei CAD was ranked lower than Patech CAD. Polymerase chain reactions, reverse transcriptase polymerase chain reactions, strand displacement amplification, and transcription amplification are examples of target amplification techniques, whereas branching DNA tests and hybrid capture are examples of signal amplification techniques. The advancement of computer-aided diagnosis software has made it possible to locate and precisely diagnose pulmonary nodular lesions. This is a significant advancement over previous techniques. According to some evidence [11–13], using templates to identify problematic areas ahead of time may aid in the detection of lung nodules in photographs. This is where the process of locating lung nodules would begin. It has previously been carried out in several countries all over the world. In their study, Bilgin and colleagues proposed a method that combines iris filtering and threshold segmentation. Given how quickly the current neural network is evolving, data demand has skyrocketed to meet the needs of the rapidly expanding neural network. This data was gathered as part of an investigation to identify the earliest characteristics that can be used to differentiate lung nodules from other lung abnormalities [11, 12]. The investigation's goal was to identify the earliest traits that could be used. Cancer's early signs and symptoms, as well as its manifestations All of these investigations resulted in the collection of 1018 distinct study samples, each of which was then included in the data set. After reviewing each patient's images, the four board-certified thoracic radiologists independently arrived at a diagnosis. Their conclusions were based on what they saw in the images of each patient. This investigation is divided into two parts, each with its own focus. Furthermore, the labeling includes information about the nodule's shape and degree of calcification, as well as its cancerous status. This section includes an illustration of the nodule's general appearance as well as these specifics [13–15].

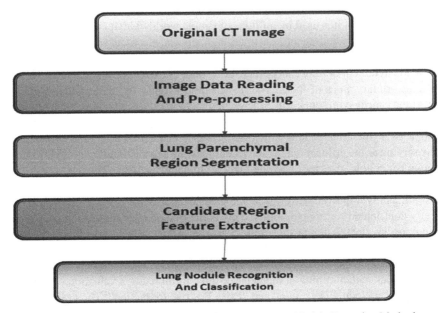

Fig. 1. Detailed Approach Incorporated into The Lung Nodule Detection Method

Extracting the features; classifying the lung nodule target; and detecting the nodule, when reaching a decision, the algorithm takes all these factors into account. The ability of the algorithm to pinpoint the specific lung nodule that requires treatment is a bonus. Figure 1 shows more information about these parts than any of the other figures. (1) The following is a list of the most used techniques for locating lung nodules. Traditional lung nodule identification systems require human intervention to construct the shape and texture of lung nodules. Differential imaging is typically one of the methods used when attempting to solve the problem of detecting lung nodules, as shown in Fig. 1.

3   Proposed Method

It is possible to attain the region of interest that will be used for further detection and classification tasks while also decreasing noise to some extent using the provided technique. The following is a condensed version of the full version that includes a summary of the key points: Is The "pydicom" toolkit can read "dicom" images, stack them into a single array, and sort the array based on the value of an "Instance Number" attribute. Because CT scans are the only ones that use the "dicom" format, this toolkit was designed specifically for reading "dicom" files that are specific to CT scans. The pixel distance, for example, is 0.75 mm on the x and y-axes but only 0.6 mm on the z-axis. Given this, the first step in standardizing pixel distances along each axis is to interpolate the lengths between pixels while keeping the 1 mm unit of measurement in mind. (iii) The organ and tissue value table can be used to determine the appropriate segmentation threshold for each given CT image. To get to the HU value, the pixel value must first go through a linear transformation. The HU value is then used to calculate the intensity of the CT radiation. (iv) Based on the testing findings, a threshold of 320Hu has been determined to be the optimal value for segmentation [16–19]. To give one example: It is possible to identify the lungs from the tissues and organs that surround them by using the Gaussian filter for segmentation and setting this threshold, along with the standard deviation, to 1. However, the segmented lung image still contains a substantial quantity of air contaminants, so we must choose the proper domain to clean up the image. After this step is done, the final image of the ROI is made by multiplying the image of the processed mask by the image of the starting points.

3.1   Methods for Identifying Lung Nodules

The focus of this paper is the presentation of a network for nodule detection shown in Fig. 2. The concepts covered in U-Net formed the basis for the network's design. U-Net was initially developed to address the problem of cell segmentation in medical imaging, but it has since proven to be a very useful tool in this field. The two distinct concepts are combined to form the completed network structure known as Nodule-Net. This model introduces the RPN network concept.

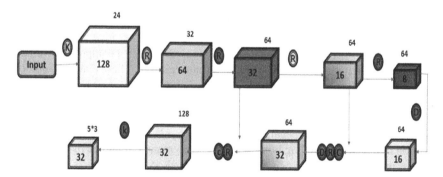

Fig. 2. The Basic Structure of a Network Designed to Identify Nodules

The U-Net structure serves as the backbone of the network, whereas the RPN structure serves as the output layer. When it is employed as a framework, U-Net can successfully capture the qualities of multi-scale data and medical imaging. All these details are crucial for finding a solution to the problem, as the nodules' sizes and attributes are widely variable. Because of this, the essential qualities are highly crucial. The RPN network can then immediately produce the specified region because of its distinctive output style [22–24]. The overall layout is understandable and unmuddled. Concurrently, it bridges the gap between the theoretical foundations of medical imaging and those of natural imaging, resulting in beneficial applications in both areas. The network's feed-forward and feedback structures can operate independently of one another. Two 3 × 3 × 3 convolutional layers, each with 24 channels, serve as an early feature extraction module in the feedforward framework. This layer is referred to as the PreBlock Layer on the internal network. The next thing to look at is a 3D array of four residual blocks, which are positioned between eight maximum pooling layers. There are three primary categories of residuals that make up each residual block: "Conv + BN + ReLU + Conv + BN" and the "skip connection". Every convolution kernel in a feedforward structure is the same size, measuring three by three by three, and there is no empty space between them. These sizing requirements are unequivocal [25–27]. Because the padding is set to 1, any errors will be obvious to the reader. Both positive and negative feedback make use of two link units and two deconvolution layers, respectively. Each deconvolution layer has a 2 × 2 kernel and a step size of 2 as well. After that, two 1 × 3D convolution operations are carried out, resulting in a total output size of 32 × 32. This is because the number of channels has increased from 64 to 15. Two separate 1 × 1 convolution algorithms control the foreground/background separation and the background border regression, respectively. Use the transform to convert the resulting four-dimensional tensor to a three-by-five matrix. The matrix's final two dimensions will show the three anchor types as well as the bounding box regression results for each anchor type.

3.2 Negative Mining

When looking for someone, it is common to find more evidence pointing to the target not existing than pointing to the target's existence. The network can correctly identify most negative samples, but a small number of them look suspiciously like nodules and may be difficult to find. Even though the network can correctly identify most negative samples, this situation is currently being subjected to hard negative mining, which is typically used to address target identification issues. To obtain a comprehensive output feature map, the network must first be fed a lung cancer image. These feature maps depict several bounding boxes, each of which is associated with a different level of certainty. (1) The initial bounding box with a value in the negative range is used as the starting point, and n boxes are chosen at random from it to create a pool of candidates. This yields a result that is in the negative number range. (2) select the examples from the collection of negative bounding boxes that pose the greatest challenge by arranging the examples in descending order of confidence. This method will allow you to identify the most difficult cases.

3.3 Refining Process

The Nodule-Net network provides access to a wide range of suggestion regions, many of which include suggestion boxes that overlap one another, as shown in Figs. 3 and 4. These two illustrations show how to do so. The results will be "post-processed," which is another word for "analyzed," with non-maximum suppression. The main goal of this strategy is to ignore the windows with the lowest level of certainty as much as possible and choose the neighborhood boxes with the highest level of certainty that are currently available. The following are the most important steps: Set B is completed by adding the remaining suggestion boxes. The confidence set S and the suggested box list B have now been generated. The detection is complete with the output of the result, D. Containers from group B with IoU of M values greater than the 0.05 cutoff during this experiment were transferred to group D. For a while, the remaining containers were allowed to dangle precariously in B. Repeat this process until all the old things have been taken out of the area marked B.

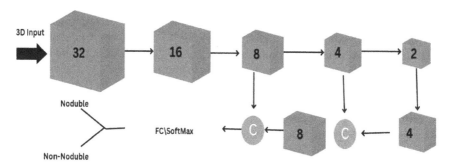

Fig. 3. The structure of the Proposed Network

Then, in the next step, one network will extract features using the leftover block, while the other network will use the dense block. These two actions will take place at the same time. The first network can extract features from the remaining block, whereas the second network cannot. Finally, standardisation is performed before adding a feature vector with 4096 dimensions to the fully linked layer. After performing a softmax on both categories, we were able to get the necessary activation value of ppred. The 3D ResNet approach produces four residual blocks. Following that, DenseNet's fully connected layer generates 4096-dimensional feature vectors, and a forecast of a final value known as ppred is formed. DenseNet is made up of four dense blocks. This is due to the U-NET structure's increased flexibility and ease of modification. Figure 4 on this page depicts the network's organizational structure graphically.

The global coordinates of photographs saved in "mhd" or "raw" formats must be translated to local coordinates. U-Net was created to address the problem of cell segmentation in medical imaging, which was one of its key goals. The two distinct ideas are combined to form the finished network structure known as Nodule-Net. A feedforward structure consists of a three-dimensional array of four residual blocks stacked between up to eight pooling layers. Use the transform to convert the resulting four-dimensional tensor into a matrix with three rows and five columns. The final two dimensions of the matrix will show the various types of anchors as well as the bounding box regression results for each type of anchor. The network can find the vast majority of negative samples correctly, but a small number of them look like nodules and may be hard to find. This enhancement is possible due to the expansion of core functionality. As a result, the public now has access to the update. The U-Net 3DCNN was chosen as the foundation for the best False Positive Reduction network since it produced the highest quality output. The weighted cross-entropy loss function was also included in this model. This conclusion was reached after extensive research. When it comes to medical imaging,

U-Nets outperform other network topologies, according to the study's findings. Consider the following as an example: The outcome confirmed that my underlying theory was correct.

4 Experiments and Result

We began our research on nodule detection with a sample size of 2,000 raw materials. The following step is to incorporate new data into the initial data set, resulting in 10,000 more samples. Following the initial division, the remaining 92% were divided into two groups: testing and training. 2% points out of the total Your attention should be drawn to the fact that the primary goal of such actions is to improve the quality of the data. The image will be rotated to fit a range of 0 to 180°, determined at random. If the data quality improves in the future, we will change the new coordinates. Please keep in mind that this is critical. As a result of our efforts, we were able to change the model's parameters. SGD is used as the optimizer to maintain the gradient throughout the experiment. The learning rate has decreased from 0.01% at the start of Stage 1 to 0.0001% by the end of Stage 3. The learning rate in the first fifty stages is 0.01 epoch, 0.001 epoch in the second fifty stages, and 0.0001 epoch in the final hundred stages. Furthermore, we use a method known as "patch learning" to focus on specific blocks to identify during training. After running a full FROC analysis, we get a score of 0.876. Figure 5 depicts one possible arrangement for displaying the test set results.

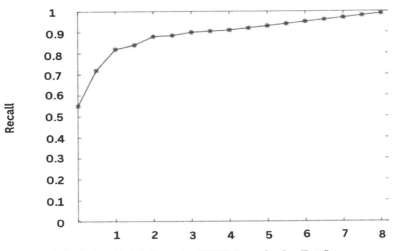

Fig. 4. The Nodule Detection FROC Curve for Our Test Set

The graph depicts the horizontal rate of correct diagnoses and the vertical rate of accurate diagnoses. One method of avoiding detection is to examine the data to see if it meets a predetermined standard or set of criteria that ensure the data's veracity. This concept can be expressed precisely and unambiguously by using phrases such as "I would rather kill a thousand by accident than let go of one". If a positive action causes an incorrect decrease in size or amount, the effect will persist even after the detection process is completed. As a result of this positive action, there was a decrease. This is since doing good has long-term consequences. To remove the FP nodules discovered in the previous phase, use the False Positive Reduction technique. During the nodule identification process, as many "real" nodules as possible must be discovered. This condition must be met. Because it takes so long to collect the remaining nodules.

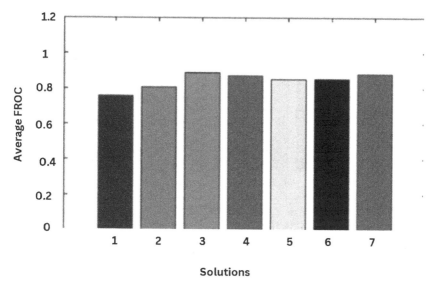

Fig. 5. A Histogram of Average FROC Values

Reasonably good detection accuracy of adherent nodules is one of the many essential benefits of our methodology, in addition to the benefits already described. Because of the extent of this benefit, it has a lot of value and is quite beneficial. This is owing to the architecture of the feature extraction network, or U-Net, utilized in this model, which integrates both low-level and high-level information. When compared to the good examples we do have, our data set's 549714 possible nodules are an excessively large number (2000 cases). So, we use data augmentation to make our positive sample bigger and downsampling to make our selected counterexample samples bigger. The sample is rotated to increase its size before being reduced back down to its original size. The scaling ratios of 0.6, 0.9, 1.2, and 1.5 are the most used. When the transposition dataset is used, the x, y, and z axes can all receive more space. Reduce the number of samples collected from a negative sample to reduce the percentage of false-negative results. As a result, the best possible negative sample is chosen at random from the pool of initial negative samples. As a result, only one positive sample was discovered for every three negative samples. To reduce the number of false positive outcomes, we conducted an experiment with a sample size of 100,000, with 80,000 used for training data and 20,000 used for test data (8:2 split). Here are some general tips to follow while modifying the settings: The mass depreciates at a rate of $1e-4$ and the momentum is 0.9. The learning rate stayed fixed at 0.01 iterations per second or 0.0001 iterations per second.

The attenuation process is also broken up into three phases, each with a batch size of 32. The following steps make up each phase: Fig. 6 shows a comparison between the architecture of the U-Net-based classification network looked at in this study and the topologies of other approaches shown at the LUNA16 conference.

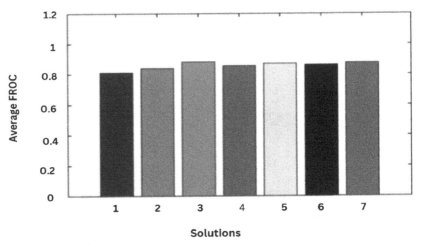

Fig. 6. A Histogram of Average FROC Values

In Fig. 6, we compare the average FROC of the 3DCNN to that of the alternative solutions. This allows us to assess the efficacy of each solution (Table 1).

Table 1. Comparative Analysis of the Proposed Method

Method	Sensitivity	Specificity	ROC_AUC
Residual Network	93	50	72
Residual Network + Support Vector Machine	93	89	93
Residual Network + Random Forest	94	92	93
Residual Network + XGBoost	95	92	94

This development is a direct result of the strategy and can be attributed to it. These qualities were then arranged in a hierarchical structure using categories. Despite the chaos, the machine learning-based classification algorithm has maintained a high level of accuracy. The XGBoost machine learning classifier has been shown to have the best speed-to-efficacy ratio. This approach cannot be considered for inclusion in the application that serves as the foundation due to its inability to provide a comprehensive solution to the problem. In the following paragraphs, we will go into greater detail about both our prompt action and the implementation of the extensive network upgrade. We have also used some secret methods and added some new data to the network to make the whole thing work better. Table 2 and Fig. 8 show comparisons of test results based on the four different research strategies.

Table 2. Comparative Analysis of the Proposed Method

Method	Sensitivity	Specificity	ROC_AUC
Residual Network + Feature Combine	91	93	92
Residual Network + Max Probability	89	91	90
Residual Network + Noise-or	94	93	93
Residual Network + Leaky Noise-or	95	96	94

Based on structural changes, lung nodules can be classified as benign or malignant.

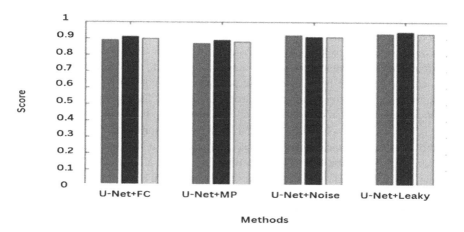

Fig. 8. Comparative Analysis of Various Methods

When compared to other methods, the "U-Net + LeakyNoise-or" approach provided the highest capacity for preventing interference, the highest specificity, and the highest ROC AUC. Based on the study's findings, these conclusions were reached. Using the model known as "U-Net + LeakyNoise", it is possible to determine whether a nodule is cancerous or not. As a result, we have a much better chance of achieving our objectives. This method has been shown to give the most accurate results when figuring out if a nodule is dangerous to touch.

5 Conclusion

The results of a thorough investigation are presented in this article. The study's goal was to look into the feasibility of using deep learning techniques on lung and thyroid cancer CT scans. The research was carried out by University of Washington academics. The authors of this article conducted the investigation. The investigational phase of this study was funded by the University of Washington in Seattle and the University of Washington in Seattle. The authors of this article put in all the necessary time and effort to collect the data used in it. The National Cancer Institute, which oversees this investigation, has been given the go-ahead to do so. Another secondary goal was to distinguish between benign and malignant nodules as well as the various lung nodules. Some researchers used deep learning on CT scans of patients undergoing lung cancer treatment. The Nodule-Net network is highly recommended because it combines the best features of both the U-Net and the RPN networks. This is because it provides advantages that both networks can benefit from. The discovery of lung nodules was the pivotal event in the chain of events that eventually resulted in the formation of this network. These lung nodules caused this network to form. This series of events acted as a catalyst for the creation of this network. Furthermore, when the proposed model was applied to the validation data, encouraging results were obtained. We were able to come to this conclusion because we had access to the data. After a thorough investigation, this was proven to be true. In comparison to the numerous other solutions submitted for consideration in the LUNA 16 competition, it has a favorable position due to the test set's final average FROC value of 0.876. This method is a versatile choice because it performs admirably throughout the entire process, from initial screening to final labeling. As a result of technological advancements, the time required to locate a nodule has significantly decreased. This advancement enabled us to address the issue of reducing false positives. This configuration can be further characterized using a weighted cross-entropy U-Net. This has resulted in the removal of a significant number of false positives. This helps keep things in perspective when there is a lot of bad news to process and a lot of information to take in. Because of its score of 0.883 on the most recent test set, the option has a significant advantage over competing LUNA16 strategies. The effectiveness of these alternative strategies cannot be guaranteed. To avoid misunderstandings, it is acceptable to use the terms FROC and TROC interchangeably. The most commonly used type of network for feature extraction in the process of attempting to distinguish between benign and malignant lung nodules is a three-dimensional U-net structure network.

Funding Statement. The research and publication of this article was not funded by any financially supporting bodies. Also the presented research didn't get any grant from any of the government bodies.

Data Availability. LUNA16 dataset publically available.

Conflict of Interest. There is no conflict of interest.

References

1. National Cancer Institute: Cancer statistics (n.d.). https://www.cancer.gov/about-cancer/understanding/statistics. Accessed 17 Oct 2022
2. Zhao, P.F.: Research on Detection and Classification of Small Pulmonary Nodules Based on Convolution Neural Network. Taiyuan University of Technology, Taiyuan (2018)

3. Choi, E., Bahadori, M.T., Schuetz, A., Stewart, W.F., Sun, J.: Doctor AI: predicting clinical events via recurrent neural networks. Proc. Mach. Learn. Healthc. **56**, 301–318 (2016)

4. Lipton, Z.C., Kale, D.C., Elkan, C., Wetzel, R.: Learning to diagnose with LSTM recurrent neural networks. In: Proceedings of the International Conference on Learning Representations (ICLR) (2016)

5. Murphy, K., van Ginneken, B., Schilham, A.M.R., de Hoop, B.J., Gietema, H.A., Prokop, M.: A large-scale evaluation of automatic pulmonary nodule detection in chest CT using local image features and k-nearest-neighbour classification. Med. Image Anal. **13**(5), 757–770 (2009)

6. Jacobs, C., Van Rikxoort, E.M., Twellmann, T., et al.: Automatic detection of subsolid pulmonary nodules in thoracic computed tomography images. Med. Image Anal. **18**(2), 374–384 (2014)

7. Tan, M., Deklerck, R., Jansen, B., Bister, M., Cornelis, J.: A novel computer-aided lung nodule detection system for CT images. Med. Phys. **38**(10), 5630–5645 (2011)

8. Lopez Torres, E., Fiorina, E., Pennazio, F., et al.: Large scale validation of the M5L lung CAD on heterogeneous CT datasets. Med. Phys. **42**(4), 1477–1489 (2015)

9. Koundal, D., Gupta, S., Singh, S.: Neutrosophic based Nakagami total variation method for speckle suppression in thyroid ultrasound images. IRBM **39**(1), 43–53 (2018)

10. Hossen, M.N., Panneerselvam, V., Koundal, D., Ahmed, K., Bui, F.M., Ibrahim, S.M.: Federated machine learning for detection of skin diseases and enhancement of internet of medical things (IoMT) security. IEEE J. Biomed. Health Inform. (2022)

11. Keserci, B., Yoshida, H.: Computerized detection of pulmonary nodules in chest radiographs based on morphological features and wavelet snake model. Med. Image Anal. **6**(4), 431–447 (2002)

12. Shao, H., Cao, L., Liu, Y.: A detection approach for solitary pulmonary nodules based on CT images. In: Proceedings of the 2012 2nd International Conference on Computer Science and Network Technology, Changchun, China, pp. 1253–1257. IEEE (2012)

13. Cascio, D., Magro, R., Fauci, F., Raso, M.G.: Automatic detection of lung nodules in CT datasets based on stable 3D mass–spring models. Comput. Biol. Med. **42**(11), 2012 (2012)

14. Bhat, S., Koundal, D.: Multi-focus image fusion techniques: a survey. Artif. Intell. Rev. **54**(8), 5735–5787 (2021)

15. Liao, F., Liang, M., Li, Z., Hu, X., Song, S.: Evaluate the malignancy of pulmonary nodules using the 3D deep leaky noisy-or network. IEEE Trans. Neural Netw. Learn. Syst. **30**(11), 3484–3495 (2017)

16. Kashyap, R.: Object boundary detection through robust active contour based method with global information. Int. J. Image Min. **3**(1), 22 (2018). https://doi.org/10.1504/ijim.2018.100 14063

17. Nair, R., Alhudhaif, A., Koundal, D., Doewes, R.I., Sharma, P.: Deep learning-based COVID-19 detection system using pulmonary CT scans. Turk. J. Electr. Eng. Comput. Sci. **29**(8), 2716–2727 (2021)

18. Sharma, A., Singh, K., Koundal, D.: A novel fusion based convolutional neural network approach for classification of COVID-19 from chest X-ray images. Biomed. Signal Process. Control **77**, 103778 (2022)

19. Malhotra, P., Gupta, S., Koundal, D., Zaguia, A., Kaur, M., Lee, H.N.: Deep learning-based computer-aided pneumothorax detection using chest X-ray images. Sensors **22**(6), 2278 (2022)

20. Yaseen, A.H., Khalaf, A.T., Mustafa, M.A.: Lung cancer data analysis for finding gene expression. Afr. J. Biol. Sci. **5**(3), 119–130 (2023)

21. Mustafa, M.A., Abdal Rahman, M.A.A., Almahdawi, Z.M.M.: Male infertility treatment unveiled: exploring new horizons with Q-well 10 - results from a pioneering medical study. Afr. J. Biol. Sci. **5**(2), 83–96 (2023). https://doi.org/10.48047/AFJBS.5.2.2023.83-96

22. Hassan, J.A., Rasheed, M.K.: Synthesis and characterization of some benzimidazole derivatives from 4-methyl ortho-phenylene diamine and evaluating their effectiveness against bacteria and fungi. AIP Conf. Proc. **2394**, 040040 (2022). https://doi.org/10.1063/5.0121766

23. Ramirez-Asis, E., et al.: A lightweight hybrid dilated ghost model-based approach for the prognosis of breast cancer. Comput. Intell. Neurosci. **2022**, 1–10 (2022)

24. Mohanakurup, V., et al.: Breast cancer detection on histopathological images using a composite dilated backbone network. Comput. Intell. Neurosci. **2022**, 1–10 (2022)

25. Parashar, V., et al.: Aggregation-based dynamic channel bonding to maximise the performance of wireless local area networks (WLAN). Wirel. Commun. Mob. Comput. **2022**, 1–11 (2022)

26. Kashyap, R.: Breast cancer histopathological image classification using stochastic dilated residual ghost model. Int. J. Inf. Retr. Res. **12**, 1–24 (2020). https://doi.org/10.4018/ijirr.289655

27. Nair, R., Bhagat, A.: Healthcare information exchange through blockchain-based approaches. In: Transforming Businesses with Bitcoin Mining and Blockchain Applications, pp. 234–246 (2020). https://doi.org/10.4018/978-1-7998-0186-3.ch014

28. Rajit, N., Vishwakarma, S., Soni, M., Patel, T., Joshi, S.: Detection of COVID-19 cases through X-ray images using hybrid deep neural network. World J. Eng. **19**(1), 33–39 (2021)

Generic Framework of New Era Artificial Intelligence and Its Applications

Brij Mohan Sharma[1], Dinesh Kumar Verma[2], Kapil Dev Raghuwanshi[3],
Shivendra Dubey[4]([✉]), Rajit Nair[5], and Sachin Malviya[4]

[1] Jai Narayan College of Technology, JNCT Professional University, Bhopal 462038,
Madhya Pradesh, India
[2] Jaypee University of Engineering and Technology, Guna 473226, Madhya Pradesh, India
[3] Parul Institute of Technology, Parul University, Vadodara 391760, Gujrat, India
kapil.raghuwanshi24672@paruluniversity.ac.in
[4] Parul Institute of Engineering and Technology, Parul University, Vadodara 391760, Gujrat,
India
shivendrashivay@gmail.com
[5] VIT Bhopal University, Kothrikalan, Sehore 466114, Madhya Pradesh, India
Rajit.nair@vitbhopal.ac.in

Abstract. Since many years ago, scholars have been interested in human-computer communication. The interface between humans as well as computers can be carried out in a variety of ways. Chatbots are a common method for carrying out a conversation. A Chabot system is a computer application that facilitates engaging and simple conversation. Current artificial intelligence techniques perform poorly even when responding to user queries in the most appropriate manner. As a result, industries currently favor rule-based Chabot systems. Artificial intelligence can correctly and consistently anticipate outcomes. The methods have been used in a variety of businesses, academic fields, and contexts. Furthermore, the majority of study has been conducted in industrialized nations, with little work from other economies published. As a consequence, an appropriate research foundation is required for AI applications to be long-term and successful. The goal of this research is to critically evaluate many studies that have used AI in various areas to create a theoretical framework guide for academics and practitioners. This framework will also help to define future research trends in the field. Additional elements of AI that affect the design and functioning of the framework model in practice are the organizational structure and technological specification. A model-based approach that maintains uniformity in research, industry, and academia is required given the present use of AI methodologies. In the present situation, we can use establishing a long-term practice may need a paradigm shift in the framework-based approach. The use case illustrated how the proposed method may be applied for educational purposes to instruct vision-based component orientation recognition using humanizer bot models. Investigating Chatbots' potential as student mentors.

Keywords: Generic framework · AI · Neural Network · Humanizer · Chatbot

M. Botto-Tobar et al. (Eds.): ICAT 2023, CCIS 2049, pp. 149–163, 2024.
https://doi.org/10.1007/978-3-031-58956-0_11

1 Introduction

A lot of web-based services, such as entertainment, e-business, and virtual help, along with others, are available in today's age. In the realm of online services, there has been significant growth, with everything now being linked to the internet. Everything is delivered to your home, which is a highly user-friendly method. Live chat support and phone support are only two of the many customer care options available. However, it takes time for any human-to-human support service to answer inquiries from customers. The longer it takes to assist each customer as the number of consumers increases, the less satisfied those customers will be in the end. One day, a computer program will support all services by listening in on phone conversations in real-time [1]. An AI assistant, equipped with advanced voice analysis capabilities, may, for instance, infer from a customer's tone that an unmentioned issue is still a problem and provide real-time feedback to guide the human next approach. AI has the potential to improve service quality in this manner, but it also has the potential for unintended downsides, especially if customers worry about the technology overhearing private conversations. Artificial intelligence (AI) bots may soon replace human receptionists as the primary point of interaction between companies and potential customers [2].

AI systems have improved during the last decades. Research has been undertaken on the application of AI systems. AI applications have especially been developed in the assembly and manufacturing industry [3, 4].

The primary aim of this research, against this backdrop, is the establishment of a framework for the use of AI, which enables the development, on the one hand, of an extra public value for our people, but on the other is adaptable to particular public sector conditions. Three key components – monitoring and regulation, economic efficiency, and technological design – need to be incorporated into the resultant framework. Therefore, it is termed an integrated public administration AI context. The research continues as follows to develop such an integrated AI framework for every aspect: First of all, the literature identifies, and classifies according to their breadth and depth and clusters the ideas, schemes, and processes related to the AI implementation, according to their standpoint [5].

This manuscript contains various sections, apart from the introduction we discuss related work about of Generic Framework of New Era Artificial Intelligence and its Applications in Sect. 2, and proposed framework towards a generic framework of artificial intelligence techniques in Sect. 3, Artificial intelligence applications of chatbots discuss in Sect. 4, Bots testing cases discuss in Sect. 5, after that discuss the results along with discussion in Sect. 5, and conclude our work in last Sect. 6.

2 Related Work

AI calls for technological investment and thus a clear choice in management must be made. Faster, accurate forecasts with greater productivity will achieve the prediction value. When data becomes more generally available and accessible, it becomes more useful to anticipate. Increased numbers and the diversity of data were allowed by the Computer Revolution. With more data available, prediction in a broader range of activities is becoming increasingly feasible [4, 6].

An inquisitive Chatbots has been developed that searches for lost information in inquiries as well as tests questions with customers to collect information needed to answer the query [5]. Missing data is identified and queried to give an accurate answer. AIML tags to define the functionality and characteristics of each tag used to create an AIML-based Chatbots [6].

Using AI and NLP techniques, it explains how "Chatbots" work, a fantastic system now under development. Users' attendance, placement cell, examination cell, admittance, academics, average grade point, and other activities are just some of the questions it may help with [7]. Using AIML files to hold question-and-answer pairs, information may be extracted from the input text by pulling out keywords using Lemmatization and POS tagging, a log file can be kept that stores the inputs which the Chatbots was unable to answer, etc. It was realized that it is often impractical to collect all the data on a single interface without having to travel through several forms and windows. It was intended that a Chabot system would provide students and staff with human-like conversational capabilities, allowing them to ask questions and get prompt, accurate responses similar to those they would receive from a person [8–18].

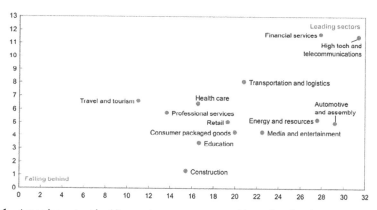

Fig. 1. Areas important in AI acceptance at present and intend to develop their asset [16]

Generally, business drivers vary linking various sectors. Production generally possible to direct the artificial intelligence technologies adoption at the range are those through the composite industry in terms of together geography and operations, whose presentation is determined through fast forecasting as well as correct decision making, or else modified client associations as shown in Fig. 1. In economic deals, there are obvious reimbursements of enhanced speed and accuracy in artificial intelligence-optimized fraud-recognition methods, predicted to sell $3 billion in 2020. We discover how this industrial driver plays out within another industry.

To look into the attempts to create psychologically-driven personalized Chatbots, a methodical re-examine of personalized Chatbots is undertaken. In light of this, we suggest a general paradigm for creating Chatbots that are character-based which is based on the fundamentals of character computing grounded in psychological theory. By choosing their chosen character traits, users will be able to construct unique chat bots personalities [20].

The level chatbot technologies have been applied in a variety of facets of education. It comprises administration (5%), development and research (19%), evaluation (6%), and advisory (4%) in addition to teaching and learning (66%).

3 Proposed AI Framework

The integrated method, however, does not case-by-case simulate specific artificial intelligence (AI) applications? Rather, a generic frame model with the different substructures is constructed, i.e. visually, an AI toolbox with each AI tool.

3.1 Evaluation of Chatbots Tools

We started by comparing Chatbots frameworks based on factors including location, cost, channels for discussion, and support for human languages. We kept an eye on each framework's price because most developers prioritize cost-effectiveness. Although all of the various systems including Dialog flow, Amazon Lex, IBM Watson, and BotPress, among others, offer a free version, many developers choose the paid versions to upgrade their Chatbots because of the limitations on the number of requests that can be created using the free versions for text or voice [20]. We also kept an eye on these Chatbots frameworks' ability to support a wide variety of human languages. More than 20 nationalities are supported by Dialog flow, compared to more than 75 nationalities [18].

3.2 Framework Design Evaluation

The approach offers a thorough analysis of the chatbot tool implementing available features online.

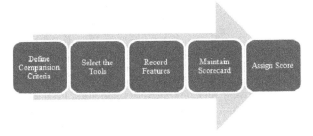

Fig. 2. Implementation procedures for chatbot tool score

The primary goal of this approach, which is focused upon that short listing of 11 chatbot methods, is to create a scoring system to assess the fundamental common electronic features that existing technologies offer to their informational stakeholders (Fig. 2), throughout our case, business organizations or users, to ensure that all interested parties from across the globe can find the problems and redesign current chatbot e-services rather than creating new ones. The initial evaluation of tools was focused on their technique, characteristics, and other specific criteria like location, cost, chat channels, and language support.

3.3 Research Assessment Framework is Being Roll-Out and Pilot Test

The suggested framework is initially evaluated using a variety of chatbot tool capabilities (Table 1). The identification of criteria set that applies to all of the tools that have been chosen and recorded as either not is described below (No) or supported (Yes).

Table 1. Chatbot tools and digital features open-source features for businesses

Features	Commercial						Open Sources				
	Wit.AI	Amazon Lex	Gupshup	Dialougeflow	Botsociety	IBMWatson	Rasa	Botkit	Pandorabots	Botpress	Microsoft Bot-Luis
Type of Chatbot											
Smart Chatbot	0	0	0	0	0	0	0	0	0	0	0
Rule – based Catbot	0	0	0	0	1	0	0	0	0	0	0
Hybrid Chatbot	1	1	1	1	0	1	1	1	1	1	1
Price											
Paid	0	1	1	1	1	1	1	0	1	1	1
Free Trial	0	1	0	0	0	0	0	0	0	0	0
Free	1	0	0	1	1	1	1	1	1	1	1
Locations											
Cloud or on platform tool storage/developments	1	1	1	1	1	1	1	1	1	1	1
In house chatbot storage or developments	0	0	0	0	1	0	1	1	0	1	0
Communication Channel											
Voice	1	1	1	1	1	1	1	0	1	1	1
Text	1	1	1	1	1	1	1	1	1	1	1
Monitoring Chatbot											
Message Metrics	0	1	1	1	1	1	1	1	1	1	1
Alert/Alarm Serice	0	1	0	0	0	0	0	0	0	1	0
User Metrics	0	1	1	1	1	1	1	1	1	1	1
Primary Features											
Call center bot	0	1	1	0	0	1	0	0	0	0	0
Device control	1	1	1	0	1	0	0	0	1	0	0
Informational control (updates, news)	1	1	1	0	1	1	1	1	1	0	1
IOT bot (Conversational and interface)	1	1	1	0	1	1	1	1	1	1	1
Enterprise productivity bots (IT, HR, Sales, Market, customer service etc.)	1	1	1	1	1	1	1	1	1	1	1
Final Score	9	14	13	9	13	12	12	10	12	12	12

The AI framework concept thus provides a generic super structure to combine the various AI solutions. This approach offers the advantages of highlighting and elaborating on structural and fundamental relationships and commencing research results and new ideas to the whole of the structure. A sophisticated and novel study topic like AI-supported customer services might benefit from the integrated AI Framework's ability to graphically or normatively describe the main elements to be examined, the essential components, constructions, or variables, and the hypothesized interrelationships between them. Because of the abstract nature of the superstructure, it is essential that the used model accurately represents reality in terms of its technical correctness and qualities. In general, when moving from an individual to a communal viewpoint, some of the original facts and results are lost since the model abstraction of the frame prevents them from being presented and expanded in a precise manner. Figure 3 shows the new era generic framework of artificial intelligence.

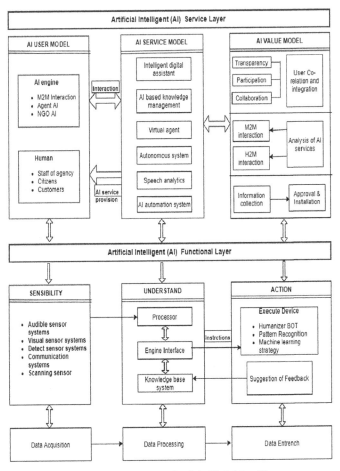

Fig. 3. Generic Framework of Artificial Intelligence

3.4 Humanizer BOT (RANS) in Education Sector

Let's look into the Humanizer-bot use case in the education system from various businesses which are shown in Fig. 4. Users can start chatting with the chatbot after initiating this admin can start the addition of data, information view, update the information as well as delete the information as per the requirement of the system. The process of establishing a system's architecture, components, modules, interfaces, and data is known as systems design. Systems design is done so that a system may meet certain criteria. In this section, the procedures that were followed to develop the chatbot for the university will be detailed in depth. These procedures include the architecture of the chatbot, its various mechanisms, and the data that is processed by the chatbot structure.

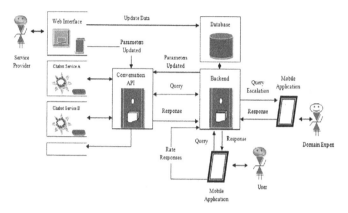

Fig. 4. Architecture Chatbot

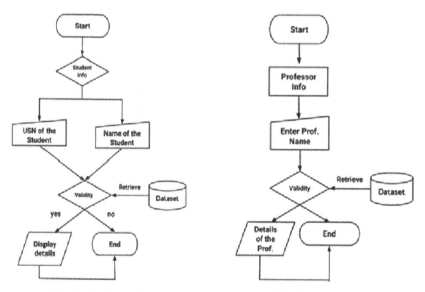

Fig. 5. Student info   **Fig. 6.** Professor info

We represent the student information retrieval in Humanizer Bot, here users can visit the bot page where they can chat with RANS which is in the react framework. RANS starts the conversation by asking for the user's name followed by many options like student information, teacher information, subject information, study materials, speech-to-text, and text-to-speech conversions through which an individual can fetch their required details. After each query option, if they wish to continue to get any other information, the bot will provide the options once again else it will reply with a "Thank you!" message.

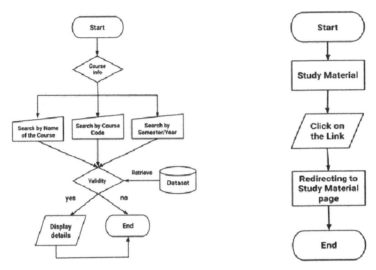

Fig. 7. Extraction of course details   **Fig. 8.** Extraction of study

Figure 5 represents the student info flow graph which is one of the components of the student retrieval system, After initiating the chat users have two options there first is the USN number and the second one is the student name to insert, we can choose one of them to insert and after that validate that data with the database system and give result as yes or no, if your data validate with the database system display the details, if not validate the data with database system will display none. Similarly, the second other component of the student trivial system is the professor info system shown in Fig. 6. It will be giving the professor information after validation with the dataset. Figure 7 represents the third component of the student retrieval system which gives the results of course details after validation based on the course name, course code, and course semester. Another component is the extraction of the study, which gives the result as a link, and that link redirects the study material as per the requirement shown in Fig. 8. Figure 9 shows the flowchart which explains how conveniently we can use the conversion technology to convert a given Text-to-Speech and vice-versa. In this paper, speech-to-text technology is used to take down important notes immediately without any difficulties, using operations like add, edit and delete. Whereas, text-to-speech technology is used to avoid eye strain from too much reading and helps in the preparation of speeches by hearing your work read aloud. To access these options all we need to do is click on conversion, choose your option accordingly and then click on the link which will redirect to that particular page.

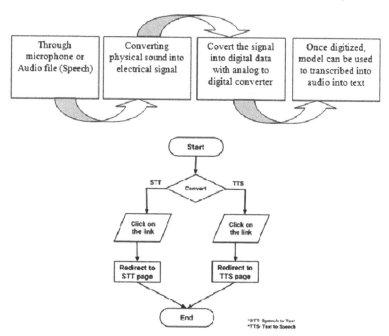

Fig. 9. Process of conversion of Speech-to-Text and vice-versa

---

Algorithm:
Create a text version of an audio file

1. 1. Import a voice recognition library
2. Starting up the recognition module to identify voices. We are making use of Google's technology for speech recognition.
3. AIFF, Wav, FLAC, and AIFF-C are among the audio file types that voice recognition can identify. I used a "wav" file in this example.
4. I've used an audible signal from such a "stolen" clip that says, "I don't know what you want or who you are, and if you're demanding extortion, I can assure you that I have no cash."
5. by default, the Google recognition system recognizes English. It accepts some different languages; further, for details, see this description.

---

4   Bot Testing

The testing of the bot has been carried out in an itinerant way while creating RANS to find technical glitches and validate if it can meet the necessities. The entire project is built on a website that can be accessed through any browser. The codes of the project are written on a text editor called ATOM. Later, RANS is viewed directly through the browser.

Fig. 10. Test case 0; Welcome to Humanizer Bot (RANS)

4.1 Test Case 0

If the database is not connected to the server, then an error with white text with red background color arises stating "SQLSTATE [HY000] [1130] Host '45.117.64.161' is not allowed to connect to this MySQL server" as shown in Fig. 10.

4.2 Test Case 1

On the login page, when the submit button is clicked without filling in any login credentials a message conveying "please fill out this field" will appear as shown in Fig. 11(a).

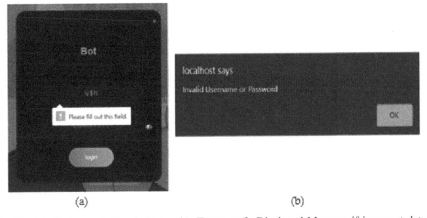

Fig. 11. (a). Test case 1; Log in Page. (b). Test case 2; Displayed Massage if incorrect details filled

4.3 Test Case 2

If any incorrect details are provided by the user, then a pop-up message saying "invalid USN or password" will show up as shown in Fig. 11(b).

4.4 Test Case 3

If the user gives inerrancy login credentials with proper database connectivity, then the page redirects to the main page from the login page.

4.5 Contact Model Test Case 4

In the contact model when send message button is clicked with empty fields; a message arises, pointing "Please fill out this field" as shown in Fig. 12.

Fig. 12. Test Case 4; Contact model details

4.6 Contact Model Test Case 5

If any invalid email id is given by the user, then an error "Please include a '@' in the email address represented in Fig. 13, 'this is mail id' is missing a '@'" is displayed.

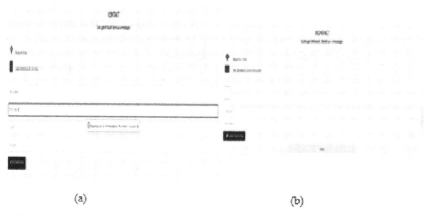

(a)   (b)

Fig. 13. (a). Test case 5; Error massage when filled incorrect details, (b). Test case 6; Feedback Massage

4.7 Contact Model Test Case 6

If all the fields are filled then the message "Thanks!" is shown indicating that the feedback is sent successfully as shown in Fig. 13(b).

4.8 RANBOT Test Case 7

By running the "npm run test" command in the command prompt the entire chatbot (RANS) is rendered and tested successfully without any errors as shown in Fig. 14.

Fig. 14. Test case 7; Chatbot on command promt

5 Results and Discussion

The result of the RANS is a combination of voice input and output that allows a simpler experience which gives information about the AI branch students and teachers, allows Speech-to-Text conversion for taking down important notes, can obtain Study Materials for all the semesters of the AI department and also facilitates to convert Text-to-Speech. When we get into the BOT page there is a chat icon at the right bottom corner where we can interact with RANS. After clicking on the icon RANS will greet you, followed by several options which are department-related that can be known which are represented in Fig. 15.

The result has some benchmarks directing towards that a chatbot could be an acceptable reservation on acting as an obliging guide for any freshman. Throughout this paper, we have brushed on some theory that has helped us gain a few skills and also have an enormous focal point on educational bona fides. Even though the users' relied on the data given by RANS, we cannot state that people trust a chatbot as much as they trust a human being. As noticed in the result, the chatbot can speed up the penetrating process in all cases. If requested for other information searches it may vary, but the results are persistent about the advantages RANS presumes for students and faculties.

Fig. 15. RANS Snapshots

Table 2. Results obtained from a Chatbot

System	No of Users	Excellent	Very Good	Good	Bad
RANS	208	123	56	08	21
Messenger	146	47	78	12	09
Web Page	77	22	27	19	08

The results presented in Table 2 were acquired in the ensuing two months, which are significant in the University for welcoming students and with the alterations made. The data has changed, but the columns, as well as the fields, have not altered. Here, more people were attained, and they evaluated the Chatbot using various mediums. In comparison to the numeral of interested parties, the percentage of negative reviews is lower. The upper-level grades follow the same pattern. When compared to the adjustments made to the Chatbot's personality and tone, these results are successful. The user's experiences have altered and the outcomes reflect this, following the updates and adjustments made to the overall system on which the Chatbot depends.

6 Conclusion

Almost the proposed AI frameworks presently employed in research and practice address both the technological foundation and the functional mode, while there is little discussion of the organizational structure of the artificial intelligence system and the regulatory and monitoring forces for AI in these studies like healthcare, industries, banking sector, education sector, and e-commerce, etc. It may thus be concluded that the scientific development of AI is carried out on a technological basis but does not transcend beyond computer science. AI research thus generates several approaches to the technological conception of information management supported by AI and case-specific solutions but does not unite and integrate such concepts at a superior level. To make RANS more interesting, we included techniques like "Speech-to-Text" and "Text-to-Speech" conversions which help the user to take down notes and listen to the text we type, for perfection. The main objectives of the project were to develop an algorithm that will be used to answer the users', related to the information that is stored. As a result, this research offers a blueprint for AI systems in public places that considers the system's outward impacts as well as its internal functioning and efficiency. According to the analysis of the findings, a user's confidence rises when they receive precise, unambiguous replies. Here, we show that there are now significantly more users using this Chatbot on the accessible channels. Due in large part to the update of the donors' phone numbers that were stored in the admissions area's database, it is also one of the texting methods that are most popular right now. With each system upgrade and advancement in Chatbot training made possible by its AI algorithms, this is anticipated to get better.

Conflicts of Interest. No potential conflict of interest was reported by the authors.

Funding Statement. No funding was received from anywhere.

References

1. Nica, E., Stehel, V.: Internet of things sensing networks, artificial intelligence-based decision-making algorithms, and real-time process monitoring in sustainable industry 4.0. J. Self-Gov. Manag. Econ. **9**(3), 35–47 (2021)
2. Enholm, I.M., Papagiannidis, E., Mikalef, P., Krogstie, J.: Artificial intelligence and business value: a literature review. Inf. Syst. Front., 1–26 (2021)
3. Wirtz, B.W., Müller, W.M.: An integrated artificial intelligence framework for public management. Public Manag. Rev. **21**(7), 1076–1100 (2019)
4. Davenport, T.H.: The AI Advantage: How to Put the Artificial Intelligence Revolution to Work. MIT Press, Cambridge (2018)
5. Reshmi, S., Balakrishnan, K.: Enhancing inquisitiveness of chatbots through NER integration. In: 2018 International Conference on Data Science and Engineering (ICDSE), pp. 1–5. IEEE (2018)
6. Carlander-Reuterfelt, D., Carrera, Á., Iglesias, C.A., Araque, Ó., Rada, J.F.S., Muñoz, S.: JAICOB: a data science chatbot. IEEE Access **8**, 180672–180680 (2020)
7. de Sá Siqueira, M.A., Müller, B.C., Bosse, T.: When do we accept mistakes from chatbots? The impact of human-like communication on user experience in chatbots that make mistakes. Int. J. Hum. Comput. Interact., 1–11 (2023)
8. Castillo, I., Argüelles, A., Piñal, O., Glasserman, L., Ramírez, S., Carreon, A.: Towards the development of complex thinking in university students supported by ideathon and artificial intelligence. Comput. Educ. Artif. Intell., 100186 (2023)
9. Dubey, S., Verma, D.K., Kumar, M.: Severe acute respiratory syndrome Coronavirus-2 Geno-Analyzer and mutagenic anomaly detector using FCMFI and NSCE. Int. J. Biol. Macromol., 129051 (2023)
10. Shi, B., Xu, K., Zhao, J.: Domain-relevance of influence: characterizing variations in online influence across multiple domains on social media. J. Big Data **10**(1), 1–20 (2023)
11. Kim, Y., Lee, H.: The rise of chatbots in political campaigns: the effects of conversational agents on voting intention. Int. J. Hum. Comput. Interact., 1–12 (2022)
12. Nti, I.K., Adekoya, A.F., Weyori, B.A., Nyarko-Boateng, O.: Applications of artificial intelligence in engineering and manufacturing: a systematic review. J. Intell. Manuf. **33**(6), 1581–1601 (2022)
13. Dubeya, S., Kumar, M., Verma, D.K.: Machine learning approaches in deal with the COVID-19: comprehensive study. ECS Trans. **107**(1), 17815 (2022)

14. Tripathi, A., Chourasia, U., Dubey, S., Arjariya, A., Dixit, P.: A survey: optimization algorithms in deep learning. In: Proceedings of the International Conference on Innovative Computing & Communications (ICICC) (2020)

15. Soni, S., Dubey, S., Tiwari, R., Dixit, M.: Feature based sentiment analysis of product reviews using deep learning methods. Int. J. Adv. Technol. Eng. Res. (IJATER) (2018)

16. Adam, M., Wessel, M., Benlian, A.: AI-based chatbots in customer service and their effects on user compliance. Electron. Mark. 31(2), 427–445 (2021)

17. Rapp, A., Curti, L., Boldi, A.: The human side of human-chatbot interaction: a systematic literature review of ten years of research on text-based chatbots. Int. J. Hum. Comput. Stud. 151, 102630 (2021)

18. Chen, J.S., Tran-Thien-Y, L., Florence, D.: Usability and responsiveness of artificial intelligence chatbot on online customer experience in e-retailing. Int. J. Retail Distrib. Manag. 49(11), 1512–1531 (2021)

19. Colabianchi, S., Tedeschi, A., Costantino, F.: Human-technology integration with industrial conversational agents: a conceptual architecture and a taxonomy for manufacturing. J. Ind. Inf. Integr. 35, 100510 (2023)

20. Suhaili, S.M., Salim, N., Jambli, M.N.: Service chatbots: a systematic review. Expert Syst. Appl. 184, 115461 (2021)

Exploring the Molecular Diversity of SARS, Ebola, MERS, and SAR-COV-2 Viruses Using Genomics Virus Classification Algorithm: ViroGen

Shivendra Dubey[✉], Dinesh Kumar Verma, and Mahesh Kumar

Department of Computer Science and Engineering, Jaypee University of Engineering and
Technology, Guna 473226, Madhya Pradesh, India
shivendrashivay@gmail.com

Abstract. As evidenced by significant mortality and transmission from the delta
and Omicron versions respectively, SARS-COV-2 mutation also causes periodic
public worry. We thoroughly examined and condensed several infection disease
like COVID-19 treatment, diagnosis, and prevention facets. The biological properties of infectious disease like COVID-19 is first described from the perspective
diagnosis. GenBank uses the file extensions .fasta and .gb to store the genomic
sequences of several viruses. There were more than 300 unique changes in the
genomic nucleotide regions of the four different viral types. Following that, the
COVID-19 preceding clinical animal models were reviewed to frame the signs
and symptoms of the disease as well as its clinical impacts from patient to patient
with the help of therapeutic options and in computational/silicon natural science.
Additionally, we looked at the potential and challenges of applying nanomedicine
and nanotechnology for identifying, evaluating, and treating infectious disease.
This article extensively discusses practically every SARS-CoV-2-associated issue
to help readers comprehend the most recent developments. We have used ViroGen
algorithm for genomics virus classification for SARS, MERS, Ebola, and SARS-
COV-2. We calculate the various performance metrics like precision, accuracy,
F1 score, and recall in terms of various model such as SVM, logistic regression,
Naïve bayes, etc. with respect to different viruses, and we get 96% accuracy for
SARS and 97% accuracy for SARS-COV-2, these suggested technique produces
good classification results.

Keywords: Genome Sequence · Infectious Disease · SARS-COV-2 · MERS ·
SARS · Ebola

1   Introduction

The most recent appearance of novel infectious diseases such as coronavirus illnesses originated in China and had been cause a universal wellbeing problem. On March 11, 2020, the Health Organization formally had recognized it as a huge pandemic. The COVID-19 pandemic is expected to cause 4,067,517 fatalities and more than 188,655,968 confirmed cases through July 2021. It has affected more than 200 territories and countries. The response of science on a global scale to the deadly disease that claimed millions of lives is unmatched. Governments and health organizations use and advise quarantine and preventative measures to minimize the dispersion and reproduction velocity of the deadly virus. Researchers are working to understand the SARS-COV-2 genome, its behavior, and its functions [1] to produce or create a long-lasting treatment or immunization. The publicly disclosed disease's primary sequence analysis was on January 10, 2020, nine days following the initial discovery of a possible COVID-19 victim.

Among the most promising research directions of COVID-19 has studied an organism's genetic structure or genomics. Genetic sequence examination enables medical professionals to create individualized therapy or diagnostic choices using information from an organism's genome. By decoding the identifying the most infected hosts and virus's genetic code, professional's expectation to shed light on community health. Adenine, Guanine, Cytosine, and Thymine are the four nucleotide bases that make up an organism's genome; they form the encoded sequence that gives nucleic acids (Adenine, Guanine, Cytosine, and Thymine) their structure. Approximately 30 KB long and divided into three groups, the unique SARS-COV-2 genome sequence is a positive sense RNA (ribonucleic acid) with single stranded as of the coronavirus family [2, 3].

Finding out which nucleotides are contained in something like a genome sequence is the process of genome sequence analysis. There is a sequence for the SARS-CoV-2 genome by many organizations worldwide and this information has helped identify various viral strains [4]. On the other hand, this interdisciplinary analysis of medical or omics data generates composite computational requirements intended for academics, clinical services, health specialists, and making it crucial to increase unique biological data for individualized treatment. Examples include measurements of vital organ systems, molecular data (genes, physiological evaluation, proteins), and data on medical images (including MRI, CT scans, etc.). Biomedical experts can forecast how these factors affect disease prevalence in the community by identifying genomic characteristics. However, it is frequently a resource- and time-consuming strategy that depends mainly on domain knowledge [5].

Toward the enhancement of genomic medicine, a primary objective of genome sequence research is to promote examining and understanding illnesses and therapies linked to gene mutations. Substantial efforts have been made to combine data sets from multiomics data collectors with clinical reports, descriptive information, and community or genomic surveys. (Such as transcriptomics, metabolomics, and proteomics) [6].

Additionally, reputable software vendors include machine learning in their genetic analysis applications and services. This work, which intends to give an artificially intelligent system for sequencing examination of SARS-COV-2 or linked viruses such as Ebola, MERS, and SARS, was inspired by the preceding discussion and the progress of machine learning in complete genome analysis. We used comparative analysis to look at the core traits of these viruses' genomic sequences before applying machine learning to categorize them [7].

2 Literature Review

AI and data analytics approaches enable investigators to analyze the behaviors, origins and other data patterns within various diseases, issues, and situations. For many types of investigations, including the risk and prediction assessments of many illnesses, statistics, machine learning, and data mining methodologies were utilized in early studies and research. The various artificially intelligent methods that researchers have developed to predict, assess, and find or identify infectious disease like COVID-19 is examined in this section. To design practical solutions for the COVID-19 epidemic, researchers have used a variety of data formats, including data sets like genomic, clinical text, clinical pictures, such as CT and X-ray images and vision-based data sets [8].

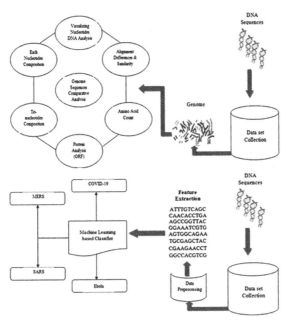

Fig. 1. The SARS-COV-2 and related viral categorization and genomic sequence analysis using artificial intelligence

A thorough description of machine learning-based methods for analyzing and predicting epidemics [9], we reviewed the big data and machine learning methodologies used in different medical procedures [10]. Others developed a prognosis prediction system using machine learning to calculate individuals' mortality probability [11]. Researchers used a variety of data sets, including genetic information, counting scientific textual information, therapeutic picture data sets, such as CT scan images, X-ray images and occasionally data sets with vision-based to offer workable answers to the COVID-19 epidemic issue. Using the reported cases from outside China, they created a regression model that predicted the rapid expansion of COVID-19 [12]. A developed healthcare monitoring technique centered on big data analytics and IOTs for assessing the COVID-19 epidemic utilizing clinical textual data sets [7]. The authors used a variety of infection symptoms to conduct analytic, expressive, predictive and prescriptive analyses in their study. Four found approaches are categorized using a specified taxonomy [14]. They highlighted the issues, and recommended that machine learning experts has improved the techniques to forecast COVID-19 incidents. The projected distribution of SARS-COV-2 across the countries could be determined using machine as well as deep learning technology [15]. Machine learning has shown the ability to predict the number of COVID-19-infected individuals [16]. That used Deep learning algorithms and surveillance data gathering to stop the SARS-COV-2 virus's dissemination and track social distance [13, 17].

For instance, some researchers [5] used sequential pattern mining with genome sequencing data sets to study the SARS-COV-2 genome. That created model with a deep learning algorithm intended for the co-infecting RNA viruses and SARS-CoV-2 categorization [18]. Researchers used a convolutional neural network for categorization and precise SARSCoV-2 detection [19]. The authors thoroughly analyzed the epidemic, looking at how could be used drone cameras; artificial intelligence, 5G, the Internet of Things, and blockchain manage and monitor COVID-19 [20].

Numerous AI-based techniques for SARS-COV-2 monitoring have been investigated [20], along with the countless problems and potential future applications. According to the summary above, researchers used a variety of data sets to identify, evaluate, forecast, and diagnose COVID-19. They also used artificial intelligence techniques. Based on prior work, we also provided a method for artificial intelligence-based classification of the sequence of SARS-COV-2 genome from supplementary diseases.

Genomics Virus Classification Algorithm: ViroGen
1	Gather genetic information about different viruses.
2	The dataset can be defined as $$D = \{(X_j, y_j)\},$$ where y_j indicates the virus type and X_j indicates genome-wide information regarding infections j.
3	For generating the vectors of features, apply the following feature extraction function: $$X_j = \varphi(X_j).$$
4	Numeral labels should be used to encode virus types: $$A = \{a_j\},$$ where a_j is the virus type i numerical label.
5	Divide this data set into sets for testing (Dtest) and training (Dtrain).
6	Using the training data, create a model $$Z(Z_j) = z_i),$$ where i represents the anticipated mark for viruses j.
7	For each tested sample, k, find the predicted label using the formula $$Z(Xtest) = \{c_{ik}\}.$$
8	Perform comparisons between true and predicted labels to calculate metrics of performance such as precision, accuracy, F1-score, and recall.
9	Display any pertinent information or features and Examine performance of the model.
10	Explain the evaluation and results, highlighting any new information and the model's performance on virus classification.
11	Use the model that has been trained to classify viruses.
12	Record every step of the method, which includes the techniques, data sources, outcomes, and specific to the domain expertise.

The ViroGen technique begins with data collection from multiple virus datasets. Next, feature selection and label encoding are required for data preprocessing. After that, data separating and training of models are completed. Subsequently, we assess the model and determine metrics for performance, calculating different metrics such as precision, recall, accuracy, and so forth. In addition, we carry out visualization and analysis using pertinent outcome features. In conclusion, we provide a summary of the evaluation and findings, which includes the model's performance, and we apply the model to different virus classifications.

3   Genome Based on Artificial Intelligence Technology

An AI-based technique for classifying COVID-19 and SARS, MERS, and Ebola based on their genetic sequences is described in this study. Figure 1 provides a detailed illustration of the entire procedure; First, we used proportional data analysis on the way to uncover internal information about these viruses of genomes, then genome sequences length, visualize nucleic acids, nucleic acid intensity within the tri-nucleotide GC, composition and DNA fraction revealing the kind that genomic sequencing has the count of Amino acids, the tremendous secure DNA, and similitude or orientation among various genome sequences.

Biologic annotations are possible thanks to the easily accessible GenBank library of gene sequences. With new sequence files added every 18 months, GenBank has substantially expanded during the last 20 years. It enables researchers from all around the world to look at any specific viral structure and function right away. International attempts to create vaccines and antiviral medications, but only falsely sensitive and specific diagnostic technologies rely heavily on the sequenced genomic data about viruses obtained from an online database.

4 Results and Discussion

The measured values of the AI-based ViroGen method, which was used to categorize genome sequencing data, are presented in this section. Although classification accuracy is a standard criterion for measuring system performance, it is insufficient for accurately/correctly evaluating algorithm performance. Here, we use many assessment criteria to gauge the strategy's viability. Several categorization criteria were used, together with true negatives and false negatives, true positives, and false positives are described in the following ways:

- For positively predicted courses, use True Positive (TP).
- False Positives (FP) are positive classes mistakenly predicted to be positive.
- True Negative (TN) designates negatively anticipated true courses.
- False negatives (FN) for sorts mistakenly predicted negatively but not accurately.

The matrices mentioned above are used to calculate the following parameters:

Classification accuracy; the percentage of correct predictions to all input samples are known as classification accuracy. If there is the same number of pieces for each class, it will operate correctly. To the assessment of categorization accuracy, the following measures remain used:

$$\text{Accuracy} = \frac{\text{True Positive}}{\text{True Positive} + \text{True Negative} + \text{False Positive} + \text{False Neagtive}}$$

Precision; A proportion concerning meaningful samples (True Positives) divided by the number of instances deemed members of a given class yields precision.

$$\text{Precision} = \frac{True\ Positive}{True\ Positive + False\ Positive}$$

Recall; Recall is calculated as follows to determine the percentage of samples anticipated to correspond to a class versus those samples that do:

$$\text{Recall} = \frac{True\ Positive}{True\ Positive + False\ Negative}$$

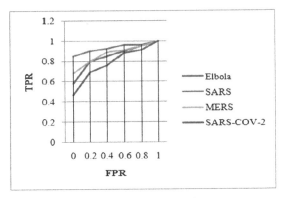

Fig. 2. Approaches to classification Different applications for genome sequence, F1 score, recall, precision, and accuracy (comparable virus SARS-COV-2)

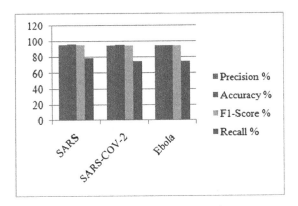

Fig. 3. SVM classification results

True Positive Rate (TPR); True positive rate (named as sensitivity) is the fraction of positively detected positive sample. The explanation is as follows:

$$\text{TPR} = \frac{True\, Positive}{True\, Positive + False\, Negative}$$

The various samples accurately classify as unfavorable, known as the true negative rate (TNR). TNR represents this given equation:

$$\text{TNR} = \frac{True\, Negative}{True\, Negative + False\, Positive}$$

FPR, also called false positive rate, acts as the proportion referring to negative class incorrectly categorized as positive.

$$\text{FPR} = \frac{False\, Positive}{False\, Positive + True\, Negative}$$

Table 1. Comparing multiple machine learning models with different parameters

S. No.	Model	Precision	Accuracy	F1 Score	Recall
1	Decision Tree	95%	95%	96%	95%
2	Random Forest	93%	94%	96%	76%
3	KNN	94%	95%	95%	77%
4	Extreme Gradient Boost	94%	92%	92%	77%
5	Logistic Regression	94%	95%	94%	70%
6	Naïve Bayes	94%	94%	95%	70%
7	SVM	97%	97%	97%	77%

We calculated recall, precision, F1-score, and accuracy as shown in Fig. 2. We note that the classifier of SVM successfully recognizes and classifies an extensive genomic sequences range, SARS (96%), including SARS-COV-2 (97%), Ebola (95%), and MERS (95%) with excellent recognition as well as classification accuracy. Recall, F1-Score, and Precision for SARS-COV-2, MERS, Ebola, and SARS are, respectively, 77%, 96%, and 96%. Using the evaluation mentioned above metrics, we generated the ROC curve depicted in Fig. 3. The curve is created using FPR data vs TPR for a specific cutoff value. Figure 3 shows that while all algorithms' efficacy has increased and nearly reached 95%, SVM's performance is still the highest. In Table 1, several machine learning methods are also looked at, and it can see that SVM classifiers are more successful than other machine learning methods.

5 Conclusions

The strategy for applying artificial intelligence to analyze the genetic sequences of the SARS, SARS-COV-2, Ebola, and MERS viruses is provided in this study.

- First, we conducted a comparative sequence analysis on SARS-COV-2 and related viruses to collect crucial information on nucleotide frequencies and distribution, DNA similarity, and genome sequence alignment. The genomic sequencing of these viruses was then examined utilizing various visualization techniques.
- The genomic sequences of different viruses can be mined for useful information via comparative data analysis. The data was finally classified using an SVM classifier based on machine learning. The Data Center repository or NCBI collects the genome sequence data and many genomic sequences. With 96% accuracy for SARS and 97% accuracy for SARS-COV-2, the suggested technique produces good classification results.

Authors' Contributions. All authors contributed equally to this research proposed the idea and implemented that idea.

Declaration
Competing Interests. There is no conflict of interest.

References

1. Marquez, S., et al.: Genome sequencing of the first SARS-CoV-2 reported from patients with COVID-19 in Ecuador (2020)
2. Laamarti, M., et al.: Large scale genomic analysis of 3067 SARS-CoV-2 genomes reveals a clonal geo-distribution and a rich genetic variations of hotspots mutations. PLoS ONE **15**(11), e0240345 (2020)
3. Leila, M., Sorayya, G.: Genotype and phenotype of COVID19: their roles in pathogenesis. J. Microbiol. Immunol. Infect. **54**(2), 159–163 (2021)
4. Lu, R., et al.: Genomic characterisation and epidemiology of 2019 novel coronavirus: implications for virus origins and receptor binding. Lancet **395**(10224), 565 (2020)
5. Dubey, S., Verma, D.K., Kumar, M.: Severe acute respiratory syndrome Coronavirus-2 Geno-Analyzer and mutagenic anomaly detector using FCMFI and NSCE. Int. J. Biol. Macromol., 129051 (2023)
6. Quazi, S.: Artificial intelligence and machine learning in precision and genomic medicine. Med. Oncol. **39**(8) (2022)
7. Ahmed, I., Ahmad, M., Jeon, G., Piccialli, F.: A framework for pandemic prediction using big data analytics. Big Data Res. **25**, 100190 (2021)
8. Khanday, A.M.U.D., Rabani, S.T., Khan, Q.R., Rouf, N., Din, M.M.U.: Machine learning based approaches for detecting COVID-19 using clinical text data. Int. J. Inf. Technol. **12**(3), 731 (2020)
9. Dubeya, S., Kumar, M., Verma, D.K.: Machine learning approaches in deal with the COVID-19: comprehensive study. ECS Trans. **107**(1), 17815 (2022)
10. Kanaujiya, A.K., Tiwari, V.: Crowd management and strategies for security and surveillance during the large mass gathering events: the Prayagraj Kumbh Mela 2019 experience. Natl. Acad. Sci. Lett. **45**, 263–273 (2022)
11. Saraei, M., Rahmani, S., Rajebi, S., Danishvar, S.: A different traditional approach for automatic comparative machine learning in multimodality Covid-19 severity recognition. Int. J. Innov. Eng. **3**(1), 1–12 (2023)
12. Li, Y., et al.: COVID-19 epidemic outside China: 34 founders and exponential growth. J. Investig. Med. **69**(1), 52 (2021)
13. Ahmed, I., Ahmad, M., Rodrigues, J.J., Jeon, G., Din, S.: A deep learning-based social distance monitoring framework for COVID-19. Sustain. Cities Soc. **65**, 102571 (2021)
14. Kamboj, V.P.: COVID-19 vaccines: speedy development and their use to be saviour of humanity. Natl. Acad. Sci. Lett. **45**, 105–109 (2022)
15. Punn, N.S., Sonbhadra, S.K., Agarwal, S.: COVID-19 epidemic analysis using machine learning and deep learning algorithms. medRxiv (2020)
16. Cafiero, C., Palmirotta, R., Micera, A., et al.: SARS-CoV-2 infection after vaccination in Italian health care workers: a case report. Natl. Acad. Sci. Lett. **45**, 249–254 (2022)
17. Ahmed, I., Ahmad, M., Jeon, G.: Social distance monitoring framework using deep learning architecture to control infection transmission of COVID-19 pandemic. Sustain. Cities Soc. **69**, 102777 (2021)
18. Mateos, P.A., Balboa, R.F., Easteal, S., Eyras, E., Patel, H.R.: PACIFIC: a lightweight deep-learning classifer of SARS-CoV-2 and co-infecting RNA viruses. Sci. Rep. **11**(1), 1 (2021)
19. Lopez-Rincon, A., et al.: Classification and specific primer design for accurate detection of SARS-CoV-2 using deep learning. Sci. Rep. **11**(1), 1 (2021)
20. Majumdar, S., Neogi, A., Gopal Dutta, R.D., et al.: Methodical approach to inactivate any microbial element like SARS-CoV2. Natl. Acad. Sci. Lett. **45**, 343–348 (2022)

Improving Dynamic Behavior of Vehicular Ad Hoc Networks by Integrating Game Theory Technique

Shobhit Mani Tiwari[1] and Anurag Singh Baghel[2]([✉])

[1] Department of Computer Science and Engineering, Faculty of Engineering and Technology, University of Lucknow, Lucknow, Uttar Pradesh, India
[2] Department of Computer Science and Engineering, School of ICT, Gautam Buddha University, Greater Noida, Uttar Pradesh, India
asb@gbu.ac.in

Abstract. In this paper, we give the focus on the continuous advancement in the domain of Vehicular ad hoc networks (VANET's) and that is developed as a tool for developing the base for platform intelligent mode in the communication (inter vehicle communications) and needful for enhanced improvement under the performance effect and traffic safety. Here, we have deployed the game theory method in the VANET domain and thereafter categorizes between the hop vehicle and the source vehicle.

The New approach to the VANET analysis we have identified and used the social parameters and hence made it look more novel approach.

"Researching vehicle ad hoc networks poses challenges due to their dynamic nature, the movement of large vehicles, unlimited energy resources, and the evolution of wireless networks. Game theory is commonly employed in wireless networks to explore the interplay between competition and cooperation. In this study, we present a system for ad hoc networks in cars, utilizing game theory to automate car groups and board elections. This approach eliminates the necessity for regular bulk updates. Furthermore, the social behavior of each car is leveraged to create clusters in the car environment. The K-means algorithm in machine learning is applied to develop social cars. The proposed system underwent testing for various characteristics, including CH lifetime, average group lifetime, average number of joins, throughput, and packet loss rate. The results demonstrate that VANET performs exceptionally well, achieving an overall performance ranging from 0.95 to 0.989".

Keywords: WECT (Wind Energy Conversion Technology) · FRT (Fault Recovery) · RTU · VANET · RSU · MANET · V2V · CH Life · Internet of Things (IoT) · ITS (Intelligent Transportation System) · VN (Vehicle Network) · V2V (Vehicle-to-Vehicle) · V2I (Vehicle-to-Infrastructure) · RSU (Roadside Unit) · GT (Game Theory) · 5G (Fifth Generation) · QoS (Quality of Service) · MAC (Media Access Control) · 4G (Fourth Generation) · MEC (Mobile Edge Computing) · V2R (Vehicle to Roadside) · TDMA (Time Division Multiple Access) · CSMA (Carrier Sense Multiple Access) · CSMA/CA (Carrier Sense Multiple Access with Collision Avoidance) · BSM (Basic Safety Message) · CBR (Channel Bit Rate) · DCC (Broadcast Data Confusion) · SU (Secondary

User) · PU (Primary User) · SINR (Signal-to-Interference plus Noise Ratio) ·
MEC (Mobile Edge Computing) · HetNet (Heterogeneous Network for Vehicles)

1 Introduction

Game Theory in the context of Vehicular Ad Hoc Networks (VANETs) involves the
study of strategic interactions among self-interested entities (such as vehicles or nodes)
to model and analyses their behavior in a networked environment. VANETs are a specific
type of ad hoc network Game Theory provides a useful framework to understand and
optimize the behavior of autonomous and self-interested entities in VANETs. Here are
some aspects of Game Theory in the context of VANETs: Cooperative Game Theory:
In VANETs, vehicles can cooperate to achieve common goals, such as improving traffic
flow sharing information about road conditions. Cooperative Game Theory can model
how vehicles form coalitions and share resources for mutual benefits.

Non-cooperative Game Theory: Vehicles in VANETs may act selfishly to optimize
their individual objectives, such as minimizing travel time or fuel consumption. Non-
cooperative Game Theory can be used to model scenarios where each vehicle acts independently, and the interactions between vehicles result in a Nash equilibrium, where no
vehicle has an incentive to unilaterally change its strategy.

Resource Allocation: Game Theory can be applied to model how vehicles compete
for limited resources, such as bandwidth for communication or access to roadside infrastructure. This is particularly relevant in VANETs where efficient resource allocation is
crucial for the overall network performance.

Security and Privacy: Game Theory can be employed to analyses security and privacy
concerns in VANETs. For example, it can model scenarios where malicious vehicles
attempt to disrupt communication or compromise the privacy of other vehicles. Game-
theoretic models can help design strategies to enhance security and privacy in such
environments.

Incentive Mechanisms: Game Theory can be used to design incentive mechanisms to
encourage cooperation and information sharing among vehicles. Incentives can include
rewards for providing useful information or penalties for misbehavior.

Routing and Traffic Management: Game Theory can assist in modeling and optimizing routing strategies in VANETs, considering the interactions among vehicles to
minimize congestion and improve overall traffic flow. By applying Game Theory to
VANETs, researchers and engineers can gain insights into the complex dynamics of
these networks, design more robust protocols and algorithms, and understand the incentives that drive the behavior of individual entities within the network. The integration
of Game Theory and Machine Learning techniques in Vehicular Ad Hoc Networks
(VANETs) aims to enhance the dynamic behavior of the network, particularly in the
context of reliable and stable routing. Let us break down the key components of this
approach:

Dynamic Behavior of VANETs: VANETs are characterized by the dynamic nature of
vehicular movements, changing network topologies, and varying communication conditions. Vehicles in VANETs need to adapt to real-time changes, such as traffic conditions,
road incidents, and intermittent connectivity.

Game Theory: Game Theory is used to model the strategic interactions among self-interested entities, such as vehicles in VANETs. Cooperative and non-cooperative game models can be employed to represent how vehicles collaborate or act selfishly to achieve their objectives.

Game Theory helps in understanding the incentives and strategies that influence the decision-making of individual vehicles.

Machine Learning Techniques: Machine Learning algorithms can be applied to predict and adapt to the dynamic behavior of VANETs. Predictive models can use historical data to forecast changes in traffic patterns, identify potential congestion points, and predict connectivity issues. Reinforcement Learning techniques can be used to enable vehicles to learn and adapt their routing strategies based on feedback from the network. Reliable and Stable Routing: The primary objective is to design routing algorithms that ensure reliable and stable communication in VANETs. Integrating Game Theory and Machine Learning helps in creating routing strategies that consider both individual vehicle incentives and the overall network dynamics. Adaptive routing algorithms can dynamically adjust to changing conditions, optimizing the use of network resources, and ensuring a more stable and reliable communication infrastructure (Fig. 1).

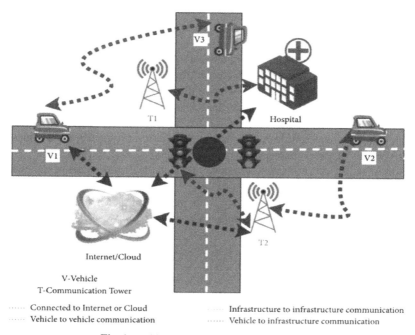

Fig. 1. Vehicular ad hoc network architecture

Benefits and Applications:

Improved Traffic Flow: Adaptive routing can help in optimizing traffic flow by dynamically adjusting routes based on real-time conditions.

Enhanced Reliability: By considering the reliability of communication links and predicting potential disruptions, the network can maintain a more stable connection.

Efficient Resource Utilization: Machine Learning algorithm scan optimize the allocation of resources, such as bandwidth, based on the evolving needs of the network.

Challenges: The integration of Game Theory and Machine Learning introduces complexities in designing and implementing algorithms. Ensuring the security and privacy of communications is crucial, especially when considering the strategic interactions modelled by Game Theory. In summary, the integration of Game Theory and Machine Learning in VANETs aims to create more adaptive, reliable, and stable routing strategies. This interdisciplinary approach considers both the strategic interactions among vehicles and the ability to learn and adapt to the dynamic nature of vehicular networks.

In Vehicular Ad Hoc Networks (VANETs), a "hop vehicle" refers to a vehicle that acts as an intermediate relay or forwarding node in the communication process between other vehicles or between a vehicle and roadside infrastructure. These hop vehicles play a crucial role in enabling communication over a multi-hop network topology.

In VANETs, communication between vehicles is often achieved through a multi-hop relay process, especially when the direct communication range between two vehicles is limited. If a vehicle is out of the direct communication range of another vehicle or roadside unit, one or more intermediate hop vehicles can relay the information to bridge the gap and facilitate communication. Here is a brief explanation of the concept of hop vehicles:

Direct Communication Range Limitations: The communication range of a vehicle's wireless communication device is limited. If two vehicles are beyond each other's direct communication range, they cannot communicate directly.

Multi-Hop Communication: To overcome the limited communication range, hop vehicles come into play. When a vehicle wants to communicate with another that is out of its direct range, the message can be relayed through one or more intermediate vehicles.

Hop Vehicle Functionality: A hop vehicle receives a message from one vehicle and then retransmits or forwards that message to another vehicle or roadside unit.

The hop vehicle serves as an intermediary node in the communication path, helping extend the effective communication range.

Dynamic Topological Network: Since Units are movable and hence due to the mobility of units the availability of hop vehicles can change rapidly as vehicles move in and out of communication range.

Routing Protocols: Routing protocols in VANETs are designed to determine the most efficient path for communication, considering the dynamic nature of the network. Hop vehicles play a role in establishing these communication paths.

The use of hop vehicles in VANETs helps in maintaining connectivity and enabling communication in scenarios where direct communication between vehicles or between a vehicle and infrastructure is not possible. This multi-hop communication is essential for disseminating information about traffic conditions, safety warnings, and other relevant data throughout the VANET.

In the context of Vehicular Ad Hoc Networks (VANETs) and Game Theory, a "cluster" refers to a group of vehicles that form a cooperative coalition to achieve common objectives or goals. Clustering is a strategic approach where vehicles collaborate with each other for mutual benefits, and Game Theory is often applied to model and analyses the interactions within these clusters. The concept of clusters is part of cooperative game models in VANETs.

Here is a breakdown of clustering in the context of Game Theory in VANETs:

Cooperative Game Theory: Cooperative Game Theory is used to model scenarios where entities (in this case, vehicles) cooperate to achieve common goals. In VANETs, vehicles can form clusters to collectively address challenges such as improving traffic flow, enhancing communication, or sharing information about road conditions.

Formation of Clusters: Vehicles in a VANET may choose to form clusters based on shared interests, geographical proximity, or specific objectives. Clusters can be dynamic and may form and dissolve based on the real-time needs and conditions of the network.

Common Objectives: Vehicles within a cluster work together to achieve common objectives, such as optimizing routing, sharing traffic information, or collectively addressing challenges like congestion.

Resource Sharing: Clusters may involve resource sharing among vehicles. Resources can include communication bandwidth, processing power, or information about the environment.

Game-Theoretic Modelling: Game Theory is applied to model the strategic interactions within and between clusters. This includes the decision-making processes of individual vehicles within a cluster and the interactions between different clusters.

Incentive Mechanisms: Game Theory helps design incentive mechanisms to encourage vehicles to participate in clusters and contribute to the common goals.

Incentives may include rewards for sharing valuable information, contributing to efficient traffic management, or assisting in the overall improvement of the VANET.

Cluster Stability: The stability of clusters is essential for their effectiveness. Game Theory can help analyses the stability of clusters over time, considering factors such as changes in network conditions, the arrival or departure of vehicles, and the evolution of shared objectives. In summary, clusters in Game Theory within VANETs represent groups of vehicles that collaborate for common goals. The application of Game Theory helps model the strategic interactions within these clusters, enabling a better understanding of how cooperation and coordination among vehicles can be optimized for the overall benefit of the VANET.

Channel (CH) selection in the VANETs domain is a critical aspect of network management, so it involves the process of choosing the appropriate communication channel for transmitting data among vehicles or between vehicles and infrastructure. The selection of channels is crucial to ensure efficient and reliable communication in the dynamic and challenging environment of VANETs. Here are some key considerations and approaches to CH selection in VANETs:

Frequency Bands: VANETs typically operate in dedicated frequency bands allocated for Intelligent Transportation Systems (ITS) communication. Common frequency bands include the Dedicated Short-Range Communications (DSRC) spectrum.

Interference and Congestion: CH selection considers the level of interference and congestion on different channels. Channels with low interference and congestion are preferred to ensure better communication performance.

Dynamic Spectrum Access: VANETs often operate in a dynamic and unpredictable environment. Dynamic Spectrum Access (DSA) techniques may be employed to adaptively select channels based on real-time spectrum availability and conditions.

Channel Quality: The quality of a channel can be assessed based on factors such as signal strength, signal-to-noise ratio, and signal stability. Channels with better quality are preferred for communication.

Traffic Characteristics: The traffic characteristics of the network, including the density of vehicles and the type of data being transmitted, influence CH selection. For example, in congested areas, channels with higher capacity may be preferred.

Cooperative Spectrum Sensing: Vehicles in VANETs can engage in cooperative spectrum sensing to share information about the quality and availability of channels. This collaborative approach can improve the accuracy of CH selection.

Game Theory Approaches: Game Theory can be applied to model the strategic interactions among vehicles in the context of CH selection. Vehicles may strategically choose channels to maximize their individual utility or collectively optimize network performance.

Centralized or Distributed Approaches: CH selection can be managed in a centralized or distributed manner. In a centralized approach, a central entity makes decisions for the entire network, while distributed approaches involve vehicles making individual or localized decisions.

Adaptive Algorithms: Adaptive algorithms can be employed to dynamically adjust CH selection based on changing network conditions. Machine learning techniques may also be used to predict and adapt to channel conditions over time.

Standardization: Standardization bodies, such as the Institute of Electrical and Electronics Engineers (IEEE), may define protocols and standards for CH selection in VANETs to ensure interoperability and consistency.

Effective CH selection in VANETs contributes to the overall reliability, efficiency, and performance of communication in intelligent transportation systems. It requires a balance between real-time adaptation to dynamic conditions and strategic decision-making for optimal network operation.

Research objectives here are indicated as mentioned below.

Stage 1: Initialize the relationship between all tools when using VANET.

Stage 2: Evaluate the relationship scores of each part of VANET and create groups of tools using k-means clustering.

Step 3: Cluster initialize nodes and specify the cluster head of each cluster using the new method from the previous step.

Step 4: Apply game evolution theory to evaluate the stability of the formation group.

Stage 5: If the partner

Stage 6: RSU to send the packet of this stage Use.

Stage 7: Send the packet to the next destination (destination); calculate the average CH lifetime upon arrival, average group member lifetime, Average member time, Transmission, and packet loss.

Description method: In this section the model of the design process is introduced. The progress of the edge of IoT data is discussed., it solves the problem of still alarm in the network and congestion in the data center by distributing the traffic outside the edge servers. But the needs of the special request of successful request require a new description process, which requires traffic-specific rules according to the user's expectations.

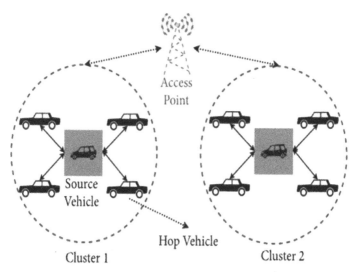

Fig. 2. Schematic representation of cluster structure

VANET Game Theory: Each interactive device possesses unique characteristics related to its environment. The network group, once again, forms a part of the relationship among similar and dissimilar devices. In this context, game theory is employed to facilitate grouping. The system is divided into three main components:

(1) Vehicle component: Represents vehicles generating messages and data for communication.
(2) Relay vehicle: Functions as a data transfer vehicle, aiding in the rapid transmission of information to the ground.
(3) Access points: All fixed points utilized in VANETs are considered as access points.

Figure 2 illustrates the schematic diagram of the cluster, where each group includes a lead vehicle and other vehicles transmitting data to and from the lead vehicle and nearby vehicles. Considering the provided information, there will be X number of cars and Y number of vehicle relays during the game. For simplicity, it is assumed that each underlying vehicle will select a vehicle relay to transmit data to. Table 1 outlines the game theory approach for relay selection.

Table 1. Indicating CH selection on Game theory-based VANET classification

Steps	Description
1	Initialization of the system
2	Number of vehicles (nodes) in the system
3	For $i = 1 : N$
4	If $S(i)\ E > 0$ means node is live
5	Cluster details and id is gathered
6	If node needs to forward the data
7	Else >> system is inactive
8	If >> social parameter score is high
9	Make the node as head for transmitting the data
10	Else >> act as hop vehicle
11	End

The entire map is shown in Fig. 3. The concept of this game starts using VANET and then divides it between locations and traffic. The subsequent analysis of each vehicle's network accuracy provides a method for VANET analysis. New and innovative approach when correlation scores are calculated, the K-group task means selecting group leaders (CHs).

The node's distribution model, the incorporation of the Global Positioning System (GPS) for nodes, and the network's scalability are all vital aspects of VANET, setting it apart from other self-participatory ventures. Additionally, the heterogeneity of VANET nodes stems from the diverse types of vehicles sharing the road at any given moment, necessitating distinct utilization based on intelligence, such as for emergency vehicles, including police. Vehicles can issue emergency warnings to oncoming vehicles, facilitated by GPS, providing real-time location and weather information to nodes. Furthermore, the organization or rearrangement of nodes is contingent on space and time, resulting in a variable number of nodes in the network corresponding to changes in vehicle speed and density.

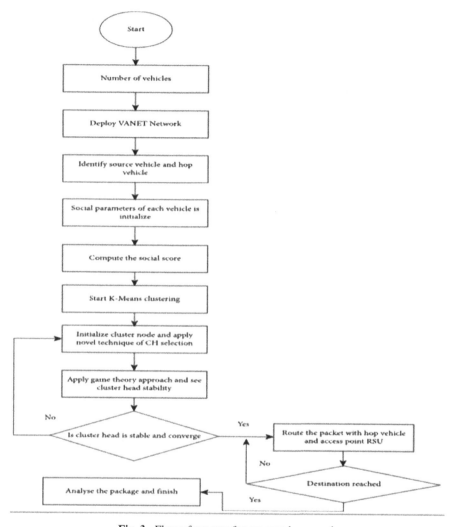

Fig. 3. Flow of process for proposed approach

References

1. Jiang, D.Y., Zhang, H., Kumar, H., et al.: Automatic control model of power information system Access based on artificial intelligence technology. Math. Probl. Eng. **2022**, 6 p. (2022). Article no. 5677634
2. Jagota, V., Luthra, M., Bhola, J., Sharma, A., Shabaz, M.: A secure energy-aware game theory (SEGaT) mechanism for coordination in WSANs. Int. J. Swarm Intell. Res. **13**(2), 1–16 (2022)
3. Yang, M., Kumar, P., Bhola, J., Shabaz, M.: Development of image recognition software based on artificial intelligence algorithm for the efficient sorting of apple fruit. Int. J. Syst. Assur. Eng. Manag. **13**(1), 322–330 (2021)
4. Zeadally, S., Hunt, R., Chen, Y.S., Irwin, A., Hassan, A.: Vehicular ad hoc networks (VANETS): status, results and challenges. Telecommun. Syst. **50**(4), 217–241 (2010)

5. Lin, Y.W., Chen, Y.S., Lee, S.L.: Routing protocols in vehicular ad hoc network a survey and future perspectives. Int. J. Inf. Sci. Eng. **26**(3), 913–932 (2010)

6. Zhang, S., Srividya, K., Kakaravada, I., et al.: A global optimization algorithm for intelligent electromechanical control system with improved filling function. Sci. Program. **2022**, 10 p. (2022). Article no. 3361027

7. Park, H.S., Park, M.W., Won, K.H., Kim, K.H., Jung, S.K.: In-vehicle AR-HUD system to provide driving-safety information. ETRI J. **35**(6), 1038–1047 (2013)

8. Cho, S.Y.: Development of an IGVM integrated navigation system for vehicular lane-level guidance services. J. Position. Navigat. Timing **5**(3), 119–129 (2016)

9. Peng, H., Liang, L., Shen, X., Li, G.Y.: Vehicular communications: a network layer perspective. IEEE Trans. Veh. Technol. **68**(2), 1064–1078 (2019)

10. Sanchez-Iborra, R., Sanchez-Gomez, J., Santa, J., Fernandez, P.J., Skarmeta, A.F.: IPv6 communications over Lora for future IoV services. In: Proceedings of the IEEE 4th World Forum Internet Things (WF-IoT), pp. 92–97, February 2018

11. Murschetz, P.C., Prandner, D.: 'Datafying' broadcasting: exploring the role of big data and its implications for competing in a big data-driven TV ecosystem. In: Khajeheian, D., Friedrichsen, M., Mödinger, W. (eds.) Competitiveness in Emerging Markets. CMS, pp. 55–71. Springer, Cham (2018). https://doi.org/10.1007/978-3-319-71722-7_4

12. Paul, P.K., Ghose, M.K.: A novel educational proposal and strategies toward promoting cloud computing, big data, and human–computer interaction in engineering colleges and universities. In: SenGupta, S., Zobaa, A., Sherpa, K., Bhoi, A. (eds.) Advances in Smart Grid and Renewable Energy. LNEE, vol. 435, pp. 93–102. Springer, Singapore (2018). https://doi.org/10.1007/978-981-10-4286-7_10

13. Li, J., Natalino, C., Van, D.P., Wosinska, L., Chen, J.: Resource management in fog-enhanced radio access network to support real-time vehicular services. In: Proceedings of the IEEE 1st International Conference on Fog and Edge Computing (ICFEC), pp. 68–74, May 2017

14. Truong, N.B., Lee, G.M., Ghamri-Doudane, Y.: Software defined networking-based vehicular adhoc network with fog computing. In: Proceedings of the IFIP/IEEE International Symposium on Integrated Network Management (IM), pp. 1202–1207, May 2015

15. Atzori, L., Iera, A., Morabito, G., Nitti, M.: The social Internet of Things (SIoT)—when social networks meet the Internet of Things: concept, architecture and network characterization. Comput. Netw. **56**(16), 3594–3608 (2012)

16. Hossen, R., et al.: BDPS: an efficient sparkbased big data processing scheme for cloud fog-IoT orchestration. Information **12**(12), 517 (2021)

17. Bharati, S., Omar, H.A., Zhuang, W.: Enhancing transmission collision detection for distributed TDMA in vehicular networks. ACM Trans. Multimedia Comput. Commun. Appl. **13**(3s), 1–21 (2017)

18. Lin, C.-Y., Chen, K.-C., Wickramasuriya, D., Lien, S.-Y., Gitlin, R.D.: Anticipatory mobility management by big data analytics for ultra-low latency mobile networking. In: Proceedings of the IEEE International Conference on Communications (ICC), pp. 1–7, May 2018

19. Rahman, M.T., Mahi, M.J.N., Biswas, M., Kaiser, M.S., Al Mamun, S.: Performance evaluation of a portable PABX system through developing new bandwidth optimization technique. In: Proceedings of the International Conference on Electrical Engineering and Information Communication Technology (ICEEICT), pp. 1–5, May 2015

20. Widiawan, A.K., Tafazolli, R.: High altitude platform station (HAPS): a review of new infrastructure development for future wireless communications. Wirel. Pers. Commun. **42**(3), 387–404 (2007)

21. Ning, Z., et al.: Blockchain-enabled intelligent transportation systems: a distributed crowd-sensing framework. IEEE Trans. Mobile Comput. (2021). https://doi.org/10.1109/TMC.2021.3079984
22. Roy, S., Shovon, A.R., Whaiduzzaman, M.: Combined approach of tokenization and mining to secure and optimize big data in cloud storage. In: Proceedings of the IEEE Region Humanitarian Technology Conference (R10-HTC), pp. 83–88, December 2017

Machine Learning to Investigate Determinants of Intention to Purchase Organic Food

Tanveer Kaur[(⊠)] [iD] and Anil Kalotra

University School of Business, Chandigarh University, Chandigarh, Punjab, India
ratantanveer@gmail.com

Abstract. The purpose of this study is to pinpoint the key variables that influence customers who have never purchased organic food previously in terms of their intention to do so. Attitude, perceived behavioural control, subjective norm, personal norm, & health awareness are the five primary components in this study. Further, this study investigates how machine learning techniques can be used to explore and identify the key determinants influencing the intention to purchase organic food. As the demand for organic products grows, understanding the factors that drive consumers' decisions to choose organic food becomes increasingly important for both businesses and policymakers. The findings revealed that only four of these five factors—attitude, subjective norm, personal norm, & perceived behavioural control were significant.

Keywords: Organic food · Consumer Behaviour · Theory of planned behaviour · Purchase intention · Machine Learning

1 Introduction

The global food sector is rapidly embracing organic goods. Due to situations involving food safety & illnesses that suddenly raise global awareness of benefits that organic goods have to offer, it has gained popularity in recent years. Numerous research has been done to investigate how customers see organic products, including studies on purchase intent, consumer decision-making patterns, consumer perception, and consumer consumption [1].

In India, demand for organic food is rising right now. The demand has been growing rapidly in India over the past several years, according to information from IFOAM from 2009, & market is thought to be developing [2]. The market for improving soil structure and fertility, using rise in organic producer numbers. Since there haven't been enough studies to clearly establish Indians' demand for organic goods, it's unknown whether these sorts of food items would be accepted there.

M. Botto-Tobar et al. (Eds.): ICAT 2023, CCIS 2049, pp. 184–193, 2024.
https://doi.org/10.1007/978-3-031-58956-0_14

2 Problem Statements

Numerous research has been conducted on the consumer side to investigate and identify the motivations behind organic consumption. Comparatively speaking to other nations, very little is known about the values, motivations, and beliefs that drive organic consumption among Indian consumers. Knowing the key elements that influence consumers' intent to buy is important from a marketing standpoint.

Out of all the elements mentioned by earlier research, this research is being undertaken to gauge determinants that impact purchasing behaviours. The study takes into account five important variables: attitude, personal norms, health awareness, subjective norms, and perceived behavioural control.

3 Literature Review

Numerous research has been carried out overseas to investigate customer purchase intentions, decision-making patterns, and perceptions of organic products.

It was shown that people buy organic products for a variety of reasons, with health ranking as the top one. Previous studies have demonstrated that consumers believe organic products are beneficial to their health, which serves as the primary driver of their purchase behaviour. The results of a study on Indian consumers with a focus on the state of Kedah showed that desire to purchase organic products is most strongly impacted by one's health [3]. Since organic goods don't include the chemicals that are commonly found in conventional agriculture products, they are more likely to be seen as healthy options. This is consistent with a study's finding that Greek consumers believed organic products to be free of chemicals, which encouraged them to have organic food. It has also been shown that Swedish consumers share this sentiment towards organic products since they think they are healthier than conventional food items. The link between good health knowledge and positive buying intent is thus established.

H1: Optimal health awareness will result in optimum purchasing intent

The strong concern for the environment is the second primary justification for buying organic products. Personal norms that are often used in behaviour connected to the environment serve as a representation of environmental concern. A cultural research that identified the environment as a key component in the rising trend of organic consumption has demonstrated this. Consumers of organic goods are typically more likely to have more environmental awareness [4]. This is a result of the nature of chemical-free, organically grown products. As a result, it has little effect on the environment and guarantees that soil fertility is not lost. The second theory is that:

H2: A favourable personal norm will result in a favourable buying intention.

Subjective norms have to do with how family, intimate friends, and relatives encourage people to act in ways that are advantageous to them. Numerous research that focused on organic food discovered that impacts from family and friends are crucial in affecting consumer behaviour, particularly when it comes to food selection. From this, the following is deduced [5].

H3: A favourable subjective norm will result in a favourable buying intention.

Since intention is the primary factor employed in the model to predict behaviour, having a positive intention will result in positive behaviour. Previous studies support this claim. One's motivations determine one's attitude. As various people might have diverse attitudes about the same subject, it varies from person to person. In the study of organic behaviour, it encounters the same challenge [6]. While each customer develops the same attitude towards the goods, the attitude itself serves each individual differently. The knowledge function occurs for consumers whose awareness of eating organic products is relatively low as they seek to learn more about it. This is consistent with the finding that consumers who care more about the environment tend to make more purchases than those who do not [7].

H4: A good outlook will result in a favourable buying intention.

When forecasting customer preferences for organic products, price is a well-known indication. Due to its limited output volume, organic farming is renowned for having low profitability & high production costs. These expenses are passed along to the consumer through marketing, making it more expensive than comparable conventional goods. Depending on the product type, the markup price can vary, although it occasionally goes up to 100% or even more [8]. The readiness of customers to pay a premium for organic items varies depending on the product category, with fruits & vegetables showing largest count of consumers who are willing to do so. Consumers in the Athens research said that they would be prepared to spend even 100% more for fundamental foods like pasta, red meat, eggs, feta cheese, & so on. Additionally, it was shown that Costa Rican consumers of organic products are becoming more willing to spend. Even though it has been found that price acts as a less significant barrier to the consumption of organic foods, it cannot be denied that price remains a significant factor, particularly in less developed nations [9]. It's crucial to realise that not all customers are ready to pay premium price for organic goods. This can be because customers from lower-income families experience budgetary limitations. The trade-off value between buying organic items and being able to purchase something more enjoyable with the same amount of money is another element that influences this. This indicates that some consumers think it is preferable to use the additional money spent on organic products for other things [10].

The obstacle to the market penetration of organic products that prevents consumers from involved in organic purchasing behaviour also includes a bad distribution channel & a lack of availability. Ineffective marketing channels have a negative impact on organic purchasing [11]. Future customers find it challenging to discover organic items on the market, and even when they do, the selection is restricted, discouraging them from doing so. In comparison to conventional items, organic ones were less favourable due to their poor physical look. Organic product markets are often less established in less developed nations [12]. Understanding customer buying behaviour also requires consideration of the market's size and degree of maturity. The quality of the items, particularly their physical appearance, & the pricing strategy of the products all have some bearing on the market's structure. In this study, perceived control behaviour is represented by the absence of availability and the cost.

4 Theoretical Framework

This study's theoretical framework is theory of planned behaviour since it has been used in many prior studies that are comparable to it. In essence, this notion has previously been validated in several marketing studies, not just for food purchases but also for other items. As a result, the theory of planned behaviour is regarded as the most well-known & well-established theory for study of behaviour, including the understanding of consumer behaviour towards organic food [13]. In addition, research on "psychology of consumer decisions" in area of organic food confirmed conclusion that Theory of Planned Behaviour applies to purchase of organic food. The underlying model for this study has been theory of planned behaviour, however there have been several changes made to the original model.

The approach is expanded with personal norms and health consciousness. A personal norm is a behaviour that a person engages in when they feel some responsibility for something or when it is consistent with their values and beliefs. The variable of environmental awareness is covered by personal norm. Since several researches have revealed a strong correlation between the intake of organic foods and health awareness, it was decided to integrate health awareness in the model [14]. Although it has been established that health awareness is closely associated to organic purchasing behaviour, the original planned behaviour theory did not take health awareness into account because it was developed for psychological research rather than for particular items. Due to prior research that demonstrate how important personal norms are in environmental-related studies for predicting behaviour, they are included in the theory along with subjective norm. Thus, in order to provide a more comprehensive conclusion for this study, the addition of personal norm & health awareness is crucial [15].

The foundation of planned behaviour theory is essentially the conviction that intention will have a direct impact on behaviour. On the other side, three beliefs—behavioral, normative, and control beliefs—are what motivate intention. An expansion of notion of reasoned action is theory of planned behaviour. The latter was frequently employed to clarify the variables at play in decision-making behaviour. The best predictor of goal behaviour, according to this model, is behavioural intention [16]. In order to more accurately anticipate behaviour, Theory of Planned Behavior was adapted from Theory of Reasoned Action. Numerous researches have also looked into the environmental concern problem and discovered that it has an influence on people's consumption of organic products. The personal norms demonstrate a knowledge of and commitment to the environment.

The degree of apparent capacity to overcome an impediment that prevents one from engaging in the desired action is known as perceived behavioural control. Price and availability will act as perceived behavioural controls in this paradigm. According to earlier surveys, availability and cost are the biggest barriers preventing consumers from buying organic products [17].

5 Methods

The information was gathered by handing out surveys to shoppers at major hypermarkets in India's Urban region. 150 customers have been chosen as respondents overall using a practical sample procedure. Only 124 of the 150 total respondents completed legitimate surveys.

Thirty-four percent of responses are men and sixty-six percent are women. The respondents who participated in this survey are highly educated, with 32% having a diploma, 48% having a degree, and 9% having a postgraduate degree. Only fresh organic vegetables and fruits are the subject of this investigation. Two sections made up the questionnaire. The respondents' demographic profile, which included information on their gender, education level, occupation, status, and age, was included in Section A. All six variables—health knowledge, attitude, subjective norm, personal norm, perceived behavioural control, & purchase intention—were covered by 40 items that made up Section B. All 40 items were rated on a 7-point Likert scale, with 1 denoting "strongly agree" and 7 denoting "strongly disagree".

6 Machine Learning Model for Finding Determinants Intention to Purchase Organic Food

1. Data Collection:
Gather a dataset that includes relevant features such as demographic information, past purchasing behavior, attitudes towards organic products, income levels, and other variables that might influence the intention to purchase organic food [18].

Label your dataset with the target variable: intention to purchase organic food. You may use surveys or online data collection methods.

2. Data Preprocessing:
Handle missing values, outliers, and normalize/standardize numerical features.

Encode categorical variables using techniques like one-hot encoding or label encoding.

Split the dataset into training and testing sets.

3. Feature Engineering:
Create new features that might be indicative of purchasing intention. For example, you could derive a feature based on the frequency of organic product searches or the proximity to organic grocery stores [19].

4. Model Selection:
Choose a machine learning algorithm suitable for classification tasks. Common choices include logistic regression, decision trees, random forests, support vector machines, or neural networks.

Experiment with different algorithms to find the one that performs best on your dataset.

5. Model Training:

Train your selected model on the training dataset.

Fine-tune hyper parameters to improve performance.

6. Model Evaluation:

Evaluate the model on the testing dataset using appropriate metrics such as accuracy, precision, recall, F1-score, or area under the ROC curve.

Use cross-validation techniques to ensure robustness of the model [18].

7. Interpretability:

Depending on the model used, consider methods for interpreting its decisions. For instance, decision trees can be visualized, and certain models support feature importance analysis.

8. Feedback Loop:

If possible, collect feedback on the model predictions and use this feedback to continuously improve the model.

9. Deployment:

Once satisfied with the model's performance, deploy it in a real-world environment. This could be integrated into an e-commerce platform, a survey system, or any other relevant application [20].

10. Monitoring and Maintenance:

Regularly monitor the model's performance in a production environment. Update the model as needed with new data to ensure its relevance over time.

7   Data Analysis

All 40 items were subjected to a reliability test, and every single one of them had a high alpha value with a value of at least 0.810 (Table 1).

Table 1. Cronbach's Alpha Value

Factor	Types of variables	Cronbach's alpha value
Attitude	Independent	.913
Subjective norm	Independent	.878
Personal norm	Independent	.810
Purchase intention	Dependent	.953
Perceived behavioural control	Independent	.893
Health awareness	Independent	.856

Source: Author created.

To determine the link between the variables, several regression analyses have been done. The autocorrelation is close to zero, according to the Durbin-Watson test result of 1.818.

In this concept, health consciousness is not relevant. Personal norm and perceived behavioural control have a strong significance level of .000 (p 0.05). A strong significant level of .001 is also demonstrated by subjective norms, which are followed by attitude at a significant level of 0.034. Since multicollinearity is virtually nil and tolerance value is more than .10, the variance inflation factor (VIF) value is less than 10 & all the data are mutually exclusive. The histograms & Q-Q plot were used to determine the residuals' normality, and it was discovered that they are normally distributed.

8 Discussion

According to the aforementioned findings, H2, H3, H4, and H5 are approved whereas H1 is disapproved. The findings indicate that Indian consumers place relatively high importance on perceived behavioural control factors like availability and price, as well as personal norms that reflect environmental awareness, attitude & subjective norms. However, they place relatively little weight on health awareness when making organic food selections. When considering whether to buy organic food, price and availability are crucial factors. This is consistent with other research done on consumer behaviour related to organic products [14]. [16, 21–23] this study demonstrates that a lack of access prevented them from becoming familiar with organic food. Due to its difficulty in obtaining, customers find it challenging to incorporate organic food into their everyday lives. In order to overcome this obstacle, producers should work more closely with hypermarkets. For consumers to conveniently get food in their region, producers may also promote their goods through chain mini-marts that are close by.

Price unquestionably plays a significant part as one of the factors influencing consumers' intentions to buy organic products. The higher cost influences customers' unfavourable choice of organic food. Even if some surveys show that customers are prepared to pay extra for organic food, the situation in India is still different. Price continues to be a top consideration for Indian shoppers [24, 25]. One of the key factors influencing Indian consumers' decision to purchase organic food is environmental consciousness. The majority of research was carried out in other nations and the results are in agreement. In order to eliminate mark-up prices by 3rd parties that raise the price of organic food above what it already is, collaboration with government agencies for marketing agricultural products like FAMA is necessary to address the higher cost of organic food. Additionally, in order to increase production and solve the pest and disease issues, growers need become involved in technology development. It is unquestionably possible to solve our production issue & thus lower cost of organic food by upgrading our organic agricultural technologies.

Since green consumerism is a popular trend right now, it is not surprising that Indian consumers weigh the environment into all of their everyday decisions, including where to buy food. A important additional element affecting purchasing intention is subjective norm [26]. This demonstrates how the community & family have a big impact on Indian consumers' decisions to buy organic food. Even if some other research did not support this conclusion, cultural differences may be a major component in this phenomenon. Since India is a country with many different ethnicities, Indians have a very different culture than studies done in Europe. This disparity in outcome is thus anticipated [27].

Attitude and intention to buy are significantly correlated. Respondents who have a favourable opinion about organic food also tend to buy organic food favourably. This is consistent with previous research that support these conclusions. It has been discovered that Indian consumers have similarly favourable attitudes regarding organic food when compared to the findings of previous studies. Since more than half of respondents have at least a bachelor's degree, their general understanding of organic food may have had an impact [28].

In these investigations, the purchase intentions of consumers varied substantially. The primary factors influencing whether someone will buy organic food include availability, cost, environmental awareness, subjective norm, and attitude. Because of this, both organic food producers and distributors need to pay attention to these issues, notably availability and cost. Since most consumers who buy organic products care about the environment, they are less likely to switch to traditional eating habits. It will help farmers and marketers of organic products learn exactly what motivates consumers to begin consuming organic products [29, 30].

According to the study's findings, consumers in all demographic groups do not all behave in the same way when it comes to making purchases. Health knowledge is not one of primary factors influencing consumer preference of organic food in the research demographic region. As a result, producers and marketers may appeal to a wider range of consumers—not just those who are health-conscious but also those who are not—to buy organic food in order to eat healthily [31]. In Urban, where there is a dearth of information on these specific items, this work makes a contribution to our understanding of consumer organic purchase behaviour. Producers may utilise the data from this study to better promote organic foods by identifying the key variables impacting consumer behaviour.

References

1. Ajzen, I.: The theory of planned behavior. Organ. Behav. Hum. Decis. Process. **50**, 179–221 (1991)
2. Cicia, G., Del Giudice, T., Scarpa, R.: Consumers' perception of quality in organic food: a random utility model under preference heterogeneity and choice correlation from rank-orderings. Br. Food J. **104**(3/4/5), 200–213 (2002)
3. Antonio, J., Gonzalez, A.: Market trends and consumer profile at the organic farmers market in Costa Rica. Br. Food J. **111**(5), 498–510 (2009)
4. Krystallis, A., Chryssohoidis, G.: Consumers' willingness to pay for organic food. Br. Food J. **107**(5), 320–343 (2005)
5. La Via, G., Nucifora, A.: The determinants of the price mark-up for organic fruit and vegetable products in the European Union. Br. Food J. **104**(3/4/5), 319–336 (2002)
6. Choo, H., Chung, J.-E., Pysarchik, D.: Antecedents to new food product purchasing behavior among innovator groups in India. Eur. J. Mark. **38**(5/6), 608–625 (2004)
7. Davies, A., Titterington, A., Cochrane, C.: Who buys organic food? A profile of the purchasers of organic food in Northern Ireland. Br. Food J. **97**(10), 17–23 (1995)

8. de Magistris, T., Gracia, A.: The decision to buy organic food products in Southern Italy. Br. Food J. **110**(9), 929–947 (2008)

9. Essoussi, L.H., Zahaf, M.: Exploring the decision making process of Canadian organic food consumers. Qual. Mark. Res., 443–459 (2009)

10. Fotopoulos, C., Krystallis, A.: Organic product avoidance. Br. Food J. **104**(3/4/5), 233–260 (2002)

11. Padel, S., Foster, C.: Exploring the gap between attitudes and behaviour. Br. Food J. **107**(8), 606–625 (2005)

12. Padel, S., Midmore, P.: The development of the European market for organic products: insights from a Delphi study. Br. Food J. **107**(8), 626–647 (2005)

13. Radman, M.: Consumer consumption and perception of organic products in Croatia. Br. Food J. **107**(4), 263–273 (2005)

14. Fotopoulos, C., Krystallis, A.: Purchasing motives and profile of the Greek organic consumer: a country wide survey. Br. Food J. **104**(9), 730–765 (2002)

15. Liao, C., Lin, H.M., Liu, Y.P.: Predicting the use of pirated software: a contingency model integrating perceived risk with the theory of planned behavior. J. Bus. Ethics, 237–252 (2010)

16. Magnusson, M.K., Arvola, A., Hursti, U.-K.K., Åberg, L., Sjödén, P.-O.: Attitudes towards organic foods among Swedish consumers. Br. Food J. **103**(3), 209–226 (2001)

17. Squires, L., Juric, B., Cornwell, T.B.: Level of market development and intensity of organic food consumption: cross- cultural study of Danish and New Zealand consumers. J. Consum. Mark. **18**(5), 392–409 (2001)

18. Tarkiainen, A., Sundqvist, S.: Subjective norms, attitudes and intentions of finnish consumers in buying organic food. Br. Food J. **107**(11), 808–822 (2005)

19. Tregear, A., Dent, J., McGregor, M.: The demand for organically grown produce. Br. Food J. **96**(4), 21–25 (1994)

20. Makatouni, A.: The consumer message; what motivates parents to buy organic foods in the UK? In: Conference Proceedings on Communicating the Quality of Organic Foods. IFOA, Florence (1999)

21. Akatouni, A.: What motivates consumers to buy organic food in the UK? Br. Food J. **104**(3/4/5), 345–352 (2002)

22. Onyango, B.M., Hallman, W.K., Bellows, A.C.: Purchasing organic food in US food systems: a study of attitudes and practice. Br. Food J. **109**(5), 399–411 (2007)

23. Rimal, A., Fletcher, S., McWatters, K.: Nutrition considerations in food selection. Int. J. Food and Agribus. Rev. **3**, 55–70 (2000)

24. Schifferstein, H., Oude Ophuis, P.: Health-related determinants of organic food consumption in the Netherlands. Food Qual. Prefer. **9**(3), 119–33 (1998)

25. Shaharudin, M.R., Pani, J.J., Mansor, S.W., Elias, S.J.: Factors affecting purchase intention of organic food in Malaysia's Kedah State. Cross-Cult. Commun. **6**(2), 105–116 (2010)

26. Tsakiridou, E., Boutsouki, C., Zotos, Y., Mattas, K.: Attitudes and behaviour towards organic products: an exploratory study. Int. J. Retail Distrib. Manag. **36**(2), 158–175 (2008)

27. Von Alvensleben, R.: Ecological aspects of food demand: the case of organic food in Germany. In: AIR-CAT 4th Plenary Meeting: Health, Ecological and Safety Aspects in Food Choice, vol. 4, no. 1, pp. 68–79 (1998)

28. Yiridoe, E., Bonti-Ankomah, S., Martin, R.: Comparison of consumer's perception towards organic versus conventionally produced foods: a review and update of the literature. Renew. Agric. Food Syst. **20**(4), 193–205 (2005)

29. Gupta, L., Kaur, T.: To examine the roadmap of organic farming in India. In: Shodhasamhita, vol. IX, Issue II (2022)

30. Bawa, S.S., et al.: A study of consumer satisfaction towards fast moving consumer goods. Webology **18**(4) (2021). http://www.webology
31. Kaur, T., Singhal, S.: Empirical study of consumer perception towards organic products. J. Xi'an Univ. Archit. Technol. **XII**(III), 5657–5672 (2020)

Influence Analysis of Driving Style on the Energy Consumption of an Electric Vehicle Through PID Signals Study

Néstor Rivera[✉], Juan Molina, David Idrovo, and Jeyson Narváez

Automotive Mechanical Engineering: GIIT Transport Engineering Research Group, Salesian Polytechnic University, Cuenca, Ecuador
nrivera@ups.edu.ec

Abstract. This research analyzes how driving style affects the energy consumption of a Kia Soul electric vehicle, studying the signals of the Identification Parameters (PID) in the city of Cuenca, Ecuador. A Real Driving Emissions (RDE) cycle including urban, rural, and highway segments is described, and it is observed that acceleration is a variable directly related to the energy consumption of the electric vehicle. This is more evident in highway areas where speed limits are higher than in urban areas, which makes the vehicle require higher energy consumption. As a result, a 31.14% increase in road consumption can be verified compared to the urban area. The unit density identifies the type of driving (conservative, normal, and aggressive) on the road by means of acceleration profiles and their distribution range. With the implementation of Machine Learning architecture, it is possible to estimate the most important variables, such as accelerator pedal open position (APS), vehicle speed sensor (VSS), and longitudinal acceleration (Ax), in relation to the state of charge (SOC), after applying an ANN to the model. This achieved a prediction with a determination factor of 0.9866 compared to the actual vehicle range.

Keywords: EV · OBD · Random Forest · ANN · SOC · RDE

1 Introduction

Climate change is a consequence of industrialization, population global increase and the growing need to burn fossil fuels leads to a reduction in air quality [1]. With the implementation of environmental policies to reduce carbon emissions from internal combustion vehicles, the use of vehicles powered by electrical sources has been incorporated [2]. In recent years, electric vehicles (EVs) have increased their position in the automotive market due to improvements in factors such as production, marketing, and innovation in response to current needs for smart and shared mobility [3]. Technological development in EVs allows competitiveness if it is compared to combustion vehicles in relation to costs [4]. To determine EV efficiency and autonomy of energy in different traffic conditions, Real Driving Emissions (RDE) cycles are implemented [5] based on a speed, power, and time profile that describes typical driving patterns in a city in real

© The Author(s), under exclusive license to Springer Nature Switzerland AG 2024
M. Botto-Tobar et al. (Eds.): ICAT 2023, CCIS 2049, pp. 194–205, 2024.
https://doi.org/10.1007/978-3-031-58956-0_15

conditions [6]. Route data obtained are acquired through the CAN bus from the OBD II connector [7]. The energy consumption estimation model for electric vehicles allows to identification of the autonomy of an EV by applying the dynamics of the car [8]. The driving modes: ecological, normal, and sport characterize the behavior of the EV's energy consumption based on the maneuvers carried out by the driver [9]. Machine Learning models' applications allow us to determine with great precision the EV power, based on the input data, the training, and the model architecture, obtaining prediction values close to the real one [10]. The signals from the sensors obtained through the onboard diagnostics port (OBD II) in the Electric vehicle indicate variables such as the state of charge, voltage, and current of the battery [11], in addition to the speed and location of the route [12]. [13] presents a methodology that describes the behavior of the obtained data by the OBD II through automatic learning techniques in real driving conditions. Several factors influence car energy consumption, including driving style, road conditions, and traffic [14]. [15] presents a Machine Learning model capable of identifying driving modes through identification parameters signals (PID's) of a vehicle based on engine performance. [16] performs an approach to the evaluation of EV performance based on driving cycles where it classifies different kinematic fragments to estimate driving patterns and forecast vehicle autonomy. [17] investigates driving parameters by patterns that influence vehicle consumption, data is extracted by GPS, driving patterns are characterized by segments of recorded driving profiles. [18] determines the main parameters such as speed, acceleration, and deceleration in addition to the use of auxiliary systems generate a significant impact on the energy consumption of the vehicle.

The paper is structured as follows: Sect. 2 describes how the on-road data acquisition is performed after the test under normal conditions and the application of the longitudinal dynamics of the vehicle. Section 3 presents the estimation of the vehicle energy consumption, the characterization of the on-road driving modes, the identification of the variables with the highest incidence in the study of vehicle autonomy, and a model capable of determining the state of charge (SOC) from these variables.

2   Materials and Methods

This study proposes an analysis of the influence of driving style on energy consumption through PID's signals of a Kia Soul electric vehicle in the city of Cuenca-Ecuador located at an altitude of 2550 m.a.s.l, by analyzing a driving cycle under real conditions. The objective of this study is to evaluate the data acquired through the OBD II identification parameters on the energy consumption of an electric vehicle as a function of the type of driving, by applying a real cycle of emissions (RDE) on urban, rural and highway roads, using standardized driving cycles. The purpose is to obtain real-time data and generate a model capable of analyzing the energy consumption of the vehicle according to the variables with the greatest impact on the state of charge (SOC). The methodology developed in the study is presented below (Fig. 1).

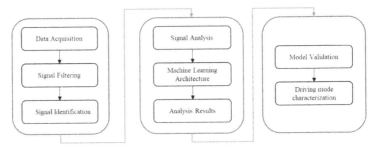

Fig. 1. Methodology

2.1 On Route Data Acquisition

Vehicle variables were obtained through the use of a Freematics ONE+ data logger which includes GPS information with a sampling frequency of 15.15 Hz, The road obtained data are stored on a micro-SD card. Table 1 shows the variables acquired during the experimental phase.

Table 1. Variables acquired on route

Variables	Nomenclature	Unit	Range
Speed	VSS	km/h	0–117
Engine Speed	RPM	rpm	0–8000
Accelerator Pedal Sensor	APS	%	0–100
Battery state of charge	SOC	%	0–100
Battery current	A	Amps	−166.1–269.8
Battery voltage	V	Volts	314.5–385

2.2 Test Route

The road test is carried out in stable environmental conditions, at an altitude of 2550 m above sea level, at an ambient temperature of 17 °C, and without rain. In addition, due to the regulations that establish speed limits on highways in Ecuador, the speed is limited to 90 km/h, which makes it difficult to exceed the limits in certain stretches [19]. The study developed in the city of Cuenca-Ecuador was carried out in a Kia Soul electric vehicle of the year 2017 SUV, then The most relevant characteristics of the vehicle are presented in Table 2.

For the experimental section, the real emissions cycle (RDE) corresponding to the EURO 6 standard is used, which establishes driving in areas: urban, rural, and highway, Fig. 2 shows the route taken through 49.82 km of road, observing the speed vector on a map where the route layout is identified through the latitude and longitude coordinates

Table 2. Kia Soul EV 2017 characteristics

Characteristics	Value
Electric motor	81.4 kW/110 Cv
Torque	285 Nm (0–2780 rpm)
Battery	Lithium polymer 27 kWh
Mass	1565 kg

acquired by GPS. For the experimental section, the real emissions cycle (RDE) corresponding to the EURO 6 standard is used, which establishes driving in areas: urban, rural, and highway, Fig. 2 shows the route taken through 49.82 km of road, observing the speed vector on a map where the route layout is identified through the latitude and longitude coordinates acquired by GPS.

Ensuring the test cycle's credibility relies heavily on adhering closely to the limitations specified in the Euro 6 regulations. These rules cover a range of elements, including speed restrictions across different road sections, designated durations for stops, and prescribed travel distances. It's pivotal to highlight that specific factors, like road speed, face constraints due to legal regulations that enforce a maximum speed limit of 90 km/h within Ecuadorian territory.

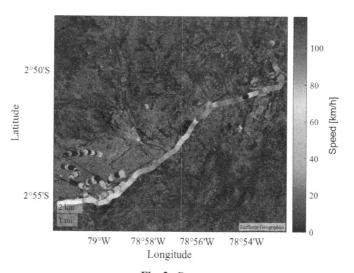

Fig. 2. Route

2.3 Longitudinal Vehicle Dynamics

The vehicle is exposed to several forces that must be overcome in order to move. The tractive force F_T depends directly on the aerodynamic resistance R_d, the rolling resistance R_x, the slope resistance R_g, and the inertia force F_i as is shown in Fig. 3.

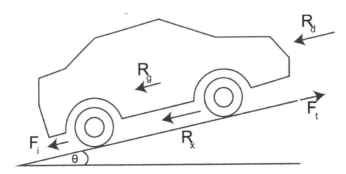

Fig. 3. Forces involved in the advance of the vehicle.

Calculous of the instantaneous power in electric vehicles (EVs) is determined by means of the speed, acceleration, and grade of the road by means of the tractive force influenced by the forces opposing the movement.

$$ma_x = F_T - F_{res} - R_g - F_{brk} \tag{1}$$

With the speed obtained by means of GPS on the route, the longitudinal acceleration [20] is calculated through:

$$a_x i = \frac{V_{GPSi+1} - V_{GPSi}}{t_{i+1} - t_i} \tag{2}$$

The rolling resistance R_x is determined through the coefficients dynamic $f_0 = 0.01$, static $f = 0.015$, and the speed V as presented in the Eq. (3).

$$R_x = f + f_0 \left(\frac{V}{100} \right)^{2.5} \tag{3}$$

The aerodynamic resistance is given by the density of the air, and the structural shape of the vehicle as the aerodynamic coefficient $C_X = 0.33$, frontal area of the vehicle $A_f = 2.05\,\text{m}^2$, and car speed acquired by the GPS with which the resistance to the slope F_{res} is obtained.

$$F_{res} = m \cdot g \cdot R_x + \frac{1}{2} \rho C_X A_f V_{GPSi}^2 \tag{4}$$

The slope resistance is calculated with the altitude obtained through the GPS based on the ascent during the route.

$$R_g = m \cdot g \cdot \sin \left(\frac{Alt_{i+1} - Alt_i}{S_{i+1} - S_i} \right) \tag{5}$$

Braking force F_{brk} is applicable when the tractive force F_T is equal to zero, this is because the brake and the accelerator cannot be activated at the same time. Aerodynamic drag and rolling force cannot be negative because they depend directly on speed. Tractive force F_T is negative due to hill climbing and braking [20].

$$F_T - F_{brk} = ma_x + F_{res} + R_g \tag{6}$$

The required power to overcome the opposing forces to the vehicle movement is given by the total resistance force to the movement in speed function.

$$P_{rueda} = F_x \cdot V [kW] \tag{7}$$

Where:

$$F_x = Opposite\ force\ to\ motion[N]$$
$$V = Speed[m/s]$$

3 Results and Discussion

3.1 Energy Consumption Calculus

The energy consumption can be calculated by relating the power (P) and the energy during the operation time (t) [21] by means of the following equation:

$$E = P \cdot t[kWh] \tag{8}$$

Since the energy consumption in the EV depends directly on the battery state of charge (SOC), this variable is analyzed during the journey in relation to the area in which it circulates. Figure 4 shows the energy consumption during the sections in urban, rural, and highway areas, where it is identified that the peaks with the highest energy consumption occur on the highway as a consequence of throttle dependence and the use of aggressive driving during that section, therefore, SOC tends to decrease progressively.

The instantaneous energy consumption obtained on the route is 23.11 kWh. Table 3 shows the obtained consumption during the circuit.

Based on the methodology (CPEM) of The Comprehensive Power-based EV Energy consumption Model, the total energy consumption (EC) is determined based on the motor power $P_{Electricmotor}$ obtained through car dynamics and the route distance d [22].

$$EC = \frac{1}{3600000} \cdot \frac{1}{d} \cdot \sum_{i=1}^{t} P_{Electric\ motor} \tag{9}$$

The energy consumption per distance traveled result is 138.8756 (Wh/km).

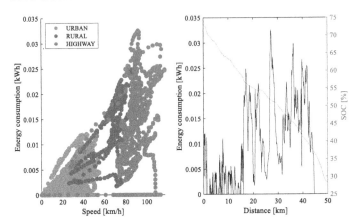

Fig. 4. Energy consumption on route

Table 3. Energy consumption by areas

Area	Energy consumption [kWh]	Percentage [%]	Average speed [km/h]
Urban	5.04	21.80	22.07
Rural	5.84	25.27	67.14
Highway	12.23	52.94	87.67

3.2   Acceleration Analysis Respect to the Route Driving Modes

Figure 5 shows the acceleration profiles for each of the driving modes using the normalized frequency of the activity within each acceleration interval [23]. The conservative mode presents a profile with high density at low accelerations with a reduced range of variation, indicating that the driver tends to accelerate and brake smoothly, maintaining a constant speed. On the other hand, the aggressive mode is characterized by a wide range of acceleration and low density in high acceleration/deceleration regions during the route, suggesting that the driver accelerates and brakes sharply, resulting in reduced energy efficiency of the vehicle. The density of driving modes refers to the frequency of activity within each acceleration range, providing insights into the driving style and its impact on energy consumption.

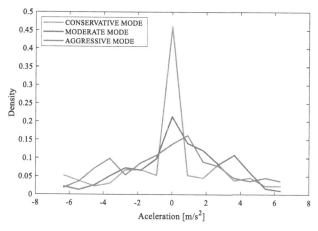

Fig. 5. Unit density as an acceleration function

3.3 Most Important Predictors in the Study from Decision Trees (Random Forest)

To estimate the battery state of charge (SOC) behavior, a Random Forest algorithm is applied which identifies the variables with the greatest influence concerning the autonomy of the vehicle, Sensors such as APS, VSS, acceleration, and power present great interaction on energy consumption during the route. The purpose of the algorithm is to find the relationship between the input variables versus the output variables, resulting in a coefficient of determination of 0.9265 (Fig. 6).

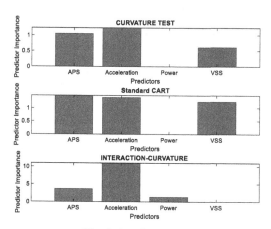

Fig. 6. Random Forest

3.4 Training and Validation of the Neural Network from the Predictors

To estimate the behavior of vehicle autonomy from the most influential variables obtained from the predictors, a neural network model (ANN) is used. In this model, the variables APS Ax and VSS are at the input, while the SOC parameter is at the output. That is, 4 input layers, 10 neurons in the hidden layer, and one output layer in the ANN are considered. The model prediction presents a high reliability of the ANN reaching a global index of 0.9866 as shown in Fig. 7 (Table 4).

Table 4. ANN Training

	Observations	Data splitting (%)	R
Training	2884	70	0.9869
Validation	618	15	0.9874
Testing	618	15	0.9840

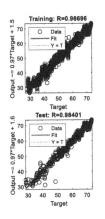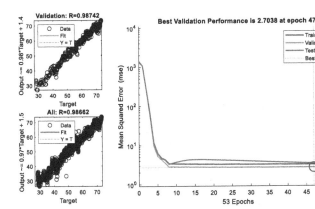

Fig. 7. Neuronal Network

With the generated model, the behavior of the autonomy of the EV is simulated through the SOC. In Fig. 8 the real SOC is presented against the SOC simulated by the ANN as a function of the distance, A general trend of the input variables with response variable can be seen, the simulated SOC presents small fluctuations with respect to the real SOC because to abrupt and sudden changes in driving conditions due to variables such as speed, acceleration and engine speed.

The difference between the actual SOC versus the simulated SOC is determined through the mean square error (MSE) in order to calculate the simulation accuracy through Eq. (10).

$$MSE = \frac{1}{N} \cdot \sum_{i=1}^{N} (Yi - \hat{y}_i)^2 \tag{10}$$

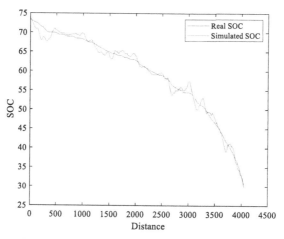

Fig. 8. Validation of the model by means of ANN

The model has an MSE of 1.3684% which indicates that the variability between observed and predicted values is relatively low, showing a strong accuracy between the simulated and real model.

4 Conclusions

This research project analyzes the influence of driving style on energy consumption by studying the PID signals of a Kia Soul electric vehicle, where the driving style is reflected in the energy consumption of the vehicle. In addition, parameters such as acceleration show a direct proportionality to energy consumption, as is the case for highway driving, where a 31.14% increase is required compared to urban driving. Through the acceleration profile, the type of driving evaluated on the road is identified, since the higher the density present at low acceleration, the lower the autonomy will be as a consequence of conservative driving. On the other hand, if the acceleration range is high, the density will be low, resulting in aggressive driving. Based on machine learning architectures, the most influential variables in the study concerning SOC are estimated, which are APS, VSS, and acceleration. Therefore, by applying an ANN to the model, a prediction of 0.9866 is achieved compared to the actual vehicle range.

It is important to note that within the context of the Ecuadorian territory, the local legislation imposes restrictions on road speed, prohibiting speeds exceeding 90 km/h. Adhering to these legal regulations is crucial to ensure compliance and safety while conducting the test cycle.

For future work, the optimization of the integration of regenerative braking and air conditioning (A/C) use in electric vehicles could be investigated. This would involve analyzing how to adjust the deceleration rate of regenerative braking and A/C power consumption based on variables such as vehicle speed, battery state of charge, environmental conditions, and driver preference. The goal would be to maximize energy efficiency by optimally utilizing both regenerative braking and A/C, providing practical guidelines for more efficient and sustainable driving.

References

1. Wee, J.H.: Contribution of fuel cell systems to CO2 emission reduction in their application fields. Renew. Sustain. Energy Rev. **14**, 735–744 (2010). https://doi.org/10.1016/J.RSER.2009.10.013
2. Li, Z., Khajepour, A., Song, J.: A comprehensive review of the key technologies for pure electric vehicles. Energy **182**, 824–839 (2019). https://doi.org/10.1016/J.ENERGY.2019.06.077
3. Sanguesa, J.A., Torres-Sanz, V., Garrido, P., Martinez, F.J., Marquez-Barja, J.M.: A review on electric vehicles: technologies and challenges. Smart Cities **4**, 372–404 (2021). https://doi.org/10.3390/SMARTCITIES4010022
4. Kameda, H., Mukai, N.: Optimization of charging station placement by using taxi probe data for on-demand electrical bus system. In: König, A., Dengel, A., Hinkelmann, K., Kise, K., Howlett, R.J., Jain, L.C. (eds.) KES 2011. LNCS, vol. 6883, pp. 606–615. Springer, Heidelberg (2011). https://doi.org/10.1007/978-3-642-23854-3_64
5. Pielecha, J., Skobiej, K., Kurtyka, K.: Exhaust emissions and energy consumption analysis of conventional, hybrid, and electric vehicles in real driving cycles. Energies **13**, 6423 (2020). https://doi.org/10.3390/EN13236423
6. Rechkemmer, S.K., Zang, X., Zhang, W., Sawodny, O.: Lifetime optimized charging strategy of Li-ion cells based on daily driving cycle of electric two-wheelers. Appl. Energy **251**, 113415 (2019). https://doi.org/10.1016/J.APENERGY.2019.113415
7. Khorsravinia, K., Hassan, M.K., Rahman, R.Z.A., Al-Haddad, S.A.R.: Integrated OBD-II and mobile application for electric vehicle (EV) monitoring system. In: Proceedings - 2017 IEEE 2nd International Conference on Automatic Control and Intelligent Systems, I2CACIS 2017, December 2017, pp. 202–206 (2017). https://doi.org/10.1109/I2CACIS.2017.8239058
8. Wu, X., Freese, D., Cabrera, A., Kitch, W.A.: Electric vehicles' energy consumption measurement and estimation. Transp. Res. D Transp. Environ. **34**, 52–67 (2015). https://doi.org/10.1016/J.TRD.2014.10.007
9. De Novellis, L., Sorniotti, A., Gruber, P.: Driving modes for designing the cornering response of fully electric vehicles with multiple motors. Mech. Syst. Signal Process. **64–65**, 1–15 (2015). https://doi.org/10.1016/J.YMSSP.2015.03.024
10. Rhode, S., Van Vaerenbergh, S., Pfriem, M.: Power prediction for electric vehicles using online machine learning. Eng. Appl. Artif. Intell. **87** (2020). https://doi.org/10.1016/j.engappai.2019.103278
11. Tseng, C.M., Zhou, W., Al Hashmi, M., Chau, C.K., Song, S.G., Wilhelm, E.: Data extraction from electric vehicles through OBD and application of carbon footprint evaluation. In: Proceedings of the Workshop on Electric Vehicle Systems, Data, and Applications, EV-SYS 2016 (2016). https://doi.org/10.1145/2939953.2939954
12. Kocsis Szürke, S., Sütheö, G., Apagyi, A., Lakatos, I., Fischer, S.: Cell fault identification and localization procedure for lithium-ion battery system of electric vehicles based on real measurement data. Algorithms **15**, 467 (2022) https://doi.org/10.3390/A15120467
13. Rivera-Campoverde, N.D., Muñoz-Sanz, J.L., Arenas-Ramirez, B.D.V.: Estimation of pollutant emissions in real driving conditions based on data from OBD and machine learning. Sensors **21**, 6344 (2021). https://doi.org/10.3390/S21196344
14. Belt, J.R.: Battery test manual for plug-in hybrid electric vehicles (2010). https://doi.org/10.2172/1010675
15. Molina Campoverde, J.J.: Driving mode estimation model based in machine learning through PID's signals analysis obtained from OBD II. In: Botto-Tobar, M., Zambrano Vizuete, M., Torres-Carrión, P., Montes León, S., Pizarro Vásquez, G., Durakovic, B. (eds.) ICAT 2019. CCIS, vol. 1194, pp. 80–91. Springer, Cham (2020). https://doi.org/10.1007/978-3-030-42520-3_7

16. Chen, F., et al.: A novel method of developing driving cycle for electric vehicles to evaluate the private driving habits. IEEE Access **9**, 46476–46486 (2021). https://doi.org/10.1109/ACCESS.2021.3049411

17. Braun, A., Rid, W.: The influence of driving patterns on energy consumption in electric car driving and the role of regenerative braking. Transp. Res. Procedia **22**, 174–182 (2017). https://doi.org/10.1016/J.TRPRO.2017.03.024

18. Badin, F., et al.: Evaluation of EVs energy consumption influencing factors, driving conditions, auxiliaries use, driver's aggressiveness. In: 2013 World Electric Vehicle Symposium and Exhibition, EVS 2014 (2014). https://doi.org/10.1109/EVS.2013.6914723

19. Molina, P.: Estimation of fuel consumption through PID signals using the real emissions cycle in the City of Quito, Ecuador. Sustainability **15**, 12474 (2023). https://doi.org/10.3390/SU151612474

20. Rivera Campoverde, N., Muñoz Sanz, J., Arenas Ramírez, B.: Modelo de bajo costo para la estimación de emisiones contaminantes basado en GPS y aprendizaje automático (2022). https://doi.org/10.5944/BICIM2022.179

21. Zhang, R., Yao, E.: Electric vehicles' energy consumption estimation with real driving condition data. Transp. Res. D Transp. Environ. **41**, 177–187 (2015). https://doi.org/10.1016/J.TRD.2015.10.010

22. Fiori, C., Ahn, K., Rakha, H.A.: Power-based electric vehicle energy consumption model: model development and validation. Appl. Energy **168**, 257–268 (2016). https://doi.org/10.1016/J.APENERGY.2016.01.097

23. Bingham, C., Walsh, C., Carroll, S.: Impact of driving characteristics on electric vehicle energy consumption and range. IET Intell. Transp. Syst. **6**, 29–35 (2012). https://doi.org/10.1049/IET-ITS.2010.0137/CITE/REFWORKS

Prediction of Academic Outcomes Using Machine Learning Techniques: A Survey of Findings on Higher Education

Priscila Valdiviezo-Diaz$^{(\boxtimes)}$ (ORCID) and Janneth Chicaiza (ORCID)

Departamento de Ciencias de la Computación y Electrónica, Universidad Técnica Particular de Loja, Loja, Ecuador
{pmvaldiviezo,jachicaiza}@utpl.edu.ec

Abstract. The growth of electronic data in educational institutions provides an opportunity to extract information that can be used to predict students' academic performance and dropout rates. This paper provides a survey to explore the current state of research on academic performance prediction using machine learning techniques. A systematic literature search was conducted to identify relevant studies published between 2019 and 2023. The review analyzed studies that used various machine learning algorithms to predict academic performance in different educational contexts. The findings indicate that machine learning models can accurately predict academic performance with a high degree of precision, using a variety of variables such as demographic data, academic history, and student interaction. The review also highlights the challenges of the current research, including the need for collection and preprocessing procedures, and the importance of considering ethical implications related to the use of student data. The findings have important implications for educators, managers, and researchers interested in using machine learning techniques to promote student success.

Keywords: machine learning algorithms · prediction of academic outcomes · survey

1 Introduction

In the context of formal education, the ability to predict academic performance is a valuable tool for identifying students' dropout risk within an educational institution. According to [1], one approach to assessing student success is predicting their performance based on their prior academic grades. Such predictions enable educators and administrators to take proactive measures to address potential academic challenges and provide targeted support to students in need, which can help to improve retention rates and foster a culture of academic achievement.

Faced with large volumes of information, Artificial Intelligence and its different branches have made it possible to analyze and extract knowledge from different data sources to help decision-making.

© The Author(s), under exclusive license to Springer Nature Switzerland AG 2024
M. Botto-Tobar et al. (Eds.): ICAT 2023, CCIS 2049, pp. 206–218, 2024.
https://doi.org/10.1007/978-3-031-58956-0_16

Considering the availability of data related to electronic learning, machine learning models have been developed to forecast students' academic performance, enabling the identification of those at risk of failure. The integration of these models into the educational context not only offers a nuanced perspective on academic outcomes but also provides educators, institutions, and policymakers with valuable insights for targeted interventions. The machine learning models allow the identification of patterns within diverse datasets, encompassing variables from socio-economic factors to individual learning behaviors. For example, in [20], academic results and behavior of engineering students are analyzed to predict their performance. Crivei et al. [12] analyze academic data in order to build supervised learning models for the prediction of student performance. In the context of distance learning systems, the work presented in [17] considers the characteristics of students' academic activity to identify those at risk of academic failure. Brahim et al. [9] describe a study focused on predicting student performance during interactive online sessions by considering a dataset extracted from educational systems [9]. Finally, in [3], a web-based system is developed to predict academic performance and so to identify students at risk of failing based on academic and demographic factors.

This paper aims to present a comprehensive review of the utilization of Machine Learning techniques in predicting academic outcomes within higher education settings. Specifically, the review focuses on identifying the factors that affect academic performance; investigating the methods and algorithms employed for academic performance prediction, and identifying metrics commonly used for assessing the efficacy of prediction models. Additionally, the paper highlights some of the main challenges related to prediction tasks. In light of these challenges, the paper also recommends relevant areas for future research.

2   Importance of Academic Performance Prediction

Academic success among university students is a highly important topic in institutions of higher education as it is considered an essential criterion for evaluating the quality of educational institutions [22]. This subject has aroused great interest among university authorities concerning the academic outcomes of their students, as it directly affects the quality of education. Analyzing academic performance enables the construction of indicators that guide decision-making in higher education. Therefore, understanding students' academic performance enables instructors to monitor students so that they can offer support and integrate training to achieve the best results.

In [34], a definition of academic success is provided by focusing on the six most important components: academic achievement, satisfaction, acquisition of skills and competencies, persistence, attainment of learning goals, and professional success. In [25], the academic performance itself is mainly based on Grade Point Average (GPA) or Cumulative Grade Point Average (CGPA), which are grading systems used in universities to assign an evaluation scale to students' academic performance [10]. Academic success has also been defined in relation to students' persistence, also called academic resilience [13], which in turn is also primarily measured through grades and cumulative grade point average.

According to [6], early prediction of student performance can assist decision-makers in providing necessary actions at the right time and planning appropriate training interventions to improve students' success rate. On the other hand, Gutiérrez et al. [15] point out that academic performance can be measured at different stages of the academic formation process, and several variables or student characteristics associated with performance can also be collected. This information can be analyzed later to make appropriate decisions and improve learning outcomes.

To analyze research related to academic performance by leveraging artificial intelligence techniques, some literature reviews have been conducted. For example, Albrei et al. [4] present a comprehensive literature review spanning from 2009 to 2021, focusing on the application of Educational data mining (EDM) techniques for the identification of students at risk of dropping out. The results of the review found that (1) several Machine Learning (ML) techniques are used to understand and overcome underlying challenges, such as predicting at-risk students and predicting student dropout; and (2) most studies use two types of datasets: university student data/databases and online learning platforms.

Delighting the same line, authors of [6] present a clear set of guidelines for using EDM to predict academic success. The authors specifically focus on the problem of predicting the academic success of higher education students.

Another research is presented in [35], where a systematic literature review was conducted on articles and conference papers published between 2011 and 2021 in the Scopus database. Here, Artificial Intelligence applications were classified into student performance, teaching, selection, behavior, and other tasks.

Finally, regarding the identification of factors that influence performance students, the study of [31] mentions that supplementing behavioral data with other more relevant data (about learning outcomes) can lead to a better analysis of the learning process, specifically, it is possible to early predict the student's final performance.

This paper aims to contribute to the existing literature on predicting academic performance, by providing details about methods, algorithms, and metrics used for academic performance prediction.

3   Methodology

This paper presents recently published articles on student academic performance and describes the purpose of these studies, the machine learning algorithms and metrics used for predicting academic performance. The steps followed are 1) literature search, 2) article selection, and 3) data analysis.

1. Literature Search: A comprehensive search was conducted on the database Scopus to identify relevant articles that address students' academic performance. Keywords such as "prediction of student academic performance",

"prediction of academic success", "prediction of academic achievement", "educational data mining", "machine learning", and "deep learning" were entered. Therefore, the following search string was used.

Search Query executed on Sep 13, 2023

TITLE–ABS–KEY((predicting AND students ' AND
academic AND performance OR predicting AND
academic AND success , OR predicting AND academic
AND achievement) AND ((educational AND data
AND mining), OR (machine AND learning) OR (deep
learning)))

As inclusion criteria, we consider the publication year (between 2019 and 2023) and language (Spanish or English). Furthermore, as exclusion criteria, we discard some document types such as book studies, book sections and conference reviews.

As a result of the filtering, 117 documents were obtained, most of which were published in the year 2022. Figure 1 shows the number of articles found according to the year of publication.

2. Article Selection: The articles were screened based on their titles, abstracts, and full texts, and only those that directly addressed the topic of the academic performance of university students were included. After this review, finally, 15 articles were selected for analysis.

3. Data Analysis: The findings of the included studies were analyzed to identify common themes related to academic performance in students, such as factors that affect academic performance, the machine learning algorithms applied for classification or clustering, metrics used to evaluate prediction quality, and some challenges found in these studies.

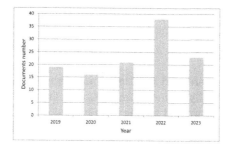

Fig. 1. Distribution of documents by year.

4   Results

This section shows a list of the articles selected for a more exhaustive review regarding the points of interest related to academic performance.

Table 1 describes the goal, the dataset used for analysis, the main features, and the target variable of each proposal. As we can see in the last column, most authors used academic data to classify student performance or predict the results of students. In addition, it was possible to determine that in most of the related work, the target variable is established in terms of labeled data or levels such as high, medium, or low; pass or fail; excellent, good, or bad. Very few studies attempt to estimate test scores or grades.

4.1 Factors Affecting the Student's Academic Performance

The results of the literature review show that there are numerous factors that can affect the academic success of students, such as socioeconomic background, academic characteristics, and motivation, among others, which should be analyzed to carry out the necessary actions for the benefit of the students. In educational institutions, it is important to examine how these factors affect academic performance as well as explore possible solutions to improve it. This section mentions the factors that were detected in the selected articles and that could affect the results of the students.

Although a wide variety of factors have been investigated in the literature regarding their impact on predicting student academic success, according to [6] the factors most widely involved in academic success are: prior academic performance, student demographics, e-learning activity, psychological attributes, and environment. According to the authors, previous academic performance and student demographics are the most important factors. Similarly, Bilal et al., in [8], mention that characteristics related to demographics, personality, socioeconomic, and environmental traits can affect student performance. Knowledge of these factors and their effect on student performance can help manage their impact.

On the other hand, *Ref.* [19] highlights that the course score is the most direct factor for evaluating student quality. If students can predict their grades in advance based on their previous academic performance, and this reminds them to study hard to avoid failing, it is of great importance in education and teaching research.

Other factors that were also mentioned in the analyzed works include parents' education level, family socioeconomic status, environment, and context. For example, academic support and teacher commitment may be important factors in academic success. Other variables that have been studied include class size, social adjustment, and self-directed learning. Overall, the results suggest that there are numerous factors that affect academic performance.

In the analyzed works, it was observed that some attributes are used to assess student performance and that they are associated with the aforementioned factors. These attributes are grouped by the target variable in predicting student success, namely grade level, year level, and course level [6]. The majority of analyzed works that have used machine learning for predicting students' performance have considered historical data related mainly to academic and interaction

Table 1. Proposals on the prediction of academic performance

Ref.	Goal	Dataset	Features	Target variable
[21]	To predict academic achievement by using students' interaction in an online learning environment.	Study sample for the academic year 2020, with factors related to individual traits.	Sex, academic specialization, academic degree, and a number of training courses.	Categorical: performance.
[2]	To predict and explain variations in course grades among students	A dataset constructed from transcripts of 650 students, and collected from Spring 2013 to Spring 2022	Course category, student course attendance percentage, gender, high-school grade, school type, GPA, & delivery mode.	Continuous: course grade (scale of 0-100)
[18]	To categorize the student's performance thus to forecast student achievements in online education.	The Kaggle student's performance assessment database (based on student's information logs).	Students' performance & behavior characteristics.	Categorical: performance (low, medium, high)
[5]	To predict students' performance by using academic performance data and social relationships features.	Students records' dataset for five consecutive years: $\geq 275K$ records for almost five thousand students.	Student's identification, gender, program, admission criteria, graduation time, instructors and course information, GPA, and grades.	Categorical: GPA (A, B, C, D).
[7]	To predict the student's performance and their several iterations.	The Kaggle dataset of high-education students' performance: 480 tuples and 17 properties.	Students' demographic and performance features	Categorical: performance (low, medium, high)
[8]	To predict students' final semester results	Data of 166 students collected from three sessions: 2010-15, 2012-17, and 2013-18	Pre-admission achievements, first-semester performance, and students' demographic features	Categorical: GPA (high or low)
[30]	To optimize Multi-Layer Perception (MLP) weights and biases for predicting student achievement	Two datasets of student performance that are available on the UCI Repository	Student's achievement, demographic, personal, social, and school-related characteristics, and family features	Continuous: student achievement
[26]	To predict performance based on behavior classification	Open University Learning Analytics Dataset (OULAD) that contains data of 6,272 learners, and their performance	Online learning behaviors: homepage, page, subpage, glossary, wiki, resource, URL, content, forum, collaborate, elluminate, external quiz	Categorical: learning performance

continued

Table 1. continued

Ref.	Goal	Dataset	Features	Target variable
[19]	To predict academic performance by using a feedforward spike neural network	Dataset of the Internet of Things major, which contains performance data for 62 courses in 6 semesters, with 26 variables related to student grades	Information of students and courses, including student ID, GPA, entrance grades, semester, course attributes, and performance in class	Categorical: grade (low, medium, and high)
[23]	To construct an appropriate education program prediction model for students in a rural school.	Academic achievement data of 1,859 students from Manchasuksa School in Thailand, during the academic year 2015-2020.	Academic results of students.	Categorical: academic achievement
[28]	To predict students' performance by using a conditional generative adversarial network in combination with a deep-layer-based support vector machine.	Records for 786 students of the Portuguese and math classes: 9 attributes are about tutoring, 24 attributes are collected via questionnaires, and the rest are from reports from the school.	Sex, age, address, mother's education and job, father's education and job, family size, course, family educational support, Internet access, free time, current health status & grades.	Categorical: academic performance.
[29]	To predict results for developing an individualized learning system.	Real-time dataset of postgraduate students undergoing the Indian higher education system. A sample of 500 students was used.	Birthdate, gender, course, high school and secondary scores, undergraduate specialization and overall score, entrance exam score, continuous assessment test, and final grade.	Categorical: student's performance.
[33]	To propose a model to predict the final exam grades of undergraduate students, taking their midterm exam grades.	Data collected from the State University in Turkey, which described 1854 students who have taken the Turkish Language-I course in the 2019-2020 fall semester.	Midterm exam grades, final exam grades, Faculty, and Department.	Categorical: grade (1,2,3,4)
[9]	To predict student performance during online interactive sessions.	The Digital Electronics Education and Design Suite dataset, with an average of 86 students. The dataset captures real-time in-class student interactions and behavior.	Time spent in types of problems in the learning environment, types of activities, number of activities, the average number of keystrokes, and grade of performance in each session	Categorical: grade performance (A, B)
[11]	To apply deep learning for predicting Portuguese high school grades.	Data from Portuguese upper secondary students. The data refer to the three final high school years and comprise 27 subjects for the 2018-19 academic year.	Gender, internet, country, father and mother's educational level, class size, teacher age and gender, lecture time, subjects, etc.	Continuous: academic achievement

factors with e-learning platforms. However, some studies use other factors that can also influence student performance, as summarized in Fig. 2.

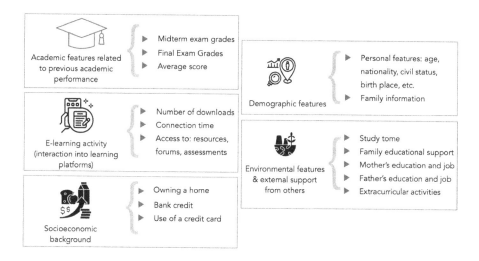

Fig. 2. Summary of factors related to academic performance.

4.2   Machine Learning Algorithms for Predicting Students' Performance

Educational institutions generate large volumes of data related to students enrolled in their majors, and the use of platforms for e-learning has increased the availability of data related to online learning. The data generated on these platforms can be transformed and analyzed, leading to meaningful information that can help managers make decisions about institutional matters and, in particular, about students and their well-being. This availability of data has encouraged researchers to develop ML models to predict student academic performance. Table 2 shows the most used algorithms in selected papers.

From the analyzed articles, the SVM and RF algorithms were the most used by the authors, followed by LR, NB, KNN, DT, and MLP. Likewise, in Table 2, we can see that RF, alone or in combination with others, offered the best performance according to different evaluation metrics. Finally, it can also be seen that current proposals are applying several algorithms based on neural networks for the prediction of academic success with the best performance.

On the other hand, from the literature review, it was also observed that the methodological quality of the studies varies in terms of design, predictive performance, and limitations. For example, some studies have adopted designs considering students' behavioral data over time and capturing changes in the predictor variables [16]. Regarding the predictive capacity of the algorithms,

Table 2. Machine learning algorithms used for student's performance prediction

Ref.	Algorithm							Best algorithm
	Trees-based	Gradient-based	K-Nearest-Neighbor	SVM	Regression	Bayesian algorithms	Neural Networks	
[21]	DT		KNN	SVM		NB		SVM based on accuracy
[2]							ANFIS	No comparison
[18]				SVM			Bi-LSTM, SPDN, CNN + WOA	CNN + WOA based on accuracy, recall, precision and F1-score
[5]	RF		KNN	SVM	LR	GNB		RF based on accuracy
[7]	RF + FCM				LR + FCM		MLP + FCM	MLP + FCM & RF + FCM based on accuracy, recall, precision and F1-score
[8]	DT, RF		KNN	SVM	LR			SVM based on accuracy, recall and precision
[30]							MLP + EGWO	No comparison
[26]			KNN (U), KNN (D)	SVC (R), SVC (L)		NB	Based on softmax	NB based on accuracy, F1-score and Kappa
[19]	DT, RF	XGBoost		SVM			SNN	SNN based on accuracy, recall, precision, F1-score
[23]	DT, RF	XGBoost						RF + XGBoost based on accuracy
[28]	ETC, RF	SGD, GBM			LR		CNN, LSTM, CGAN + SVM	CGAN + SVM based on recall, specificity and AUC
[29]	DT, RF		KNN	SVM	LR	NB		RF based on accuracy
[33]	RF		KNN	SVM	LR	NB	NN (Not specified)	NN based on AUC, accuracy and F1 score, and RF based on accuracy and precision
[9]	RF			SVM	LR	NB	MLP	RF based on accuracy, recall, precision, F1-score and AUC
[11]					MLR	NB	MLP	MLP based on MSE, MAE and R2

Nomenclature: ANFIS - Adaptive Neuro-Fuzzy Inference Systems, DT - Decision Tree, ETC - Extra Tree Classifier, LR - Logistic Regression, GBT - Gradient Boosted Trees, GBM - Gradient Boosting Machine, GNB - Gaussian Naive Bayes, WOA - Whale Optimization Algorithm, SPDN - Sparse Probabilistic Dynamic Network, LSTM - Long Short-Term Memory, Bi-LSTM - Bi-directional LSTM, EGWO - Elastic Grey Wolf Optimization algorithm, SGD - Stochastic Gradient Descent, CGAN - Conditional Generative Adversarial Network.

some studies have achieved high levels of predictive performance, highlighting the effectiveness of certain machine learning models. These models, such as those based on neural networks, have demonstrated abilities to capture complex patterns and improve prediction accuracy [7,11,18]. Other studies face limitations in predictive accuracy, especially those that depend on traditional variables such as previous outcomes and demographic characteristics. Likewise, others may lack diversity in the samples, affecting the applicability of the findings to different educational contexts.

4.3   Challenges of Machine Learning for Academic Performance

Educational institutions can implement machine learning algorithms to predict students' learning behavior and academic achievement, giving them the opportunity to detect at-risk students early and then develop strategies to help them overcome their weaknesses [24]. However, despite the benefits associated with machine learning techniques, there are some challenges that could affect their implementation in the prediction of academic events. Some of them are related to:

Diversity in the Academic Performance: The academic performance of students can be measured in different ways, including grades, graduation rate, attendance, and activity participation. Each measure can have different predictors, making the prediction more complex.

Data acquisition: To build a prediction model, machine learning algorithms are based on data to learn and predict academic events. However, the acquisition of these data is not easy or may be limited, which may affect the validity of the results. The larger the data, the better the reliability of the prediction [14].

Selection of variables: Identifying the most relevant and significant variables to predict academic performance is a challenge. Variables can be academic, socioeconomic, demographic, ability, and attitudinal. Choosing the right variables can be critical to the accuracy of the prediction.

Ethical implications: Other challenges in ML algorithms are the definition of parameters used to obtain the target variable considering specific input data. These parameters are not determined by human intelligence, instead, they are learned from input data [27].

According to [32] there are also privacy concerns about the data used to train models, for example, the use of ML algorithms to infer sensitive, personal data about users based on non-sensitive data. Likewise, the accuracy of the predictions of ML systems may also present risks.

5   Conclusions

The literature review revealed that there are a variety of factors that affect the academic performance of university students. Factors that can have a significant impact on the academic performance of students are socioeconomic background, motivation, academic features, and environmental and demographic features.

Analysis of these data, using machine learning techniques, provides a solid foundation for developing effective predictive models. In addition, the inclusion of contextual variables, such as social interaction and educational support, during the analysis can improve the accuracy of predictive models. This suggests that academic performance is not only determined by individual characteristics but also by the environment in which the student acts.

For educational institutions and teachers, the findings related to the prediction of academic performance are a valuable base for identifying possible difficulties and designing personalized support strategies. Predictive models can help educators intervene early and provide additional resources to students in need to help them pass the courses and thus avoid a possible dropout.

However, it is essential to keep in mind that the prediction of academic performance is a constantly evolving field and that there are still challenges to overcome. Among them are the acquisition and adequate selection of predictor variables, as well as the need for additional research to validate and improve existing models.

In the context of this research, the next steps include considering the incorporation of socio-emotional variables in the models for predicting academic performance and investigating how these variables affect student performance. Advanced machine learning techniques, like deep learning, could be examined to improve the accuracy and predictive power of academic performance.

References

1. Abdul, B., et al.: Imbalanced classification methods for student grade prediction: a systematic literature review. IEEE Access **11**, 1970–1989 (2023). https://doi.org/10.1109/ACCESS.2022.3225404
2. Abou Naaj, M., Mehdi, R., Mohamed, E.A., Nachouki, M.: Analysis of the factors affecting student performance using a neuro-fuzzy approach. Educ. Sci. **13**(3) (2023)
3. Alboaneen, D., Almelihi, M., Alsubaie, R., Alghamdi, R., Alshehri, L., Alharthi, R.: Development of a web-based prediction system for students' academic performance. Data **7**(2) (2022). https://doi.org/10.3390/data7020021
4. Albreiki, B., Zaki, N., Alashwal, H.: A systematic literature review of studentâ performance prediction using machine learning techniques. Educ. Sci. **11**(9) (2021). https://doi.org/10.3390/educsci11090552
5. Alhazmi, E., Sheneamer, A.: Early predicting of students performance in higher education. IEEE Access **11**, 27579–27589 (2023). www.scopus.com
6. Alyahyan, E., Düştegör, D.: Predicting academic success in higher education: literature review and best practices. Int. J. Educ. Technol. High. Educ. **17**(1), 3 (2020). https://doi.org/10.1186/s41239-020-0177-7
7. Baig, M.A., Shaikh, S.A., Khatri, K.K., Shaikh, M.A., Khan, M.Z., Rauf, M.A.: Prediction of students performance level using integrated approach of ml algorithms. Int. J. Emerg. Technol. Learn. **18**(1), 216–234 (2023)
8. Bilal, M., Omar, M., Anwar, W., Bokhari, R.H., Choi, G.S.: The role of demographic and academic features in a student performance prediction. Sci. Rep. **12**(1) (2022)

9. Brahim, G.B.: Predicting student performance from online engagement activities using novel statistical features. Arab. J. Sci. Eng. **47**(8), 10225–10243 (2022). https://doi.org/10.1007/s13369-021-06548-w

10. Choi, N.: Self-efficacy and self-concept as predictors of college students' academic performance. Psychol. Sch. **42**(2), 197–205 (2005)

11. Costa-Mendes, R., Cruz-Jesus, F., Oliveira, T., Castelli, M.: Deep learning in predicting high school grades: a quantum space of representation. Emerg. Sci. J. **6**(Special Issue), 166–187 (2022)

12. Crivei, L.M., Czibula, G., Ciubotariu, G., Dindelegan, M.: Unsupervised learning based mining of academic data sets for students' performance analysis. In: 2020 IEEE 14th International Symposium on Applied Computational Intelligence and Informatics (SACI), pp. 11–16 (2020). https://doi.org/10.1109/SACI49304.2020.9118835

13. Finn, J.D., Rock, D.A.: Academic success among students at risk for school failure. J. Appl. Psychol. **82**(2), 221–234 (1997)

14. Geurts, P., Irrthum, A., Wehenkel, L.: Supervised learning with decision tree-based methods in computational and systems biology. Mol. Biosyst. **5**, 1593–605 (2009). https://doi.org/10.1039/b907946g

15. Gutierrez-Monsalve, J.A., Garzón, J., Segura-Cardona, A.M.: Factores asociados al rendimiento académico en estudiantes universitarios. Formación universitaria **14**, 13–24 (2021)

16. Kannan, K.R., Meena Abarna, K., Vairachilai, S.: Graph neural networks for predicting student performance: a deep learning approach for academic success forecasting. Int. J. Intell. Syst. Appl. Eng. **12**(1s), 228–232 (2024). https://www.scopus.com/inward/record.uri?eid=2-s2.0-85173776870&partnerID=40&md5=fd9ef67ead33fb72cb3903e4a12aeec5

17. Karalar, H., Kapucu, C., Gürüler, H.: Predicting students at risk of academic failure using ensemble model during pandemic in a distance learning system. Int. J. Educ. Technol. High. Educ. **18**(1), 63 (2021). https://doi.org/10.1186/s41239-021-00300-y

18. Khalaf, M.H.R., Abdel Azim, Z.M.: Predicting student's performance in online education through deep learning model. Inf. Sci. Lett. **12**(3), 1619–1630 (2023)

19. Liu, C., Wang, H., Yuan, Z.: A method for predicting the academic performances of college students based on education system data. Mathematics **10**(20) (2022). https://doi.org/10.3390/math10203737

20. Nahar, K., Shova, B., Ria, T., Rashid, H., Islam, A.: Mining educational data to predict students performance: a comparative study of data mining techniques. Educ. Inf. Technol. **26** (2021). https://doi.org/10.1007/s10639-021-10575-3

21. Nasser Alsubaie, M.: Predicting student performance using machine learning to enhance the quality assurance of online training via maharat platform. Alex. Eng. J. **69**, 323–339 (2023). https://doi.org/10.1016/j.aej.2023.02.004

22. National Commission for Academic Accreditation & Assessment. Standards for Quality Assurance and Accreditation of Higher Education Institutions (2015)

23. Nuankaew, P., Nuankaew, W.S.: Student performance prediction model for predicting academic achievement of high school students. Eur. J. Educ. Res. **11**(2), 949–963 (2022)

24. Onyema, E.M., et al.: Prospects and challenges of using machine learning for academic forecasting. Comput. Intell. Neurosci. **2022**, 5624475 (2022). https://doi.org/10.1155/2022/5624475

25. Parker, J.D.A., Summerfeldt, L.J., Hogan, M.J., Majeski, S.A.: Emotional intelligence and academic success: examining the transition from high school to university. Pers. Individ. Differ. **36**(1), 163–172 (2004)
26. Qiu, F., et al.: Predicting students' performance in e-learning using learning process and behaviour data. Sci. Rep. **12**(1) (2022)
27. Rashidian, N., Hilal, M.A.: Applications of machine learning in surgery: ethical considerations, vol. 2, no. 1, pp. 18–23 (2022). https://doi.org/10.20517/ais.2021.13
28. Sarwat, S., et al.: Predicting students' academic performance with conditional generative adversarial network and deep SVM. Sensors **22**(13) (2022)
29. Sassirekha, M.S., Vijayalakshmi, S.: Predicting the academic progression in studentâs standpoint using machine learning. Automatika **63**(4), 605–617 (2022). https://doi.org/10.1080/00051144.2022.2060652
30. Song, Y., Meng, X., Jiang, J.: Multi-layer perception model with elastic grey wolf optimization to predict student achievement. PLoS ONE **17**(12) (2022)
31. Villagrá, C., Durán, F.J., Rosique, P., Llorens, F., Molina-Carmona, R.: Predicting academic performance from behavioural and learning data. Int. J. Des. Nat. Ecodyn. **11**, 239–249 (2016). https://doi.org/10.2495/DNE-V11-N3-239-249
32. W3C Group: Ethical Principles for Web Machine Learning (2022). https://www.w3.org/TR/webmachinelearning-ethics/
33. Yağcı, M.: Educational data mining: prediction of students' academic performance using machine learning algorithms. Smart Learn. Environ. **9**(1) (2022)
34. York, T.T., Gibson, C., Rankin, S.: Defining and measuring academic success. Pract. Assess. Res. Eval. **20**(5), 1–20 (2015)
35. Zafari, M., Bazargani, J.S., Sadeghi-Niaraki, A., Choi, S.M.: Artificial intelligence applications in k-12 education: a systematic literature review. IEEE Access **10**, 61905–61921 (2022). https://doi.org/10.1109/ACCESS.2022.3179356

Identification of Factors and Teacher Profile Associated with Student Performance Using Fuzzy Techniques and Data Mining

Luis Barba-Guaman[✉] and Priscila Valdiviezo-Diaz

Universidad Técnica Particular de Loja, San Cayetano Bajo, Loja, Ecuador
{lrbarba,pmvaldiviezo}@utpl.edu.ec
http://www.utpl.edu.ec

Abstract. The academic performance of students is one of the most relevant indicators in the quality of higher education, as well as the importance of the teacher profile in academic activity. This document explores the link between academic performance and the behavior of Engineering students and determines the teacher's profile based on personality traits. Demographic, academic, and enrollment data of 2001 students were collected, in addition to analyzing the personality traits of four teachers with fuzzy techniques and the Big Five model. The results indicate that academic performance is largely linked to academic factors and specific course activities, and does not depend solely on demographic variables. The teacher's profile showed a higher percentage in the personality trait of openness to experiences, which can play a crucial role in the academic success of students.

Keywords: student performance · data mining · teacher profile · big five model

1 Introduction

In the face of the availability of learning-related data, studies have been developed to analyze and predict students' academic performance. For example, a study proposed by Nahar et al. [14] analyzes the academic results and behavior of some engineering students with the aim of predicting student performance. On distance learning systems, in [8] the academic activity characteristics of students are taken into account to identify those at risk of academic failure. In [1], factors affecting students' academic performance are identified in order to determine students at risk.

A Brooks study [5] highlighted that peer support during difficult times is essential for students to continue, pass, and complete their degrees. In addition, the authors of the paper [16], described a "genuine" relationship between the tutor and students, which "buffered" academic challenges and helped minimize falling behind or dropping out. Teaching intervention has been shown to be

© The Author(s), under exclusive license to Springer Nature Switzerland AG 2024
M. Botto-Tobar et al. (Eds.): ICAT 2023, CCIS 2049, pp. 219–230, 2024.
https://doi.org/10.1007/978-3-031-58956-0_17

a fundamental factor in improving the effectiveness of students' learning processes; therefore, it is necessary to have teaching evaluation processes that allow improving teachers' competencies based on the results obtained.

The teaching profile can have a significant influence on the academic performance of students, since the teaching skills of the teacher as well as the use of different teaching strategies can facilitate a better understanding of the course contents. Therefore, teaching performance is a key factor in the educational quality and academic performance of students.

On the other hand, the large amount of information available in academic systems makes it possible to use data mining techniques to discover information to support decision making. The purpose of this study is to analyze and understand the factors and the teacher's profile that are associated with the academic performance of students in a higher education institution. It is proposed to use fuzzy and data mining techniques to identify factors that intervene in the academic performance of students, considering socio-demographic and academic variables; and analyzing the teacher profile based on their evaluation, interaction and contents in their respective subject.

For this purpose, the data of the students of the Information Technology (IT) career of a Higher Education Institution is taken as a reference. With this information, managers could make more informed decisions regarding the early detection of problems related to student performance and thus implement support measures.

2   Related Works

While a wide variety of factors have been investigated in the literature regarding their impact on predicting students' academic success, according to Alyahyan et al. [3] the factors most widely involved in academic success are prior academic performance, students' demographic information, e-learning activity, psychological attributes, and environment. Similarly, Bilal et al. [4] mention that characteristics related to demographics, personality traits, socioeconomic and environmental traits can affect student performance. In [9] they determine that student background and social activities are important factors in predicting academic performance. Alboaneen et al. [1] develop a web-based system to predict academic performance and identify students at risk of failing through academic and demographic factors. Other factors such as environment and context can influence academic performance. For example, an optimal educational environment, with excellent communication channels between teachers and students, is a prerequisite for ensuring quality education.

In [11] discusses the relationship between students' personality traits and their academic performance, the authors showed that there is a relationship in three main ways, these being behavioral tendencies (personality traits), cognitive ability and evaluation criteria. To analyze these personality traits, the researchers used the Big Five model [6,12]. This model is based on five personality dimensions (see Fig. 1) and is used in the classification of personality traits through lexicographic (everyday language) and factorial (relationship of personality factors) linkage.

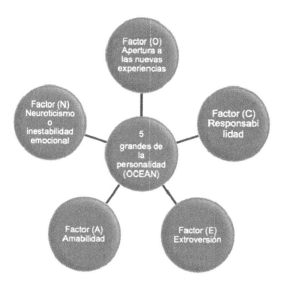

Fig. 1. Dimensions of Big Five model [6, 12]

Thus, there are a variety of factors that affect the academic performance of college students. These factors include socioeconomic status, motivation, academic characteristics, environmental characteristics, and teaching style, all of which can have a significant impact on students' academic performance.

Identifying factors that influence academic success can help improve the quality of teaching and promote an inclusive and equitable educational environment. Factors affecting academic performance combined with data analysis and machine learning techniques have provided a solid basis for developing effective predictive models.

Most of the analyzed works that have used machine learning on student performance have considered historical data mainly related to academic and e-learning platform interaction factors, however, there are other characteristics that can also influence student performance such as demographic data.

Table 1 presents a summary of some factors that are related to students' academic performance.

On the other hand, the teacher's profile can also have an influence on academic performance, either through his or her pedagogical skills, teaching style, personality and openness with students. In [17] they present an action-research project that seeks to improve educational guidance practices in Mexico. Its goal is to create peaceful environments and transform teachers' thinking in order to achieve inclusive, fair, equitable and non-violent school environments.

Table 1. Factors related to academic performance identified in the literature

Factors	Attributes	Descriptions
Academic characteristics	Grades of partial examinations Final exam scores Grade Point Average	Previous academic performance attributes
Student demographic information	Gender Nationality Place of birht Marital status Disability Locality	Student demographic attributes, including family and personal characteristics
E-learning activity	Number of visits Number of downloads Connection time Access to resources, forums, quizzes and assignments.	Student learning platform interaction attributes
Socioeconomic background	Own house Bank credit Payment of tuition fees Credit card	Socioeconomic attributes
Personality traits	Responsibility Introversion-Extraversion Emotional Instability	Describes the subject's capacity and ability (e.g., effectiveness, commitment, efficiency, etc.)
Environmental	Family Educational Support Study Time Tutor and Parent Work Extracurricular Activity	Academic support and teacher commitment can be important factors in academic success

According to [15] mentions that through IBM Watson's Personality Insights service it is possible to describe the personality of tutors through linguistic analysis in social networks, messages, forums among other documents. In this study, two traits of the Big Five model were used, being these concentration and kindness, then through fuzzy techniques they present the personality traits of the tutors.

The paper presented by [18] demonstrated a trajectory of advances in automatic personality detection, covering a wide range of psychological and psycholinguistic approaches, as well as the latest development in natural language processing. The technique used for obtaining personality trait information is based on the use of questionnaires. The representation of the model is shown in Fig. 1 below.

According to the literature review there is no consensus on how to measure and evaluate teaching performance, some authors mention that teaching performance is related to training, pedagogical innovation, motivation, communication and interaction with students [7, 10, 13].

Finally, it is required to develop tools and methods for the evaluation of teaching performance that provide valuable information to ensure that students receive relevant and useful educational content for their professional training.

3 Methodology

This research starts with a literature review of previous studies that include the identification of factors related to academic performance. Then, an analysis and preparation of the data is carried out for the application of data mining techniques to identify hidden patterns and trends in the students' academic data. The results obtained can provide valuable information for decision making and educational quality improvement. The identification of patterns provides important information about factors that influence academic performance. Next, through the use of different technological tools from the use of questionnaires, text processing APIs and the use of fuzzy logic libraries, the teacher profile model was generated based on the answers entered by the students.

The following research question is posed:

What are the main factors that influence the academic performance of information technology students?

To answer this question, two data sources were used, the first contains demographic and academic characteristics related to the academic performance of students and the other data source was obtained to determine the teaching profile. The information is detailed below.

3.1 Academic Performance Dataset

The dataset used for the analysis and identification of factors related to academic performance, contains data of the students of the Information Technology (IT) career of a Higher Education Institution corresponding to 4 academic periods during the years 2020–2022. This dataset refers to 2001 student records and 60 variables related to:

– Socio-demographic data of the students.
– Academic information, such as grade history in each of the components that make up the subjects. Example: autonomous component, practical-experimental and in contact with the teacher.
– Information about the subjects in which the students are enrolled.

Table 2 shows the variables considered for the identification of factors affecting academic performance using data mining.

Table 2. Type of variables

Type of variables	Variable name
Socio-demographics	Edad
	Sexo
	Provincia
	Cantón
	Discapacidad
	Formas de pago
	Porcentaje de beca
Academics	Periodo_admisión
	Materiales
	Notas parciales por cada componente:
	Aprendizaje autónomo, Aprendizaje práctico
	experimental, y en contacto con el docente
	Notas finales de cada bimestre
	Status
	Tasa de aprobación
	Número de reprobacions

3.2 Teaching Profile Data

Four teachers of the following subjects participated: a) Intelligent Systems, b) Discrete Structure, c) Hardware Fundamentals and d) Computing and Society of the Information Technology career.

The number of students who entered information through the questionnaire was 324, the type of questions are related to the communicative capacity, the content, and the evaluation of the subject.

To obtain the personality of a teacher according to the Big Five model, a questionnaire was implemented as a dataset to load it to a dataframe and process it with the GrammarBot API to ensure data consistency. Subsequently, the Symanto API and its two endpoints were invoked to obtain the personality traits and emotions expressed. The results obtained were entered into the fuzzy logic model developed with the *skfuzzy* library implemented in the Python programming language, and presented on screen through a graph with the option of generating a report to be sent (Fig. 2).

3.3 Data Preparation

Based on the students' grades, a new variable called "status" was created, which indicates whether the student passed or failed the subject. This is obtained from the final grade, if this is greater than or equal to 7 points it is recorded as "PASSED", otherwise it is recorded as "FAILED". On the other hand, if the student has not yet taken any of the subjects, a blank value is left for that subject. The number of failures is calculated for each subject; if the student

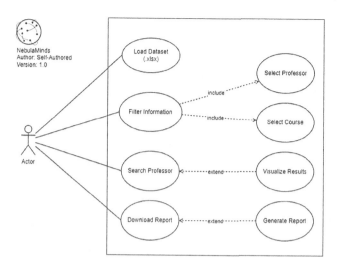

Fig. 2. Use cases

has not failed the subject on any occasion, a value of 0 is entered. Variables with unique values and those that do not contain relevant information about the student such as subject codes, periods, and payment details are eliminated.

4 Results

4.1 Identification of Factors Affecting Academic Performance

Considering that academic performance is one of the main indicators of efficiency in higher education, we proceed to analyze the socio-demographic and academic factors of the students, considering data mining techniques to identify trends and patterns in the data.

A correlation analysis is used to identify how closely related the variables are to each other.

Figure 3, shows a correlation map of quantitative variables, applying Pearson's correlation coefficient. The correlation analysis was performed considering only information from students studying information technology, in order to identify which variables are most related to academic performance (as measured by final grades).

As a result of the correlation analysis, the variables related to the components of autonomous learning, in contact with the teacher and experimental practice have a high positive correlation with the final grade and the passing rate. While age does not present a significant relationship with the academic performance variables. Likewise, it can be observed that the disability variables present an almost null correlation with the passing rate and the final grade. Between the variables number of failures and bimonthly grades, a moderate correlation can be observed.

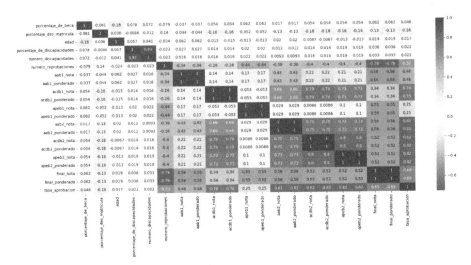

Fig. 3. Diagram of correlation between variables

From Fig. 3 it can also be observed that variables such as scholarships and tuition discounts present a very low correlation with respect to the academic performance variables.

Therefore, we can conclude that the socio-demographic variables are not predominant factors in the academic performance of the students of the information technology career, while the academic factors do have a more direct relationship with the final grade and the passing rate of the students, this is evidenced through a positive relationship between the components of autonomous learning, experimental practical and in contact with the teacher with the final grade, and this in turn with the passing rate. There is also a high correlation between the number of failures and the final grade. As expected, students who obtain a high final grade achieve better pass rates in the subjects.

Scatter plots are also used to identify patterns and trends. From Fig. 4(a) there is no linear pattern between the variables scholarship percentage assigned to the student with the final grade, likewise in Fig. 4(b) there is no linear trend between age and final grade, which corroborates what was mentioned in the correlation analysis.

The analysis also determined that gender and province are not variables that affect academic performance; the number of passing or failing grades in each province is related to the number of students belonging to each province.

In response to the research question, the Table 3 summarizes the determinants of academic performance that were identified during the analysis of the data of the information technology students.

In comparison with the study presented by [2] who analyze the profile of students and its relationship with their GPA (grade point average) by selecting four main attributes: department, grade, city, and gender, in our work we consider the grades of each learning component and data associated with age,

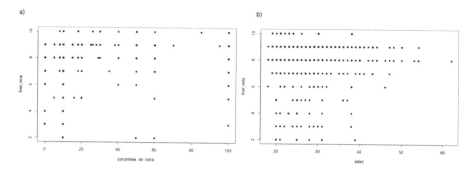

Fig. 4. Scatter plots

Table 3. Factors related to the academic performance of IT career students.

Factor	variable
Autonomous learning component (first and second periods)	aab1_nota, aab2_nota
Teacher contact component (first and second periods)	acdb1_nota, acdb2_nota
Practical experimental component (first and second periods)	apeb1_nota, apeb2_nota
Number of failures	numero_reprobaciones
Approval rate	tasa_aprobacion

disability, and enrollment. Similarly to the authors of the previously mentioned study, we found a greater association with the academic variables than with the socio-demographic attributes.

4.2 Identification of the Teaching Profile as a Factor of Academic Performance

The research analyzed five subjects of the Faculty of Engineering and Architecture, in order to obtain relevant information, the process of answering the questionnaire was carried out during the teachers' tutoring hours. The subject of Computers and Society was not well received by the students; therefore, it was not considered in the study. Table 4 presents the percentage of the variables corresponding to the teachers' personality trait.

The information entered was used to generate the teachers' personality reports using the Big Five model. Figure 5 shows the report format.

It is important to mention that the dimensions of the Big Five model are not mutually exclusive, and that each individual may possess different degrees of each. In addition, it is important to note that the poles do not have a positive or negative connotation, but rather describe the opposite extremes of each dimension from a quantitative perspective. This is because the poles are measured

Table 4. Identified personality traits

Subject	Kindness	Emotional	Responsibility	Outgoing (%)	Experience opening (%)
Estructuras discretas - A	54.88	45.67	63.02	59.17	68.71
Estructuras discretas - B	48.99	59.56	46.15	64.71	81.31
Sistemas Inteligentes	58.23	50.42	54.97	50.05	63.26
Fundamentos de Hardware	56.31	49.54	48.98	49.36	43.74

through a scale of variables, which makes it possible to establish a correlation between each person's position on the scale and the dimension in question.

The teacher profile showed a higher percentage in the personality trait of openness to experiences, that is, the teacher is creative, curious, receptive to change and tolerant, which can play a crucial role in the academic success of students.

The report in Fig. 5 gives teachers a much more complete understanding of the various profiles, which translates into a better relationship between them and, as a consequence, generates a more positive atmosphere within the classroom.

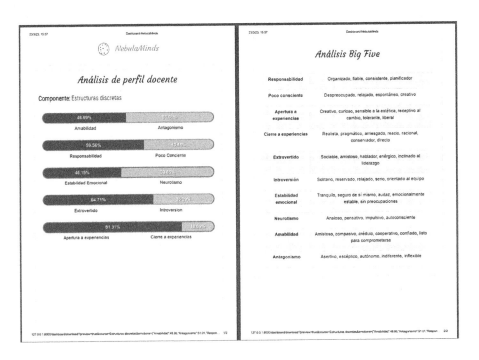

Fig. 5. Teacher profile report

5   Conclusions

From the literature review it was determined that more research is needed to better understand how these factors relate to and contribute to the academic performance of college students. In addition, from the analysis conducted on a set of academic data of information technology students, it was determined that academic performance does not necessarily depend on socio-demographic variables but rather on academic factors related to activities specific to each subject.

Knowing the teacher's personality through student comments is a valuable tool to improve the work environment and student performance. By having a clear idea of the teacher's personality, it is possible to identify areas where the teaching style can be improved and adapted to the needs of the students, which can improve the quality of teaching and foster a more positive relationship between the teacher and the students.

By obtaining the results of teachers' personalities, it is possible to expand the filtering options with academic periods to evaluate different cycles and how the behavior has contributed to a better relationship with students. This would allow a more complete and accurate assessment of teaching behavior in the classroom.

One of the limitations of this study is the availability of data related to interaction, social and psychological factors, which makes it difficult to find significant relationships with academic performance.

As future work, one of the pending tasks of the research is to evaluate the relationship between teachers' personality traits and academic factors that influence students' performance.

Finally, the result of this study may help educational institutions in the prediction of academic performance in order to identify early on students who may be facing difficulties in their learning and with the support of teachers improve the possibility of academic success.

References

1. Alboaneen, D., Almelihi, M., Alsubaie, R., Alghamdi, R., Alshehri, L., Alharthi, R.: Development of a web-based prediction system for students' academic performance. Data **7**(2) (2022). https://doi.org/10.3390/data7020021
2. Alkayed, M., Almasalha, F., Hijjawi, M., Qutqut, M.H.: Factors analysis affecting academic achievement of undergraduate student: a study on faculty of information technology students at applied science private university (2023). https://doi.org/10.1109/ICBATS57792.2023.10111100
3. Alyahyan, E., Düştegör, D.: Predicting academic success in higher education: literature review and best practices. Int. J. Educ. Technol. High. Educ. **17**(1), 3 (2020). https://doi.org/10.1186/s41239-020-0177-7
4. Bilal, M., Omar, M., Anwar, W., Bokhari, R.H., Choi, G.S.: The role of demographic and academic features in a student performance prediction. Sci. Rep. **12**(1) (2022)
5. Brooks, R.: Friends, peers and higher education. Br. J. Sociol. Educ. **28**(6), 693–707 (2007)

6. Digman, J.M.: Personality structure: emergence of the five-factor model. Annu. Rev. Psychol. **41**(1), 417–440 (1990)
7. Escribano Hervis, E.: El desempeño del docente como factor asociado a la calidad educativa en américa latina. Revista educación **42**(2), 717–739 (2018)
8. Karalar, H., Kapucu, C., Gürüler, H.: Predicting students at risk of academic failure using ensemble model during pandemic in a distance learning system. Int. J. Educ. Technol. High. Educ. **18**(1), 63 (2021). https://doi.org/10.1186/s41239-021-00300-y
9. Kiu, C.: Data mining analysis on student's academic performance through exploration of student's background and social activities. In: 2018 Fourth International Conference on Advances in Computing, Communication & Automation (ICACCA), pp. 1–5 (2018)
10. Martínez Chairez, G.I., Esparza Chávez, A.Y., Gómez Castillo, R.I.: El desempeño docente desde la perspectiva de la práctica profesional. RIDE. Revista iberoamericana para la investigación y el desarrollo educativo **11**(21) (2020)
11. Martínez De Ibarreta Zorita, C., Redondo Palomo, R., Rua Vieties, A., Fabra Florit, E.: Factores de personalidad (big five) y rendimiento académico en asignaturas cuantitativas de ade. Anales de ASEPUMA **19**, 1–19 (2011)
12. McReynolds, P., Rosen, J.C., Chelune, G.J., John, O.P.: The search for basic dimensions of personality: a review and critique. Adv. Psychol. Assess. **7**, 1–37 (1990)
13. Monsivais, C.L.R., Hernández, R.V.R.: La influencia docente y el rendimiento académico en estudiantes de una universidad pública mexicana. Dilemas contemporáneos: Educación, Política y Valores (2021)
14. Nahar, K., Shova, B., Ria, T., Rashid, H., Islam, A.: Mining educational data to predict students performance: a comparative study of data mining techniques. Educ. Inf. Technol. **26** (2021). https://doi.org/10.1007/s10639-021-10575-3
15. Rosario Vázquez, M., Zavaleta Carrillo, P.: Modelo para caracterizar perfiles de tutores académicos a través del uso de técnicas softcomputing. J. Educ. Innov./Revista Innovación Educativa **20**(83) (2020)
16. Ross, J., Head, K., King, L., Perry, P.M., Smith, S.: The personal development tutor role: an exploration of student and lecturer experiences and perceptions of that relationship. Nurse Educ. Today **34**(9), 1207–1213 (2014)
17. Sánchez Alba, B., Escobedo Orihuela, S.: Educación emocional para la paz. una propuesta para la práctica en la orientación educativa. Innovación educativa **19**(81), 67–88 (2019)
18. Štajner, S., Yenikent, S.: A survey of automatic personality detection from texts. In: Proceedings of the 28th International Conference on Computational Linguistics, pp. 6284–6295 (2020)

Predictive Model for Accurate Horticultural Product Pricing Using Machine Learning

Davis Alessandro Suclle Surco$^{(\boxtimes)}$, Andres Antonio Assereto Huamani$^{(\boxtimes)}$,
and Emilio Antonio Herrera-Trujillo

Faculty of Engineering, Universidad Peruana de Ciencias Aplicadas, Lima, Perú
{U201919462,U201912529,pcsieher}@upc.edu.pe

Abstract. The trade of horticultural products is a crucial sector in the local economy of Lima, Peru. Microenterprises dedicated to this activity face various challenges, including demand volatility. This volatility can decrease the likelihood of generating profits and impact the stability of the business, primarily due to the challenges associated with adjusting selling prices. To address this issue, our proposal is based on implementing the XGBoost algorithm, which has the capability to handle heterogeneous data and variables of different types. This algorithm leverages historical data to provide accurate and up-to-date price recommendations for horticultural products. This, in turn, enables micro-entrepreneurs to make informed decisions when setting prices, thereby achieving expected benefits and enhancing their competitiveness. The integration of our project with microenterprises in Lima has the potential to mitigate the risk of economic losses by offering greater accuracy in predicting future market prices. Through the development of our project, we have achieved a high level of accuracy in forecasting future prices, reaching a minimum of 90% when compared to actual prices.

Keywords: Horticultural Products · Price Prediction · Machine Learning · Sale Risk · Recommendation System

1 Introduction

The Peruvian horticulture sector is one of the most important in the country, generating billions of dollars in revenues and employing millions of people. However, at present, microenterprises in horticulture, which represent 90% of the agricultural sector, are facing a series of factors that are affecting their commercial performance and a significant decrease in their profits. Among the causes of this situation are the variation in prices, the volume demanded, and the increase in the cost of transportation. In addition, the shortage of fertilizers and disinfectants, together with the effects of the El Niño phenomenon and the coastal El Niño, limit the production of quality and can have a strong influence on their quality and, therefore, on the variation of their selling price. Additionally, the prices of horticultural products are highly volatile and can fluctuate significantly, making it difficult for microenterprises to plan their businesses effectively. It is interesting and important to study this problem because, in addition to the above, it can affect the national economy as a whole. These microenterprises play a crucial role in providing employment and producing fresh, healthy food for Peruvian consumers. In addition, the horticultural sector is vital for food security and nutrition in Peru, as it provides a large quantity of fresh and nutritious fruits and vegetables. The problem is complex, due to the interconnectedness of economic, climatic, and production factors involved in the commercial performance of the aforementioned. In addition, previous approaches to proposed solutions have focused on addressing a single factor, which has proven to be insufficient to effectively solve the problem. In this context, the need arises to address the problem comprehensively and propose innovative solutions that contribute to the sustainable development of the companies in question. Our project approach focuses on conducting an exhaustive analysis related to pricing and the variables involved, and based on this, propose an innovative approach to improve the management of the factors identified and achieve a sustainable commercial balance. The impact of this approach on the performance of microenterprises will also be evaluated. The results have a significant impact on the implementation of support programs for these enterprises, contributing to the strengthening of the sector and the sustainable development of the country.

2 Related Works

In the current context, artificial intelligence has experienced notable growth, showcasing its ability to make improvements in the business environment. One of the most outstanding areas is price prediction, where machine learning algorithms play a key role in obtaining benefits and optimizing strategies. That is why in the presented article, we delve into research related to machine learning applied to price prediction.

In [1], the authors discuss the agricultural product supply chain in China, which presents numerous deficiencies, such as multiple stages, low efficiency, and high inventory wastage. One possible solution to address these shortcomings is to establish a direct link between farms and supermarkets, reducing costs and resources while ensuring product quality. However, implementing this solution on a large scale is a considerable challenge, especially given the continued growth of agricultural production and the potential for new deficiencies in the future.

Similarly, in [2], the authors highlight the essential nature of the agricultural product issue for economic progress. The ability to predict the future prices of these products has a significant impact on market and economic stability. Currently, the futures market is highly leveraged and presents investment risks influenced by complex factors such as national policies, macroeconomics, industrial economics, and investor psychology.

Furthermore, in the paper [3], the authors propose a model based on the LSTM network that utilizes historical data and influencing parameters to predict prices. This model can be highly beneficial for farmers in making informed decisions about crop selection, maximizing profits.

Finally, another technique used for price prediction is LSTM, as proposed in the paper [4] the authors suggest a method for pre-predicting vegetable prices that combines the STL temporal decomposition approach with an attention mechanism-based long-term memory neural network (LSTM-AT). This method has proven more effective than other time series models in predicting vegetable prices.

Currently, [9] has observed that microenterprises engaged in horticulture in Peru have faced various challenges negatively impacting their business performance. This has led to decreased profits in their sales activities, stemming from multiple factors, one of which is the volatility in horticultural product prices. In recent years, there has been a marked fluctuation in prices, attributed in part to the overproduction of these products, resulting in an approximate variation of $\pm 15\%$ in the production rate.

Another important factor affecting this scenario is the variation in the volume of demand for horticultural products in the Peruvian market. This variation is closely related to the laws of supply and demand, fluctuating according to market conditions and, consequently, influencing price variability [10, 11].

Several factors influence these indicators; for example, according to the journal [5], the rise in fuel prices is the variable with the greatest impact on the direct increase in horticultural products due to the increased cost of transportation. Another influencing variable is the shortage of fertilizers and disinfectants involved in the production of horticultural products. Additionally, the varied climate of Peru has a marked influence on the quality of the mentioned product, leading to product degradation, inappropriate pricing, and potential failure [6].

As mentioned above, this generates many negative consequences for microenterprises dedicated to horticulture in Peru. For example, a decrease in profits leads to a financial burden, forcing microenterprises to take loans that may become unpayable, even leading to their disappearance [7]. Another consequence is the deterioration of product quality, influencing future prices and demand, which is a significant factor [1]. Moreover, it can lead to poor inventory management, bringing further consequences such as dissatisfied customers and low business profitability [8].

For this project, the terminologies we will use are "Horticultural Products," "Machine Learning," "Predictive Models," and "Artificial Intelligence". There is a need to address the problem holistically and present novel approaches that contribute to the sustainable growth of horticulture-related microenterprises in Peru. It should be noted that the approach proposed in this project focuses on identifying the key components (price and volume) to solve the problem and achieve a sustainable commercial balance.

Although we have previously reviewed works related to the prediction of prices for horticultural products, we will proceed to conduct a review of the most commonly used models for this prediction. In this regard, the following characteristics have been considered, and they are detailed below:

- **Model application:** According to [12], the application of the model is an important factor to consider, since it can determine the type of model needed, depending on the type of problem. For example, if the model is intended for critical decision-making, an accurate and reliable model is needed.
- **Response time:** According to [12], response time is crucial for real time applications. For example, a model that is used to predict the price of some product must be capable of generating predictions quickly so that informed decisions can be made.
- **Training speed:** According to [12], training speed is vital for projects with tight deadlines. For example, a model employed to predict the price of certain products must be able to be trained quickly to stay updated with the most recent data.

- **Prediction accuracy:** According to [12], accuracy is the most fundamental aspect for any prediction model. However, it is important to keep in mind that not all applications require the same level of accuracy. For example, a model used to classify images of cats and dogs does not need to be as accurate as a model used to diagnose diseases.

3   Main Contribution

The research aims to develop and adapt an Intelligent Recommendation System for micro-entrepreneurs in Lima, who are engaged in the sale of horticultural products in the Gran Mercado Mayorista de Lima (GMML). The proposed solution will support micro-entrepreneurs in decision-making related to pricing. To achieve this goal, a machine learning algorithm based on XGBoost is implemented, which is especially suited to address complex classification and regression problems on heterogeneous data and variables of various types. This algorithm ensures that the recommender system can leverage the collected information and provides the corresponding guidance to microentrepreneurs. Additionally, the system utilizes decision trees and can reduce the error in each iteration to enhance the accuracy of results in supervised learning. The XGBoost algorithm is formulated as follow:

$$f(x) = \sum_{\{i=1\}}^{T} \Omega_i h_{i(x)}$$

- $f(x)$ is the model prediction for a set of x features.
- T is the number of trees in the set.
- $h_{i(x)}$ the prediction of the i-th tree in the set for the set of x features.
- Ω_i is the weight assigned to the i-th tree in the set.

$$L^t = \sum_{\{i=1\}}^{n} l\left(y_i, \widehat{y}_l^{t-1}\right) + f_j(x_i) + \Omega\left(f_j\right)$$

- "L" is the missing function.
- "y_i" is the actual value of the target of the i-th observation.
- "$y_i^{(t-1)}$" is the model prediction up to the previous iteration t-1 for the i-th data point.
- "$\sum_{i=1}^{n}(ecuación)$" is the summation notation, which indicates that you sum over all data points in your training set.
- "$f_j(x_i)$" The prediction made by the new weak model (tree) at iteration j for the i-th data point.

In our research, the XGBRegressor algorithm will be trained using historical data from the year 2013 to the year 2023, which was collected from the Sistema de Abastecimiento y precios (SISAP) page. This platform provides historical price data for various horticultural products, such as red head onion, yellow potato and serrano white green peas. Based on this information, prices and volumes of these horticultural products will be considered to generate accurate and updated forecasts.

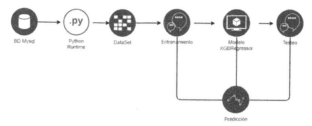

Fig. 1. XGBRegressor Process

According to the flow in Fig. 1, all the acquired data will first go through a cleaning process in which data with no value will be considered as "0". Afterward, this data will be stored in our MySQL database which through the Python language will select the necessary data and the XGBRegressor algorithm will be used to train the data which will be updated every day. Additionally, a test of the effectiveness of this model will be conducted.

4 Methodology

The methodology used in the research follows the Cross Industry Standard Process for Data Mining (CRISP-DM) approach. This approach assists in analyzing information and data to predict future losses, comprising six main phases: [1] business understanding, [2] data understanding, [3] data preparation, [4] modeling, [5] evaluation, and [6] deployment (Fig. 2).

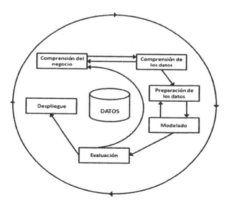

Fig. 2. Business Understanding Conceptualization Process for Information Exploitation Projects.

The step-by-step approach used in the CRISP-DM methodology ensures a logical and coherent explanation of how the results are achieved. By applying the XGBRegressor algorithm and following the CRISP-DM methodology, a price prediction with an accuracy of over 90% was achieved. Providing micro-entrepreneurs with precise information about future prices enables them to make more informed decisions regarding the purchase and sale of their products, which will be enhancing the profitability and stability of their businesses. Our solution features an architecture that begins by extracting data from SISAP (Supply and Price Information System available to the public by the Ministry of Agrarian Development and Irrigation). This system provides us with the date, volume and price of the products that have been selected. Subsequently, our virtual machine in Azure proceeds to transform the data and stores it in a database called MySQL. This database not only contains the transformed data, but also processes the final data to enable the corresponding predictions. The transformed data is consumed by Jupyter Notebook to make predictions using the Python language. Then, this database is utilized by Power BI to generate reports that will be sent to our website built in React. This way, the micro-entrepreneur can view the price predictions for the current day or the day after, as well as make comparisons directly from their computers through the dashboard (Fig. 3).

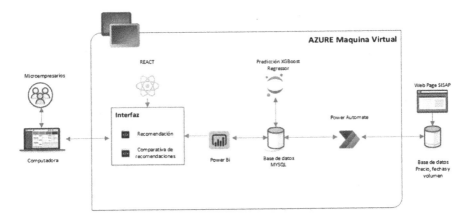

Fig. 3. System Architecture

5   Experiments

After loading the data, we can access it and make predictions using a proprietary code containing machine learning algorithms associated with XGBoost in an environment with Jupyter and Python software. These predictions are then inserted into the MySQL database. This code requires importing specific libraries for Machine Learning variables and database connection to function, such as: "pymysql", "pandas", "numpy", "sklearn.model_selection", "XGBRegressor" and "datetime". Upon executing the main code and collecting the actual data and predictions, we export the information to charts previously created in Power BI, which is an application that allows us to visualize variations between the actual prices, the predicted prices and the accuracy of our predictions. Finally, we export the Power BI graphs to the front-end of the web page. When visualizing the results of the predictions, with the objective of achieving an accuracy of greater than or equal to 90%, calculated by dividing the predicted price by the actual price of each day, we notice a significant variation in actual prices each passing day. To analyze the results of the predictions more effectively, a table was prepared containing the actual price of the mentioned products (Red Head Onion, Yellow Potato and Green White Serrano Pea) and the effectiveness of the prediction. We made predictions for the month of May 2023, which is visualized below, but first, we will visualize the data, both collected and predicted:

To obtain the predicted data, initially the libraries mentioned above had to be imported, and once this first part was completed, the model flow is explained as follows:

1. Connection to the database:
   A connection to a local MySQL database is established with details of the host, user, password, and database. Then, a cursor is created to query the database.
2. SQL query:
   An SQL query is executed to obtain information on date, minimum and maximum prices, volume, etc. The results of the query are stored in a variable.
3. Creation of the Data Frame:
   The variable, which contains the results of the SQL query execution, is converted into a DataFrame using the "DataFrame" function of the "pandas" library.
4. Manipulation of Dates and Preparation of Incoming and Outgoing Data:
   The date data is converted to date format using the "to_datetime" function of the "pandas" library, then the DataFrame is sorted by date. Additional columns are created for the day, month, and year of the date. Then, the input characteristics 'Day', 'Month', 'Year' of a date and volume are selected as "X". The outputs of interest are the Actual Minimum Price as "Y" and the Actual Maximum Price as "W".
5. Division of Data into Training and Test Sets:
   The data are split into training and test sets using the "train_test_split" function of the "sklearn.model_selection" library for both input and output features.
6. XGBoost Model Creation and Training:
   Two XGBoost models are created, one to predict the Minimum Real Price (model_xgb_y) and one to predict the Maximum Real Price (mode-lo_xgb_w). Then, the XGBoost models are trained using the training sets defined above (X_train, y_train and w_train) together with the "fit" function of the "XGBRegressor" library.
7. Predictions and printout of results:
   Price predictions are made using the models trained on the test data. The minimum and maximum price predictions are stored in variables. Then, the date of the day to be pre-predicted is calculated from the last record in the defined DataFrame. Then, another DataFrame is created with similar characteristics to the set of data, but with the date of the next day. Finally, the predictions are printed as the predicted prices for the previously selected day with the "predict" function of the "XGBRegressor" library, executing it on the 2 trained models. Having the maximum and minimum price data, we average them to obtain the average predicted price.

Table 1. Data Collected and Data Predicted for Red Head Onion, Yellow Potato and White Serrano Pea for the Month of June 2023.

Fecha	Cebolla Cabeza Roja						Papa Amarilla						Arveja Verde Blanca Serrana					
	Precio Mínimo Real	Precio Promedio Real	Precio Máximo Real	Precio Mínimo Predicho	Precio Promedio Predicho	Precio Máximo Predicho	Precio Mínimo Real	Precio Promedio Real	Precio Máximo Real	Precio Mínimo Predicho	Precio Promedio Predicho	Precio Máximo Predicho	Precio Mínimo Real	Precio Promedio Real	Precio Máximo Real	Precio Mínimo Predicho	Precio Promedio Predicho	Precio Máximo Predicho
30/06/2023	4.50	4.70	5.00	4.04	4.53	5.01	1.30	1.40	1.50	1.33	1.40	1.48	3.00	3.38	3.50	2.29	2.89	3.49
29/06/2023	4.50	4.78	5.00	3.89	4.36	4.82	1.30	1.41	1.50	1.42	1.55	1.68	3.00	3.33	3.50	2.86	3.28	3.69
28/06/2023	4.00	4.60	5.00	3.92	4.21	4.51	1.30	1.43	1.50	1.42	1.51	1.60	3.50	3.68	3.80	3.67	3.83	3.99
27/06/2023	4.00	4.58	5.00	4.05	4.46	4.86	1.30	1.40	1.50	1.37	1.46	1.55	3.50	3.73	4.00	3.47	3.65	3.82
26/06/2023	4.00	4.63	5.00	3.99	4.46	4.94	1.30	1.40	1.50	1.55	1.69	1.83	3.20	3.40	3.60	3.91	4.16	4.41
25/06/2023	4.00	4.38	5.00	3.92	4.34	4.76	1.30	1.40	1.50	1.38	1.48	1.59	3.00	3.25	3.50	3.20	3.44	3.68
24/06/2023	4.00	4.38	5.00	3.93	4.19	4.45	1.30	1.40	1.50	1.37	1.48	1.60	3.00	3.25	3.50	2.74	2.94	3.14
23/06/2023	4.00	4.20	4.50	3.91	4.12	4.33	1.30	1.43	1.50	1.61	1.62	1.63	2.60	2.85	3.00	2.92	3.08	3.24
22/06/2023	4.00	4.20	4.50	3.88	4.14	4.41	1.40	1.53	1.60	1.63	1.65	1.67	2.80	3.00	3.20	2.68	2.78	2.88
21/06/2023	4.00	4.33	4.50	3.85	4.09	4.33	1.50	1.58	1.60	1.63	1.68	1.73	2.50	2.68	2.80	2.75	2.82	2.89
20/06/2023	4.00	4.25	4.50	3.79	4.08	4.36	1.50	1.63	1.70	1.97	2.23	2.49	2.90	3.08	3.20	2.87	3.08	3.29
19/06/2023	4.00	4.25	4.50	3.41	3.67	3.94	2.00	2.08	2.20	1.53	1.77	2.01	2.80	3.05	3.20	2.31	2.47	2.62
18/06/2023	3.50	3.73	4.00	3.45	3.69	3.93	1.70	1.85	1.90	1.68	1.89	2.10	3.00	3.18	3.50	2.87	3.12	3.37
17/06/2023	3.50	3.73	4.00	2.90	3.22	3.53	1.70	1.85	1.90	1.69	1.72	1.75	3.00	3.18	3.50	2.18	2.32	2.46
16/06/2023	3.30	3.55	3.80	2.84	3.08	3.33	1.80	1.88	2.00	1.37	1.52	1.68	2.20	2.38	2.50	2.41	2.55	2.69
15/06/2023	3.30	3.53	3.80	2.83	3.15	3.47	1.80	1.85	2.00	1.47	1.56	1.64	2.50	2.60	2.70	2.76	2.71	2.66
14/06/2023	3.00	3.33	3.50	2.73	3.04	3.34	1.40	1.48	1.60	1.64	1.77	1.89	2.80	3.00	3.20	2.94	2.90	2.87
13/06/2023	3.00	3.20	3.50	2.77	3.00	3.23	1.20	1.28	1.40	1.36	1.48	1.60	2.60	2.73	2.80	2.12	2.53	2.93
12/06/2023	3.00	3.30	3.50	2.86	3.00	3.14	1.20	1.30	1.40	1.47	1.52	1.57	2.80	2.93	3.00	2.41	2.69	2.98

(continued)

Table 1. (*continued*)

Fecha	Cebolla Cabeza Roja						Papa Amarilla						Arveja Verde Blanca Serrana					
	Precio Mínimo Real	Precio Promedio Real	Precio Máximo Real	Precio Mínimo Predicho	Precio Promedio Predicho	Precio Máximo Predicho	Precio Mínimo Real	Precio Promedio Real	Precio Máximo Real	Precio Mínimo Predicho	Precio Promedio Predicho	Precio Máximo Predicho	Precio Mínimo Real	Precio Promedio Real	Precio Máximo Real	Precio Mínimo Predicho	Precio Promedio Predicho	Precio Máximo Predicho
11/06/2023	3.00	3.28	3.50	2.86	2.89	2.92	1.20	1.28	1.40	1.52	1.58	1.63	3.00	3.33	3.50	2.45	2.49	2.52
10/06/2023	3.00	3.28	3.50	2.72	2.89	3.06	1.20	1.28	1.40	1.53	1.55	1.57	3.00	3.33	3.50	2.57	2.61	2.65
9/06/2023	3.00	3.28	3.50	2.90	3.09	3.28	1.20	1.28	1.40	1.55	1.60	1.65	2.70	2.88	3.00	1.76	2.39	3.02
8/06/2023	3.00	3.23	3.50	2.84	3.05	3.25	1.20	1.33	1.40	1.67	1.69	1.72	2.80	3.00	3.20	2.15	2.29	2.44
7/06/2023	3.00	3.18	3.50	2.64	2.83	3.03	1.20	1.33	1.40	1.60	1.73	1.86	2.80	3.03	3.30	2.36	2.74	3.12
6/06/2023	2.80	3.00	3.20	2.24	2.41	2.57	1.40	1.50	1.60	1.61	1.68	1.75	2.80	3.03	3.30	1.52	1.56	1.60
5/06/2023	2.20	2.33	2.50	2.20	2.38	2.55	1.40	1.53	1.60	1.66	1.77	1.88	1.40	1.58	1.80	1.48	1.66	1.84
4/06/2023	2.20	2.30	2.50	2.13	2.37	2.61	1.50	1.60	1.70	1.49	1.73	1.97	1.30	1.53	1.80	1.28	1.35	1.42
3/06/2023	2.20	2.30	2.50	1.98	2.25	2.52	1.50	1.60	1.70	1.57	1.62	1.66	1.30	1.53	1.80	1.60	1.58	1.57
2/06/2023	2.20	2.30	2.50	2.02	2.26	2.50	1.40	1.53	1.60	1.81	1.94	2.06	1.40	1.63	1.80	1.57	1.64	1.72
1/06/2023	2.20	2.33	2.50	1.60	1.81	2.02	1.60	1.69	1.80	2.06	2.09	2.11	1.50	1.78	2.00	1.99	1.86	1.72

6 Results

After testing our predictive model, we have determined its effectiveness, where we calculated the division of the predicted price by the actual price and the result must be greater than or equal to 0.90 (90%), as the difference between prices is between 0.0 and 0.20 cents. To better comprehend this, we have made some graphs related to the prediction's effectiveness and price variation for each listed product, which are visualized as follows:

1. Prediction results for the product "Cebolla Cabeza Roja" (Fig. 4):

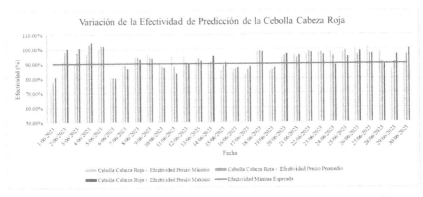

Fig. 4. Variation of the Predictive Effectiveness of the Cebolla Cabeza Roja

According to the graph, the following analysis was made:

- Regarding the variation in the effectiveness of the Minimum Price prediction, we can notice that there are days where the effectiveness varies significantly, due to the volatility of the real prices occurring approximately every 4 days on average. However, on more than two-thirds of the predicted days the effectiveness exceeds 90%. In summary, considering Table 1, the mean of the minimum predicted and actual prices was 3.10 and 3.35 respectively, and the daily effectiveness was 92.74%.
- Regarding the variation in the effectiveness of the Maximum Price prediction, it is noticeable that there are days when the effectiveness varies notably, again due to the volatility of the real prices occurring approximately every 5 days on average. However, on more than two-thirds of the predicted days the effectiveness exceeds 90%. In summary, considering Table 1, the average of the minimum predicted and actual prices was 3.63 and 3.89 respectively, and the daily effectiveness was 93.31%.
- Regarding the variation of the Average Price predictions, there is not much to say, as this is the result of the average of the Minimum and Maximum Prices.

2. Product prediction results "Papa Amarilla" (Fig. 5):

According to the graph, the following analysis was made:

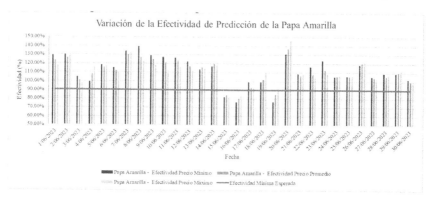

Fig. 5. Variation of the Predictive Effectiveness of the Papa Amarilla

- Regarding the variation in the effectiveness of the Minimum Price prediction, we can notice that there are days when the effectiveness varies notably, due to the volatility of the real prices occurring approximately every 2 days on average. However, in the great majority of the predicted days the effectiveness exceeds 90%. There are occasions where the effectiveness exceeds 100% (even reaching more than 115%), which raises a point for evaluation. In summary, considering Table 1, the average of the pre-stated and actual minimum prices was 1.57 and 1.41 respectively, and the average effectiveness was 110.74%.
- Regarding the variation in the effectiveness of the Maximum Price prediction, it is noticeable that there are days when the effectiveness varies notably, due to the volatility of the real prices occurring approximately every 3 days on average. However all the predictions exceed 90% effectiveness. There are occasions where the effectiveness exceeds 100% (even reaching more than 110%), which raises a point to evaluation. In summary, considering Table 1, the average of the minimum predicted and actual prices was 1.77 and 1.61 respectively, and the average effectiveness was 109.65%.
- Regarding the variation of the Average Price predictions, there is not much to say, since this is the result of the average of the Minimum and Maximum Prices.

3. Product prediction results "Arveja Verde Blanca Serrana" (Fig. 6):

   According to the graph, the following analysis was made:

- Regarding the variation in the effectiveness of the Minimum Price prediction, we can notice that there are days when the effectiveness varies significantly, due to the considerable volatility of the real prices occurring approximately every 2 days on average. However, in more than half of the predicted days effectiveness exceeds 90%. There are some cases where the effectiveness exceeds 100%, which raises a point to evaluation. In summary, considering Table 1, the mean of the minimum predicted and actual prices was 2.47 and 2.62 respectively, and the mean effectiveness was 94.15%.
- Regarding the variation in the effectiveness of the Maximum Price prediction, we can notice that there are days when the effectiveness varies significantly, due to the considerable volatility of the real prices occurring approximately every 2 days on average. However, in more than half of the predicted days effectiveness exceeds 90%.

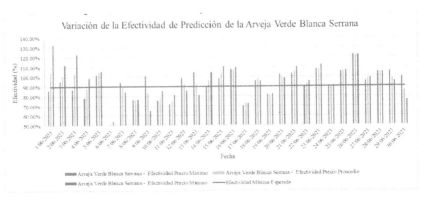

Fig. 6. Variation of the Predictive Effectiveness of the Arveja Verde Blanca Serrana

There are some cases where the effectiveness exceeds 100%, which raises a point to evaluation. In summary, considering Table 1, the average of the minimum predicted and actual prices was 2.82 and 3.03 respectively, and the average effectiveness was 93.13%.

- Regarding the variation in Average Price predictions, there is not much to say, since this is the result of the average of the Minimum and Maximum Prices.

After testing our predictive model for its effectiveness, the model has been tested in a real environment to verify its support in decision-making for pricing. These tests were conducted based on surveys in the Gran Mercado Mayorista de Lima with a segment of 21 micro-entrepreneurs, aiming to achieve more than 50% approval. For these surveys, 7 questions were asked, associating them with 3 indicators in relation to a Recommendation System, which is based on our predictive model (Table 2):

To show the results, we will first make use of the Likert scale, which is suitable for this type of test because of its simplicity of understanding for microentrepreneurs and the ease of interpreting the results (Table 3):

It should be emphasized that, out of the 21 microentrepreneurs evaluated, the sample will be derived from applying the formula for calculating the sample size, which will be explained below:

$$n = \frac{N * Z^2 * p * (1 - p)}{E^2 * (N - 1) + Z^2 * p * (1 - p)}$$

Where:

- n is the required sample size.
- N is the size of the total population. For the case we are evaluating, n is 10.
- Z is the critical value of the standard normal distribution corresponding to the desired confidence level. In this case, we aim for a 50% confidence level in the total results, the Z would be 0.
- p is the estimated proportion of the population that possesses the characteristic under study. We will use 0.5 to obtain the most conservative sample size.
- E is the margin of error you are willing to tolerate, expressed as a fraction. For this case, we aim for a margin of approximately 50%, which would be 0.5.

Table 2. Questions associated with indicators.

Indicators	Description	Code	Questions
Reliability	Indicator related to the security provided by the results of the Recommender System	Q1	Did you feel confident before trying the Recommender System?
		Q2	Did you feel confident after trying the Recommender System?
		Q3	How useful is the Recommendation System in helping you decide on prices?
Usability	Indicator related to user navigation in the Recommender System	Q4	How easy is it to use the Recommender System to get information about recommendations?
		Q5	How easy is it to use the Recommender System to get information about comparisons?
Accuracy	Indicator related to the accuracy of the Recommender System results	Q6	Do you think the Recommender System is very accurate in its predictions?
		Q7	Has the Recommender System ever given you a recommendation that seemed to be better than it really was?

Table 3. Likert Scale

Alternativas	Score
Very bad	1
Bad	2
Fair	3
Good	4
Very Good	5

Applying the values to the formula, we obtain a sample size of 0. Therefore, it is recommended to analyze the entire population, which in this case consists of 21 microentrepreneurs. The results are shown below (Table 4):

Verifying the results, it should be noted that, based on the responses of the 21 microentrepreneurs surveyed, scores between 4 and 5 are considered "Good", while scores between 1 and 3 are considered "Fair". With this understanding, the goal is to achieve an approval rate exceeding 50% of the total responses, which should consist of "Good" ratings. The results are then analyzed in the form of a graph (Fig. 7).

Table 4. Responses from the 21 microentrepreneurs on the 7 questions.

Microentrepreneurs	Q1	Q2	Q3	Q4	Q5	Q6	Q7
M01	4	5	5	5	4	5	3
M02	5	4	3	5	4	3	4
M03	5	3	3	3	3	3	5
M04	2	5	3	5	4	3	4
M05	5	3	4	4	4	2	3
M06	5	4	5	4	4	3	2
M07	3	3	4	5	4	4	4
M08	5	5	4	4	4	5	4
M09	5	4	3	4	3	5	3
M10	5	3	4	5	4	4	4
M11	4	3	2	4	3	4	4
M12	5	5	4	4	3	3	2
M13	4	3	4	5	5	4	5
M14	2	4	4	5	5	5	4
M15	5	5	4	3	3	5	5
M16	4	4	4	4	5	4	2
M17	2	4	5	5	5	5	2
M18	5	5	4	3	4	4	4
M19	5	4	5	4	4	4	4
M20	5	4	3	4	4	3	3
M21	3	5	4	3	3	4	4

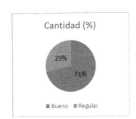

Fig. 7. Graph of the segmented results of microentrepreneurs' responses

Taking stock of the total of all the results, it has been determined that, out of the 147 responses, 105 were "Good" and 42 were "Fair". This significantly exceeded the targeted half approval rate of 71%.

7 Conclusion and Perspective

In conclusion, it is evident that the effectiveness of our prediction approach must undergo rigorous and careful evaluation. Clear limits must be established to assess effectiveness, especially when it exceeds 100%. Therefore, our approach will continue to involve exhaustive tests in the range of 90% to 110% effectiveness. Delimiting the effectiveness within this range would significantly contribute to other predictions, enhancing the accuracy of the predictions. This accuracy plays a crucial role in the generation of forecasts for several fundamental horticultural products in the Peruvian market, such as potato, pumpkin, garlic, among others.

It is crucial to highlight the necessity of daily updates to the price and volume database with new information. This continuous update enhances the effectiveness of the predictions by feeding new data into the learning process of our model. We are committed to continuously improve our predictive capabilities.

Finally, it has been determined that a more accurate prediction can be achieved by considering another variable. The quality of the horticultural product. However, acquiring this data poses a challenge due to the diverse nature of product quality. To address this, it is advisable to specify predictions for a particular microenterprise and consider its product inventory. Additionally, the application of another Artificial Intelligence technology, such as Deep Learning, can provide more detailed insights into product quality, enabling more precise evaluations.

In this context, detailed consideration of product inventory allows us to enhance the quantity and quality of data for more accurate predictions. This integrated approach will enable us to continually improve our forecasts, delivering significant value to the Peruvian horticultural market.

References

1. Minghui, D., Libo, L.: Risk assessment of agricultural supermarket supply chain in big data environment. Sustain. Comput. Inform. Syst. Food Policy **28**(100420) (2020). https://doi.org/10.1016/j.suscom.2020.100420
2. Sourav, P., Sibarama, P., Prabira, S., Sante, B.: Time series forecasting of price of agricultural products using hybrid methods. Appl. Artif. Intell. **35**, 1388–1406 (2021). https://doi.org/10.1080/08839514.2021.1981659
3. Banerjee, T., Sinha, S., Choudhury, P.: Long term and short-term forecasting of horticultural produce based on the LSTM network model. Appl. Intell. **52**, 9117–9147 (2022). https://dl.acm.org/doi/abs/10.1007/s10489-021-02845-x
4. Helin, Y., Don, J., Yeon, H., Chang, J., Sang, K., Seong, J.: STL-ATTLSTM: vegetable price forecasting using STL and attention mechanism-based LSTM. Agriculture **10**, 1–17 (2021). https://doi.org/10.3390/agriculture10120612
5. Rodriguez, M.: Alza en los vegetales desde febrero: ¿Qué factores afectan el incremento en los precios de frutas y verduras? 26 de marzo de 2022. Revisado el 22 de marzo del 2023. El Comercio. https://elcomercio.pe/economia/alza-en-los-vegetales-desde-febrero-que-factores-afectan-el-incremento-en-los-precios-de-frutas-y-verduras-canasta-basica-en-peru-incremento-de-precios-mercado-noticia/?ref=ecr
6. Manrique, R.: Los cambios del clima y su impacto en el campo peruano. Redagricola, 13 de junio de 2022. https://www.redagricola.com/pe/el-clima-bajo-lupa/

7. Zambrano, F., Sánchez, M., Correa, S.: Análisis de Rentabilidad, endeudamiento y liquidez de microempresas en Ecuador. Artículos destinados al monográfico **11** (2021). https://doi.org/10.17163/ret.n22.2021.03

8. Vendty: Efectos de un mal inventario (2023). https://www.vendty.com/blog/efectos-de-un-mal-inventario#:~:text=La%20falta%20de%20control%20en,no%20les%20est%C3%A1s%20brindando%20un

9. Castillo, M.: La Agricultura Peruana, Situación Post COVID-19 y Perspectivas. Agricultura, seguridad y soberanía alimentaria (2021). https://library.fes.de/pdf-files/bueros/peru/18971.pdf

10. EMMSA: Gran Mercado Mayorista de Lima: Serie Histórica por volumen de los principales productos (2022). http://old.emmsa.com.pe/emmsa_spv/rpEstadistica/rpt_Histo_Volumen_Principales_Productos.php

11. EMMSA: Gran Mercado Mayorista de Lima: Volumen de Precios Diarios (2022). http://old.emmsa.com.pe/emmsa_spv/rpEstadistica/rptVolPreciosDiarios.php

12. Burkov, A.: The Hundred-Page Machine Learning Book (2019). http://ema.cri-info.cm/wpcontent/uploads/2019/07/2019BurkovTheHundred-pageMachineLearning.pdf

Analysis of Driving Style and Its Influence on Fuel Consumption for the City of Quito, Ecuador: A Data-Driven Study

Paúl Molina[1]([✉]) [ID], Ricardo Parra[1,2] [ID], and Felipe Grijalva[3] [ID]

[1] Grupo de Investigación en Ingeniería Del Transporte (GIIT),
Universidad Politécnica Salesiana, Quito 170146, Ecuador
pmolinac1@ups.edu.ec, rparrab@est.ups.edu.ec

[2] Empresa Pública Metropolitana de Agua Potable y Saneamiento (EPMAPS) -
Agua de Quito, Quito 170519, Ecuador
ricardo.parra@aguaquito.gob.ec

[3] Colegio de Ciencias e Ingenierías "El Politécnico", Universidad San Francisco
de Quito USFQ, Quito 170157, Ecuador
fgrijalva@usfq.edu.ec

Abstract. The constant increase in vehicles and their consequent production of pollutant emissions from mobile sources is a global predicament. In response, efforts are underway to mitigate fuel consumption. This metric is influenced not only by the vehicle type and fuel choice but also by strategic decisions such as maintenance, route selection, and driver behavior. Driving style is a parameter that is often ignored but has great repercussions on energy costs. Moreover, Ecuador lacks studies on driver behavior in real conditions. This study conducted dynamic tests to gather data through a data logger device. Subsequently, the collected data underwent a preprocessing stage to extract relevant features. These predictors were then employed to train a decision tree model for discerning between normal and aggressive driving styles. Our findings reveal that during urban driving, the aggressive style results in an average consumption of approximately 15% higher than the normal style. In rural settings, this difference is around 13%, with aggressive driving consuming 0.644 l/h more. However, during highway driving, no significant difference in average fuel consumption was observed between the two driving styles.

Keywords: fuel consumption · decision tree · driving style

1 Introduction

The constant increase of vehicles causes a degradation in air quality due to pollutant emissions generated by mobile sources [13]. According to estimates made by the World Health Organization (WHO), it was found that in 2016, exposure to these pollutants caused around 4.2 million premature deaths worldwide [10]. For

2018, the transport sector reported a demand of 29% of the world's energy and 92% of this was obtained from petroleum products and it is expected to double by 2050 [12]. In Ecuador, according to the balance presented by the Ministry for the Coordination of Strategic Sectors, the transportation sector is the largest consumer of petroleum derivatives [17]. Furthermore, according to data reported by the public hydrocarbons company Petroecuador EP, to supply the internal demand for derivatives, it was necessary to import 16 million barrels of derivatives, representing an increase of 15% compared to 2022, used for the production of naphtha and Diesel 2 [14]. Based on the report presented by the Secretariat of Mobility, there has been a considerable increase in the number of vehicles in Quito in recent years. This resulted in a growth of approximately 17539 vehicles added annually to Quito's vehicle fleet, representing an average annual increase of 4.9% [5]. Fuel consumption is not only influenced by the size of the vehicle and the type of fuel used for its operation, it is also related to strategic decisions such as maintenance and selection of the unit, route chosen, and driver behavior [18]. Fuel consumption is a complex and non-linear phenomenon that encompasses many parameters and is, therefore an open topic for research [8, 19]. This work focuses on analyzing the driving style under real conditions due to differences found in tests carried out on vehicles on chassis dynamometers and others through the application of on-road driving cycles [3, 11]. In addition, several studies have established that reductions of around 10% in fuel consumption and pollutant emissions can be obtained by varying the driving style [9, 15, 19]. To address this problem, Dia et al. conducted a study in the city of Georgia, USA, collecting over 100,000 km of data from bus operations in two types of services: a local urban service with frequent stops and an express service with high speeds. The results showed that fuel consumption can be reduced by 5% in local transit service and 7% in bus service by changing driving style, and modifying factors such as acceleration, brake use, gear shifting, and idling time [4]. Other research identified that driving characteristics during acceleration are responsible for 56.5% of total fuel consumption, while deceleration only contributes less than 5.7% of total fuel consumption. Mae et al attributed that an aggressive driving style, characterized by hard acceleration and high engine revolution, significantly increases fuel consumption, by driving more efficiently, the amount of resources needed to propel the car can be reduced [7]. Rodriguez et al., in a study in Bogotá, Colombia, conducted tests on a 10 km urban circuit that included different types of roads and traffic conditions; where two different professional drivers drove test vehicles consisting of 78 vehicles in total, 64 petrol engines and 14 vehicles modified with petrol and CNG. This study aimed to examine vehicle emissions in various traffic conditions and road types by examining their relationship with variables such as speed, acceleration, and vehicle load [16].

This study centers on an in-depth analysis of driving styles and their impact on fuel consumption in the city of Quito, Ecuador. To achieve this goal, we have established a hierarchical decision structure based on a decision tree. This decision tree takes various factors into account, including road characteristics, altitude conditions, traffic situations, and the driver's individual driving style. These factors converge to classify the driving style as either 'aggressive' or 'normal,' subsequently influencing fuel consumption. The structure of this article is as follows: Following the introduction and literature review in Sect. 1, Sect. 2 outlines the methodologies and materials employed in the experimental phase. Section 3 details the results obtained through post-processing of the collected vehicle data. Finally, in Sect. 4, we present the study's key findings and conclusions.

2   Material and Methods

The vehicle diagnostic system also known as OBD (On Board Diagnostics) is widely used in modern vehicles. These devices are designed to monitor and diagnose vehicle performance by collecting a variety of data about various parameters such as throttle position, speed, among others. The information collected by OBD is used to detect and troubleshoot mechanical problems and to improve vehicle performance. However, the data obtained by OBD is also useful for analyzing driving behavior and looking for ways to improve fuel efficiency. The testing and training procedure for a driving style and fuel consumption classification model proposed in this study involves several steps, as described in Fig. 1.

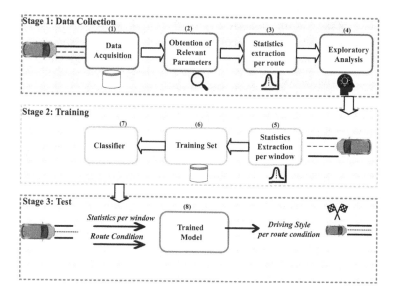

Fig. 1. Our proposed methodology has three stages: data collection from an OBD, training a machine learning model and test the model on new routes.

Data is acquired using the Freematics One+ data logger. Subsequently, the information is preprocessed to extract significant parameters based on statistical metrics from signals such as acceleration, speed, RPM, fuel flow, accelerator pedal position, absolute intake manifold pressure, and velocity per positive acceleration. An exploratory analysis examines statistical characteristics concerning manual driving style labeling. Next, statistics are extracted by window, where information from all routes is consolidated into a single matrix, divided into ten-second segments. From each segment, statistical characteristics are selected based on signals during specific time intervals of interest. These characteristics are grouped by the range of speeds in the Real Driving Emissions (RDE) cycle, establishing a comprehensive database to train the classification model. Once trained, the model classifies driving styles based on RDE cycle conditions (urban, rural, and motorway), indicating the driver's behavior in each stage.

2.1   OBD Signal Acquisition

The signals captured by the Freematics One+ data logger are obtained in digital form while the vehicle is being driven under real road conditions. For this case study, the signals extracted via OBD II are shown in Table 1 [2].

Table 1. Parameter IDs acquired

Parameter	Symbol	Min	Max	Unit
Throttle Position	TPS	0	99	[%]
Manifold Absolute Pressure	MAP	17	75	[kPa]
Intake Air Temperature	IAT	32	54	[°C]
Engine Coolant Temperature	ECT	82	94	[°C]
Vehicle Speed	VSS	0	61	[km/h]
Engine Speed	RPM	608	4102	[RPM]

2.2   Test Vehicle

The Changan CS15 SUV 4X2 was utilized for data acquisition and subsequent classifier model testing. The technical specifications of the vehicle are detailed in Table 2. It is important to highlight that the vehicle underwent preventive maintenance, conducted in accordance with the manufacturer's specifications, prior to the tests.

Table 2. Technical specifications of the test vehicle

Parameter	Value
Year	2021
Engine	1.5 l
Maximum speed	161 km/h
Power	105 HP
Torque	145 Nm

2.3   Road Tests

Data acquisition tests were conducted in various sectors of the Metropolitan District of Quito, encompassing the north, south, and valleys. These routes covered diverse traffic conditions, roads, and highways, aiming to capture a broad spectrum of driving situations representative of different styles. During the tests, drivers were instructed to replicate both normal and aggressive driving behaviors. For the normal style, drivers maintained a reserved approach with smooth accelerations, moderate accelerator use, and controlled driving. In contrast, the aggressive style involved dynamic maneuvers, including sharp accelerations and braking, intensive accelerator use, and an overall energetic driving style. These driving styles exhibit specific measurable parameters such as acceleration and braking magnitudes, throttle response, and other indicators related to driver behavior. Details regarding the number of routes, distance covered, and the maintained driving style for each test are summarized in Table 3.

Table 3. Test routes (N-Normal, A-Aggressive)

Route	Label	Distance [km]	Route	Label	Distance [km]	Route	Label	Distance [km]	Route	Label	Distance [km]
1	A	14.61	13	N	19.22	25	A	28.52	37	N	18.95
2	N	19.11	14	N	0.36	26	N	14.61	38	N	299.33
3	N	3.93	15	N	14.97	27	A	14.71	39	A	20.25
4	N	1.91	16	A	22.78	28	A	29.32	40	A	19.60
5	N	3.48	17	A	27.71	29	N	19.06	41	N	2.72
6	N	14.14	18	N	19.40	30	N	0.38	42	A	20.03
7	N	0.92	19	N	5.29	31	A	1.91	43	N	0.83
8	A	13.82	20	N	19.13	32	N	19.08	44	N	0.44
9	A	27.88	21	N	0.88	33	N	3.07	45	A	13.90
10	N	2.32	22	N	1.97	34	N	17.20	46	N	13.05
11	N	19.09	23	A	19.99	35	A	29.33	47	N	1.34
12	N	11.80	24	N	19.10	36	N	12.88	Distance		904.32

2.4   Exploratory Analysis of Variables

An input variable is used as a predictor or cause in a model or experiment. In the case of this study, those parameters previously shown in Table 1 are considered to be of interest. Additionally, variables such as acceleration are calculated through velocity variation, fuel flow established through the pressure found in the intake manifold, Velocity times Positive Acceleration (VPA), and Relative Positive Acceleration (RPA) are derived from acceleration. Parameters such as RPA need an evaluation threshold. This is because the majority of recorded accelerations throughout the entire route either are or tend to be close to zero. Therefore, it has been considered to set a threshold at accelerations greater than 0.1 to distinguish and analyze the most significant positive accelerations [1].

Test with Normal Driving. In this phase, the level of correlation between the most relevant parameters and fuel consumption is examined for both a normal route and an aggressive route. For the normal route, the results of the correlation matrix are presented in Fig. 2. This matrix shows the relationships between the variables of interest with fuel consumption (denoted as flux in the matrix) on a route with a normal driving style.

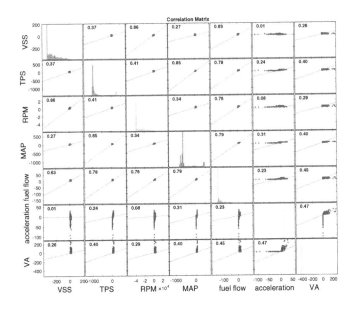

Fig. 2. Correlation matrix of a normal driving style route

When analyzing the correlation matrix based on fuel consumption, the following relationship between the variables and fuel consumption can be observed: The VSS sensor and RPM have a moderate positive correlation with fuel consumption, indicating that as vehicle speed and engine revolutions increase, fuel consumption also tends to increase. The MAP sensor and TPS show a high positive correlation with fuel consumption, indicating that as manifold pressure and throttle position increase, fuel consumption also tends to increase.

Road Test with Aggressive Driving. A correlation analysis of the variables of interest with fuel flow on an aggressive route was developed. The purpose of this was to test the data and determine if there are changes in the level of correlation as the driving style is modified. The results of the correlation matrix for a route with an aggressive driving style are shown in Fig. 3. The results provide a detailed view of the correlation index between the variables of interest and their association with fuel flow on the aggressive route.

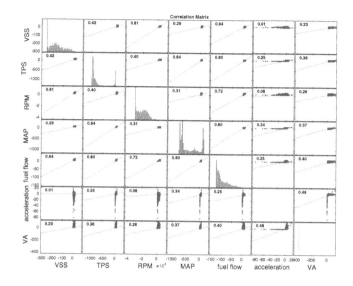

Fig. 3. Correlation matrix of an aggressive driving style route

Examining the correlation matrix for the aggressive route about fuel consumption, the following relationships between the variables and fuel consumption can be identified: VSS sensor and RPM show a moderate positive correlation with fuel flow, indicating that as vehicle speed and engine revolutions increase, fuel consumption tends to increase.

2.5   Data Classification

T-SNE of Driving Style. The t-SNE visualization in Fig. 4 reveals a clear clustering of the route statistics according to normal and aggressive driving styles. This confirms that the statistical measures calculated per route are crucial for the differentiation between aggressive and normal driving.

Classification Model. After conducting the exploratory analysis and collecting data from all the routes used, we compiled a database that served as input for a classification model. Specifically, we opted for a decision tree model due to its ease of interpretability. This model classifies driving styles, categorizing them as either 'normal' or 'aggressive,' across various conditions. We applied the methodology used in real driving emissions (RDE) during the construction of route sections, encompassing urban, rural, and highway driving. For this purpose, the database consists of time signal statistics recorded in 10-second segments. Within each segment, the standard deviation and mean of variables that were determined to be relevant in the exploratory analysis such as fuel flow, acceleration, RPM, TPS, MAP, and VA are calculated; by extracting these statistical characteristics, information is obtained that can be used to train the classification model. These features represent important aspects of the vehicle's behavior

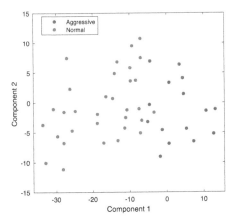

Fig. 4. The t-SNE visualization shows that the driving styles tend to cluster into aggressive and normal styles.

during these time intervals and can be used as attributes or predictor variables in the model. This process aims to enrich the database and provide more quantitative information that allows the classification model to learn distinctive patterns and characteristics of each driving style (normal or aggressive).

3 Results and Discussions

3.1 Relationship Between Variables of Interest and Driving Style

Understanding the most important predictors that cause the fuel consumption process can identify which variables have the greatest influence on dynamic driving conditions. This allows a better understanding of the variables that affect the process and provides useful information to optimize vehicle performance in terms of fuel efficiency.

Fuel Flow. The analysis of the box plot shown in Fig. 5 indicates a statistically significant difference in fuel flow between aggressive driving and normal driving with an average difference of 1 l/h.

Engine Revolutions. A statistically significant difference between the average and standard deviation of engine revolutions is identified for the aggressive and normal driving styles. This difference is relevant in the context of fuel consumption, as the previous correlation analysis identified a strong relationship between RPM and fuel consumption (see Fig. 6).

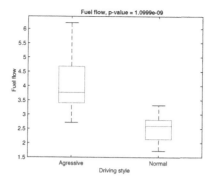

Fig. 5. Box plot fuel consumption vs. driving style

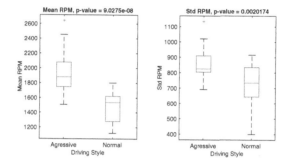

Fig. 6. Box plot RPM vs. driving style

VA 95th Percentile. The analysis shows that there is a statistically significant difference in the 95th percentile of the VA index between normal and aggressive driving styles as shown in Fig. 7. This is important in the context of fuel consumption because it confirms the correlation shown above.

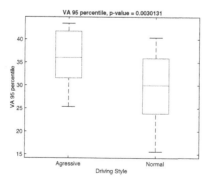

Fig. 7. Box plot VA 95 percentile vs. driving style

3.2 Differences in Fuel Consumption

For the final stage of the study, a t-test was performed to analyze whether there was a statistically significant difference in average fuel consumption between the aggressive driving routes and the normal driving routes. This analysis was carried out taking into account the different speeds associated with each of the RDE cycle conditions and using the average fuel consumption calculated per 10-second segment. The results can be seen in the Table 4.

Table 4. Fuel consumption by driving style and RDE condition.

Route	Average fuel consumption by driving style		Difference in consumption	p-value
	Aggressive	Normal		
Urban	3.101	2.344	0.757	0.0001
Rural	5.813	5.169	0.644	2,73E-146
Highway	4.593	4.511	0.082	0.1833

In the urban stage, it is observed that the average fuel consumption of the aggressive driving style is significantly higher than the average consumption of the normal driving style, with a difference of approximately 0.757 l/h. In the rural stage, the average fuel consumption of the aggressive driving style is higher than the average consumption of the normal driving style, with a difference of approximately 0.644 l/h, which is confirmed by a p-value of less than 0.05. At the highway stage, the statistical analysis shows that there is no significant difference in average fuel consumption between the aggressive driving style compared to the normal driving style, due to the higher traffic speeds. Additionally, the differences in driving behaviour are attenuated due to the difficulty of maintaining a constant driving pattern.

3.3 Development of the Calculation Algorithm

To verify the driving style, a decision tree was trained using a database containing the most important predictors. These predictors were calculated for each 10-second segment of the routes, and also included driving on urban, rural and motorway sections as an additional predictor. To validate the model, a 5-fold cross-validation was used. Subsequently, we used Bayesian optimisation to find the best combination of hyperparameters for the model. Once the optimal model has been trained, the confusion matrix is computed and presented in Fig. 8.

3.4 Testing the Classifier Model on a Normal Route

To evaluate the effectiveness of the model, a route that was not used during training was selected. The results of the driving style classification and the fuel

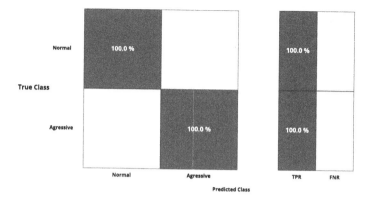

Fig. 8. Calculation of the confusion matrix. TPR and FNR stand for True Positive Rate and False Negative Rate, respectively.

consumption at each stage of the route, according to the conditions set according to the RDE cycle, are presented in the Table 5.

Table 5. Test route

Test route		Driving area		
Parameter	Unit	Urban	Rural	Highway
Driving style	Normal/Aggressive	Aggressive	Normal	Aggressive
Mean fuel consumption	l/h	3.277	7.159	7.222
Total distance	Km	28.87		

The classifier model correctly identified the driving style at each stage of the test route. At the urban stage, it was classified as aggressive, while the rural stage style was identified as normal, and at the motorway stage, it was classified as aggressive. This indicates that the model was able to distinguish between more aggressive and normal driving styles with reasonable accuracy. Regarding fuel consumption, it was observed that average fuel consumption varied according to driving style and stage of the cycle. In the urban stage, where an aggressive driving style was identified, the average fuel consumption was 3.277 l/h. In the rural stage, with a normal driving style, the average fuel consumption was 7,159 l/h. On the highway stage, again with an aggressive driving style, the average fuel consumption was 7,222 l/h. These results show that a more aggressive driving style tends to result in higher fuel consumption compared to a normal driving style. The classification process of the decision tree is illustrated in Fig. 9. The classification criteria start with the mean value of the speed, if this value is less than 5.79 m/s, the driving style is classified as normal, otherwise the standard deviation of the speed is examined. If the standard deviation is less than 1.17

m/s, it is classified as normal. If this condition is not fulfilled, the average fuel consumption is analyzed. If the average fuel consumption is less than 8.78 l/h, the driving style is classified as normal, otherwise, it is classified as aggressive.

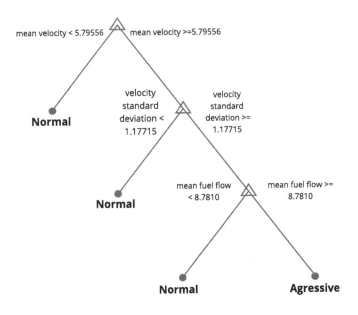

Fig. 9. Decision tree and nodes

3.5   Classifier Model Testing in an RDE Cycle

The classification model was used to determine the driving style in each of the stages of an RDE route designed in the metropolitan district of Quito, this route was designed from the sector of Conocoto to the Mariscal Antonio José de Sucre International Airport. The results of the driving style classification and the average fuel consumption in each stage of the RDE cycle of the test route are presented in the Table 6.

Table 6. Model testing on an RDE route

Test route		Driving area		
Parameter	Unit	Urban	Rural	Highway
Driving style	Normal/Aggressive	Normal	Normal	Aggressive
Mean fuel consumption	l/h	2.380	6.258	6.812
Total distance	Km	50.876		

In the urban stage, the model classifies the driving style as normal, indicating that the driver adopts a moderate and controlled approach to driving. In addition, the average fuel consumption during this stage is 2.380 l/h. In the rural stage, the driving style is again classified as normal, suggesting that the driver maintains a similar behavior to the urban stage, adapting to road conditions in less urbanized areas. The average fuel consumption in this stage is 6.25 l/h, however, in the highway stage, the model classifies the driving style as aggressive, implying that the driver adopts a more dynamic and higher speed approach to driving. As a result, an increase in average fuel consumption is observed during this stage, reaching 6.812 l/h.

4   Conclusions

The results of our study, as determined through multiple linear regression analysis, shed light on the intricate relationship between various driving variables and fuel consumption. Notably, certain factors such as engine revolutions, throttle pedal position, absolute intake manifold pressure, speed, as well as the RPA and VA indexes, exhibited a positive correlation with fuel flow, implying that an increase in these variables corresponded to higher fuel consumption. Conversely, other factors, like the standard deviation of acceleration and the average value of the VA index, displayed a negative influence, signifying that their increase was associated with a reduction in fuel flow.

Our analysis unequivocally demonstrates the significant impact of driving style on fuel consumption. A statistically significant difference was observed in engine revolutions and the 95th percentile of the VA index between normal and aggressive driving styles, affirming the intrinsic relationship between these variables and fuel consumption. On the other hand, no statistically significant difference emerged regarding the RPA index or the standard deviation of acceleration. These findings underscore the importance of considering driving style as a key factor in fuel consumption analysis.

For the urban stage, the aggressive driving style shows a mean fuel consumption approximately 15% higher than the normal driving style, supported by a difference of 0.757 l/h and a p-value of less than 0.05. In the rural setting, the difference is approximately 13% with a higher average consumption in the aggressive driving style of 0.644 l/h and a p-value of less than 0.05. However, on the highway stage, no significant difference in average fuel consumption was found between the two driving styles. These findings highlight the importance of considering driving style to promote more efficient practices and reduce fuel consumption and associated emissions.

An optimized decision tree model was trained using cross-validation and Bayesian hyperparameter optimization. The model achieved a true positive rate of 100% in the confusion matrix. The trained model was used to make predictions on new routes. The model used to classify driving style and predict fuel consumption has proven effective and accurate. The model was able to correctly identify the driving style at each stage of the test route, distinguishing between aggressive and normal driving styles with reasonable accuracy. In addition, it was found that a more aggressive driving style is associated with higher fuel consumption compared to a normal driving style. Our study's practical implications extend to driver education, emphasizing the importance of adopting less aggressive driving styles for fuel efficiency. Incorporating these findings into educational programs can empower drivers with a better understanding of how their behavior influences fuel consumption. This knowledge may also serve as a motivational tool for individuals to contribute to cost savings and environmental impact reduction.

The sample size employed in our study is a potential limitation, and we recognize the importance of expanding our dataset to incorporate a more diverse range of vehicle types and longer travel distances. This extension will provide a more comprehensive understanding of driving styles across various vehicular contexts. Additionally, we acknowledge the necessity of enhancing the reliability of driving style labeling by incorporating a larger pool of drivers in our study. A more extensive participant pool will introduce greater variability in the data, enabling our machine learning model to better generalize across diverse driving behaviors. Furthermore, future investigations may benefit from including micro routes in the analysis, as these routes are potentially more conducive to capturing nuanced characteristics of aggressiveness in driving behavior. These proposed avenues for future research aim to address the identified limitations and contribute to a more robust and applicable model for assessing driving styles and their impact on fuel consumption.

In future works, we intend to explore advanced machine learning techniques, including neural networks, to enhance our analytical capabilities further. An additional critical avenue for future investigation involves a comprehensive exploration of the influence of traffic conditions on our selected routes. Moreover, we aspire to expand our dataset through the application of generative machine learning methods, such as Generative Adversarial Networks (GANs), which have exhibited notable success in modeling similar time-series data [6], albeit in distinct contexts.

References

1. Barlow, T., Latham, S., McCrae, I., Boulter, P.: A reference book of driving cycles for use in the measurement of road vehicle emissions. TRL Published Project Report (2009)
2. Campoverde, P.A.M., Campoverde, N.D.R., Espinoza, J.E.M., Fernandez, G.M.R., Novillo, G.P.: Influence of the road slope on NOx emissions during start up. Mater. Today Proc. **49**, 8–15 (2022)
3. Costagliola, M.A., Costabile, M., Prati, M.V.: Impact of road grade on real driving emissions from two euro 5 diesel vehicles. Appl. Energy **231**, 586–593 (2018)
4. Dia, H., Panwai, S.: Impact of driving behaviour on emissions and road network performance. In: 2015 IEEE International Conference on Data Science and Data Intensive Systems, pp. 355–361. IEEE (2015)

5. DMQ: Plan de metropolitano de desarrollo y ordenamiento territorial 2015–2025 (2015). https://gobiernoabierto.quito.gob.ec/wp-content/uploads/documentos/interactivos/movilidad/downloads/publication.pdf

6. Grijalva, F., Ramos, W., Perez, N., Benitez, D., Lara-Cueva, R., Ruiz, M.: ESeismic-GAN: a generative model for seismic events from cotopaxi volcano. IEEE J. Sel. Top. Appl. Earth Obs. Remote Sens. **14**, 7111–7120 (2021)

7. Ma, H., Xie, H., Huang, D., Xiong, S.: Effects of driving style on the fuel consumption of city buses under different road conditions and vehicle masses. Transp. Res. Part D: Transp. Environ. **41**, 205–216 (2015)

8. Molina Campoverde, P.A.: Estimation of fuel consumption through PID signals using the real emissions cycle in the city of Quito, Ecuador. Sustainability **15**(16), 12474 (2023)

9. Orfila, O., Saint Pierre, G., Messias, M.: An android based ecodriving assistance system to improve safety and efficiency of internal combustion engine passenger cars. Transp. Res. Part C Emerg. Technol. **58**, 772–782 (2015)

10. World Health Organization: Burden of disease from household air pollution for 2012 (2017)

11. Ortenzi, F., Costagliola, M.A.: A new method to calculate instantaneous vehicle emissions using OBD data. Technical report, SAE Technical paper (2010)

12. Páez, C.F.T., Guayanlema, V., Mera, A.G.C.: Estimation of energy consumption due to the elimination of an environmental tax in Ecuador. Energy Sustain. Dev. **66**, 92–100 (2022)

13. Parnell, S.: Defining a global urban development agenda. World Dev. **78**, 529–540 (2016)

14. Petroecuador: Informe estadístico subgerencia de planificación y control de gestión (2023). https://www.eppetroecuador.ec/wp-content/uploads/downloads/2023/04/INFORME-ESTADISTICO-MARZO-2023.pdf

15. Rivera, N.D., Molina, P.A., Bermeo, A.K., Bermeo, O.E., Figueroa, J.L.: Driving style analysis by studying pid's signals for determination of its influence on pollutant emissions. In: Rocha, Á., López-López, P.C., Salgado-Guerrero, J.P. (eds.) Communication, Smart Technologies and Innovation for Society: Proceedings of CITIS 2021, pp. 321–331. Springer, Cham (2022). https://doi.org/10.1007/978-981-16-4126-8_30

16. Rodríguez, R.A., Virguez, E.A., Rodríguez, P.A., Behrentz, E.: Influence of driving patterns on vehicle emissions: a case study for Latin American cities. Transp. Res. Part D: Transp. Environ. **43**, 192–206 (2016)

17. Sierra, J.C.: Estimating road transport fuel consumption in Ecuador. Energy Policy **92**, 359–368 (2016)

18. Sivak, M., Schoettle, B.: Eco-driving: strategic, tactical, and operational decisions of the driver that influence vehicle fuel economy. Transp. Policy **22**, 96–99 (2012)

19. Zhou, M., Jin, H., Wang, W.: A review of vehicle fuel consumption models to evaluate eco-driving and eco-routing. Transp. Res. Part D: Transp. Environ. **49**, 203–218 (2016)

Preventing Drug Interactions in Diabetic Patients: The Role of a Mobile Conversational Agent

Carlos Armijos[1], Juan Cambizaca[1], Victoria Abril-Ulloa[2(✉)],
and Mauricio Espinoza-Mejía[2,3]

[1] Faculty of Engineering, University of Cuenca, Cuenca, Ecuador
{carlos.armijos,juan.cambizaca}@ucuenca.edu.ec
[2] Technologies Applied to Health Research Group, Faculty of Medical Sciences,
University of Cuenca, Cuenca, Ecuador
{victoria.abril,mauricio.espinoza}@ucuenca.edu.ec
[3] Computer Science Department, University of Cuenca, Cuenca, Ecuador

Abstract. This paper presents the development of a conversational agent embedded in a mobile application aimed at improving the safety of medication use in patients with diabetes, a highly prevalent chronic disease. One of the main challenges in the management of diabetes is the prevention of drug interactions and the understanding of how food can affect treatment.

The conversational agent uses a database of drug, food, and pharmacological interaction information to provide both preventive and informative recommendations. In the first scenario, it alerts users to possible interactions between the medications they are planning to take. In the second scenario, it provides information on contraindications, suggests food alternatives, and points out possible drug-food and drug-drug interactions. The design of the conversational agent allows it to understand and answer questions in natural language, making it easier for users to intuitively access relevant information. The usability of the tool was evaluated, resulting in an overall positive perception by users. In addition, the system identifies drug-drug and drug-food interactions and provides useful recommendations as indicated by experts.

Although areas for improvement were identified and specific adaptations are needed to fully meet the needs of users, the implementation of the agent through a mobile application has the potential to prevent dangerous interactions for patients with diabetes and significantly improve their quality of life.

Keywords: Conversational agent · Drugs interactions · Mobile app

1 Introduction

Over-the-counter medications, also called non-prescription medications, are medications that can be obtained without a doctor's prescription. These drugs are

M. Botto-Tobar et al. (Eds.): ICAT 2023, CCIS 2049, pp. 262–276, 2024.
https://doi.org/10.1007/978-3-031-58956-0_20

usually intended to treat minor symptoms or conditions and do not pose a significant risk of abuse or serious adverse effects. While these drugs are generally safe when used as directed by the manufacturer, their availability without a prescription may encourage self-medication. This practice may be driven by a variety of reasons, including lack of access to medical services, a desire to save time and money, or a belief that certain health problems do not require medical attention [12].

One of the main concerns about self-medication is that it can lead to health complications such as risky drug interactions, antibiotic resistance, and negative side effects. In addition, it can mask symptoms of more complex pathologies, delaying proper medical care and ultimately worsening the patient's health [11]. As mentioned in [2], the elderly population is considered highly vulnerable to health complications due to the high consumption of drugs, both prescribed and self-medicated, which can lead to the phenomenon of polypharmacy. The work described in [9] also concludes that drug interactions can be a cause of morbidity and mortality because they can interfere with the effectiveness of a treatment a person is following, accumulate the active ingredient of the drug, or reduce its effect. Importantly, these risks are often not recognized by doctors, pharmacists or patients themselves. It is therefore essential to increase awareness of drug-drug and drug-food interactions and to promote more effective management of drug treatments, especially in the elderly population.

A considerable amount of evidence has highlighted the potential benefits of conversational agents for health-related purposes [7]. For example, the work described in [3] discusses how healthcare chatbots, as part of AI technologies, are helping to revolutionize the management of medication-related issues by providing patients with accurate information, enabling them to actively manage their health and make informed decisions. AI algorithms used in chatbots can also benefit healthcare providers by providing critical information about medication prescriptions and dosing recommendations, helping to minimize medication errors and maximize treatment effectiveness. However, to the best of our knowledge, there no proposals for conversational agents that focus on identifying drug-food and drug-drug interactions for patients with diabetes. This is the strength of this study, as it is the first prototype designed for this purpose.

In this context, considering the current technological trends and the availability of pharmacological databases, this work proposes the implementation of a conversational agent that provides recommendations to avoid possible drug-food and drug-drug interactions in patients with diabetes. This type of conversational agent is mainly defined as a computer program or artificial intelligence capable of conversing with humans through natural language processing (NLP) [10]. Our focus is on diabetic patients because in recent years Ecuador has reported a significant increase in mortality attributed to type 2 diabetes, with it becoming the leading cause of death in 2013, resulting in 4,695 deaths [1]. For the year 2020, the number increased to 7,900 deaths, and the latest data indicate that this disease is among the top 5 causes of death in the country [6].

To reduce the risk of drug-drug or drug-food interactions in diabetic patients, our proposal is based on the modeling of a database fed with information on drugs, foods, and drug interactions. Due to the proposed scope, only specific drugs for diabetes are included; from the most commonly used or common drugs, and the drugs that the user consumes for other clinical conditions. Based on the selected sample of drugs, the system is able to make recommendations focused on two scenarios: preventive and informative. In the preventive scenario, the user informs the conversational agent of the intention to take a different medication than the one he/she has been taking, the conversational agent analyzes the drug-drug interactions of the medication, and provides an alert if such interactions exist. In the informative scenario, the focus is on alerting the user to potential interactions resulting from the ingestion of food or medication, with an eye toward a possible subsequent interaction. In addition, the conversational agent focuses on warning about contraindications, food consumption alternatives, and possible drug-food and drug-drug interactions, since studies such as [15] state that the simultaneous or sequential use of multiple drugs can alter the effectiveness of a drug due to interactions with other drugs.

The main challenge in creating a conversational agent is its ability to access the information stored in the database through natural language questions. In this context, the objective of this work was to develop a first approximation of a conversational agent integrated into a mobile application with the purpose of ensuring the safe use of medication by users suffering from diabetes. In addition, an evaluation of the usability of the tool was carried out and another to measure the opinion of experts on the accuracy of the conversational agent's responses in predefined situations.

The rest of the paper is organized into three sections. Section 2 presents the materials and methods used in this work. Section 3 describes and discusses the results of the evaluation of the proposed conversational agent. The results of the expert verification of the interactions detected by the conversational agent are also presented. Finally, Sect. 4 draws final conclusions and provides future lines of work.

2   Materials and Methods

This section provides a comprehensive account of the architecture of the Conversational Agent, including its operation and components. Additionally, it covers the design of the database, which stores information about drug-drug and drug-food interaction. The proposed architecture is based on the sequentially implemented components outlined below, as depicted in Fig. 1.

2.1   Data Store

One of the first steps in creating the conversational agent was to identify the sources and platforms that would be used to manage pharmacological information for patients with diabetes. The data to populate the information on *drugs,*

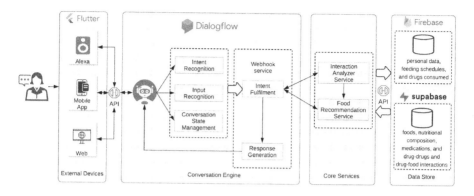

Fig. 1. Conversational agent architecture.

and *drug-food and drug-drug interactions*, was obtained from the DrugBank platform via web scraping, and this choice was based on its extensive set of drug information [14]. Although Vademecum[1] was considered as an alternative, it was ultimately discarded due to its limitation in providing details of drug-food interactions, unlike DrugBank, which provides more comprehensive information in this regard. All data in DrugBank are derived from public, non-proprietary sources. Nearly every data item is fully traceable and explicitly referenced to its original source. This is critical to ensuring access to reliable and up-to-date data on medications, drug interactions, and recommendations related to this disease. A limitation of the database is that it does not contain information on the specific compounds in the foods that are responsible for the interaction, which limits the possibility of identifying other foods or preparations containing these compounds that may cause interactions.

To ensure secure and scalable storage, the Firebase[2] and Supabase[3] platforms were chosen.

Firebase provides the ability to manage the persistence of the user's session, as well as store personal data, feeding schedules, and records of medications consumed. In addition to the above, Firebase adds value with its real-time services, which allow notifications to be generated for users based on their meal times. When a meal time is approaching, a notification is sent to the user reminding them that they can consult the application before eating to check if any food interacts with the prescribed medication.

Supabase is used to manage a relational model that contains information about foods, nutritional composition, medications, and drug-drug and drug-food interactions. The following is a description of the main relational tables that make up the model and their usefulness within the system.

---

[1] https://www.vademecum.es/.

[2] https://firebase.google.com/.

[3] https://supabase.com/.

- *Food.* This is the core element of the relational model and includes the Glycemic Load (GL), Glycemic Index (GI), and Carbohydrates per 100 g fields, as well as the group to which the food belongs. All information is taken from the table of foods, glycemic index and glycemic load described in [8]. These data are essential for the *recommendation service* (described in Sect. 2.3).

  It is important to note that in the diet of a patient with diabetes, GI, carbohydrate, and GL are critical to blood glucose control. The GI indicates how a food affects blood glucose and insulin levels after consumption. Foods with a low GI raise blood glucose slowly, while processed foods tend to have a high GI. Carbohydrates are also important because they can affect blood glucose. The GL combines the GI and the amount of carbohydrate in a serving to give a more complete picture of how a food affects blood glucose levels. A high GL indicates a greater impact on blood glucose levels, and a low GL is preferable for maintaining adequate diabetes control. Therefore, these factors help patients make more informed dietary decisions and better manage their disease.

  Regarding the group to which a food may belong, eight major groups have been established based on the food pyramid, such as: dairy products, vegetables, fruits, nuts, cereals and tubers, legumes, proteins, and alcohol [4].

- *Nutritional Composition.* Stores information about the nutritional composition and ingredients of foods, allowing these components to be categorized and organized. This makes it easier to evaluate the nutritional quality of foods and to make personalized recommendations according to the user's needs.

- *Drug.* Contains information about various drugs, it is used to organize and store data related to drugs used in diabetes-related medical practice. For each drug, it also stores the trade names by which a particular drug is known.

- *Drug-Food and Drug-Drug Interactions.* These relational tables contain information about drug interactions, both between drugs and foods and between different drugs. For drug-food interactions, detailed information is provided on the description of the interaction, the food involved and its composition, and the food group to which it belongs. For drug-drug interactions, the relationship between two drugs is recorded in each entry and details of possible interactions, including potential adverse effects, are included. This information is essential for the *recommendation service*, as it helps to identify dangerous combinations or contraindications when several drugs are taken simultaneously.

2.2   Conversation Engine

This component, the core of the architecture, handles the interaction between the user and the conversational agent. The *conversation engine* processes the user's input, queries the *data store* and the *core services* through the *webhooks*[4]

---

[4] Webhooks are services that host your business logic or call other services.

to determine the most appropriate response for the user. To implement this component, we chose Dialogflow CX[5], a robust and versatile platform for building chatbots and dialog systems.

Input Recognition. Given input text (such as transcribed voice commands or free text messages), this module performs natural language processing (NLP) through several stages, including: normalization, filtering, grammatical tagging, and encoding.

The *normalization* process is responsible for ensuring that the user's text input is interpreted consistently by applying transformations such as capitalizing the first letter and converting the rest of the text to singular. The *filtering* and *grammatical tagging* processes identify relevant words and phrases by assigning grammatical tags to words in a sentence to identify their function (noun, verb, adjective, etc.). *Encoding* converts words and phrases into numerical vectors, facilitating machine understanding by models that consider the full context of a sentence.

To train the machine learning model in DialogFlow, we used sets of representative sentences covering requests for information about medications and food (preventive mode) as well as advice about the user's condition (informative mode). An example of the sentences used to train the model in preventive and informative modes is shown in the list below. These sentences are designed not to be too complex to avoid overfitting the model.

- Preventive Mode
    - I want to take a medicine?
    - I am thinking about eating a food, can you help me?
    - Can you help me with my medication?
    - I need information on medication
    - I need help
    - Hey, I have a question about a medication
- Informative Mode
    - I don't know what's wrong with me, my body hurts
    - I feel sick
    - I have a sharp pain in my stomach
    - I have a toothache and I am diabetic
    - I have difficulty breathing

Intent Recognition uses pre-built dialog flows to deliver meaningful interactions and accurate, relevant responses. When a user writes or says something, it compares the expression to training phrases for each intent to find the best match. To compute intents, our approach uses a supervised machine learning technique. The agent has been trained with datasets containing intents, intent training phrases, and examples of interactions; these datasets ensure that the system evolves and continuously improves its ability to understand and effectively respond to user requests.

---

[5] https://cloud.google.com/dialogflow.

Conversation State Management. This module tracks the state of the conversation between the user and the conversational agent and determines follow-up intentions. Within the conversational agent, several pages[6] have been defined that are responsible for retrieving data that allows interaction and continuation of the conversation. In the case of the proposed conversational agent, two essential flows are proposed; preventive and informative. The preventive scenario recommends to the user if the medicine or food that he/she intends to consume is suitable for his/her condition. If the user indicates a preference for food information, several options are presented, such as providing general details about a food, specifying a particular food, or indicating that no further information is needed. After providing information about the food, the user is asked if he/she would like information about another food before the interaction is completed.

The informative scenario focuses on situations where the user has taken a drug that is not part of his or her usual regimen or has consumed a food that could cause an interaction. The goal is to evaluate the occurrence of these two situations: the first is when the user tries to understand why he/she feels bad, and the second is related to the user's exploration of food intake to identify possible interactions. In both cases, relevant information is collected and guidance is provided as needed.

Intent Fulfillment. The *intent fulfillment* module acts as a router, connecting the user's natural language input to the *core services*. Using the *conversation state management* along with the user's intent and messages, this module decides whether the conversational agent should ask a follow-up question or proceed to fulfill the user's request.

This functionality is implemented using a *webhook service*. A webhook in the Dialogflow context enables asynchronous, event-driven communication with the conversational agent. This means that the webhook is called only when necessary, i.e. when relevant events are generated in the conversation. Setting up a webhook in Dialogflow CX is relatively simple compared to setting up a WebSocket connection. Using a webhook requires providing a URL to which Dialogflow CX can send HTTP requests, while using WebSockets requires additional server configuration and implementation of event handling logic at both ends.

Response Generation. This component is responsible for generating messages to the user as a result of interactions. During each interaction, the user makes a request that the conversational agent processes and uses to generate and send a response.

The end-user interaction is designed to be both voice and text based[7]. A mobile application allows users to make requests via chat. In addition, basic

---

[6] Pages have the ability to guide an entire conversation around topics for which the flow has been designed.

[7] It is important to note that due to specific technical limitations of certain platforms, such as Android, voice functionality may present some challenges.

Alexa support has been added using its SDK, allowing basic interaction with the conversational agent.

After the request is parsed, it is sent to the webhook, which is responsible for connecting to the *core services*. First, it goes to the database, which is responsible for storing the user's information. This extracts the relevant information, such as food or medication, and then sends it to the *API*. The API interacts with the database that stores interaction information, parses the request, and looks for any relevant food or drug interactions. After querying the interaction database, the system returns a response about the interactions to the system via the webhook. The intent of the response is then determined and the response is sent to the front-end, which is responsible for presenting the information either through the mobile app or Alexa.

2.3   Core Services

This system element provides the details of the domain with which the conversational agent interacts. The *Interaction Analyzer Service* extracts the necessary data to check for possible drug interactions. Then the Webhook is responsible for orchestrating the process and finally the *Food Recommendation Service* is responsible for providing an alternative in case of a drug-food interaction. Each component is described below in order of importance.

Interaction Analyzer Service. This component is essential in this work as it is dedicated to query and check drug-drug and drug-food interactions.

In the preventive scenario, the system collects data on drugs and foods that the user plans to consume and compares them with the information in the database to detect possible interactions. In the informative scenario, the system analyzes recently consumed drugs and foods to determine whether symptoms may be the result of an interaction. In this scenario, the system asks detailed questions. The first scenario focuses on anticipation, while the second focuses on retrospective evaluation of interactions. Both are aimed at ensuring user safety.

In situations where an interaction is not detected, our approach goes beyond basic analysis and attempts to provide additional information to the user. For drug-food interactions, two types of checks are performed. The first checks for direct interaction of the food with the drug. If no interaction is found at this level, the interaction with the food group to which the food belongs is checked. If still no interaction is found, it is checked against the nutritional components of the food. If an interaction is found, the description of the interaction and the drug involved is returned to the conversational agent. Otherwise, it proceeds to the second check, which analyzes the glycemic load of the food.

The glycemic load of the food is calculated based on the glycemic index and the amount of carbohydrates in the food. Although the end user does not receive explicit information about the glycemic load, it is translated into three categories of messages:

- "You can consume cautiously...", if the glycemic load is between 0 and 9;

– "Consume with caution...", if the glycemic load is between 10 and 19, and;
– "Alert do not consume..." if the glycemic load exceeds 20.

The portion size is also taken into account when calculating the glycemic load, and conversion factors are used for this. This is important because people may describe the amount of a food in different ways. For example, it is not the same to say "one loaf of whole wheat bread" as "one slice of whole wheat bread". The Conversational Agent includes various conversion processes to detect and handle these variations.

Food Recommendation Service. This component comes into operation when an interaction between a food and a drug is detected. The service plays a critical role in finding a viable and safe alternative for the user, ensuring that the suggested new food does not interact with the medication he/she is taking. This is achieved through the use of a content-based filtering algorithm that analyzes and selects a suitable food option, taking into account the absence of negative drug interactions.

It is important to note that in the context of this work, recommendations are generated only when a drug-food interaction is identified, thus acting preemptively to mitigate potential health risks to the user.

A neural network using TensorFlow[8] was trained to predict similar foods in terms of carbohydrate content, glycemic index, and glycemic load. The Sequential class of TensorFlow was used to create a three-layer neural network. The first layer has 64 neurons and uses the ReLU activation function[9]; the second layer has 32 neurons also with ReLU; and the third output layer has three neurons equal to the number of input features and uses a linear activation function. The data source for training the model was extracted from [8] and 80% of the data was used for training and 20% for validation, for 17 epochs.

The *food recommendation service* uses the trained model to identify foods with carbohydrate content, glycemic index, and glycemic load similar to the user's preferences, while avoiding interactions with user-reported medications. A process is performed beforehand to normalize the attributes entered by the user so that they are on the same scale as the data used to train the model.

As a result, the service provides a list of at least three foods that, according to the available information, are similar to the original food provided by the user and do not present interactions with the medications the user is taking.

2.4   External Devices

Extending the platform to external devices was a key aspect of the project planning. Although the mobile application is functional, interoperability testing with web platforms and Alexa devices still presents challenges related to user

---

[8] https://www.tensorflow.org/.
[9] The Rectified Linear Unit (ReLU) function is a nonlinear function that outputs the input value if it is positive and zero otherwise.

authentication. This has limited the full functionality of the system on these platforms.

The user interacts with the conversational agent through a unified interface. The conversational agent uses this API to deliver responses and recommendations to the user, and key parameters include the user's message, the session ID to differentiate user sessions, and a Firebase key to enable user identification.

Mobile Application. The mobile application is compatible with iOS and Android and was developed in Flutter, which allows for the creation of cross-platform applications. The application provides voice and text interaction. Two libraries have been included to improve the user experience in voice interaction: Speech To Text (v6.1.1)[10] and Text To Speech (v3.6.3)[11]. The first converts speech to text, focusing on command recognition and short sentences. The second converts text to speech, allowing the conversational agent to communicate verbally with users. The integration of these libraries into the mobile application provides a more natural and versatile interaction, improving the user experience.

The graphical user interface (GUI) design focused on achieving good usability for the user and includes: welcome, authentication, medication and meal plan registration, requesting and visualizing recommendations, notifications, and food registration. Figure 2 shows an example of three GUIs designed for the system. Figure 2a shows the GUI created to log the user's medication intake. Once authenticated, users have the option to request recommendations through the chat interface, Fig. 2b shows the message that starts the conversation with the user in preventive mode. The application offers the possibility to customize the alerts, allowing the user to enable or disable the notifications according to his preferences, Fig. 2c shows the alert sent before the meal time that the user notified.

3 Results and Discussion

A conversational agent that helps to prevent drug-food and drug-drug interactions is a valuable tool in the pharmacological field. In order to obtain a complete and objective view of the implemented system, two types of complementary evaluations were carried out: a usability evaluation and an evaluation based on expert judgment.

---

[10] https://pub.dev/packages/speech_to_text.
[11] https://pub.dev/packages/flutter_tts.

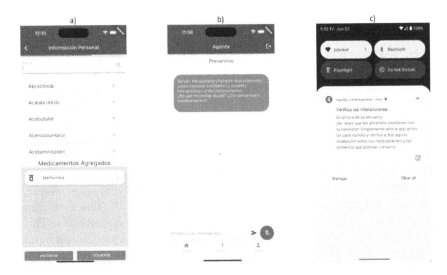

Fig. 2. Conversation Agent Screenshots. a) The GUI that logs the user's medication intake. b) The GUI that starts the chat in preventive mode. c) The GUI that displays a notification to the user before a meal to warn them of possible interactions.

3.1   Usability

This evaluation was conducted using the Chatbot Usability Questionnaire (CUQ). The CUQ is a tool specifically designed to evaluate the usability of chatbots, and consists of 16 questions that address various aspects of user experience (UX) [5].

To tailor CUQ to the needs of our conversational agent, we selected 11 relevant questions that are rated on a five-point Likert scale. The questionnaire was distributed online and involved 26 students of nutrition and dietetics at an institute of higher education, mostly women. The main findings are described below.

Positive Aspects. In general, users agreed that the conversational agent interface was intuitive and easy to use. In addition, most found the process of registering information to be simple and straightforward. Evaluators expressed mixed opinions about whether the conversational agent understood the requests correctly. This suggests that there is room for improvement in the conversational agent's ability to interpret and respond appropriately to user requests.

Regarding the clarity and conciseness of the information provided by the conversational agent, most users indicated that the responses were clear and concise. With regard to the ability of the Conversational Agent to provide food consumption alternatives, the results showed a variety of responses. Some users felt that the Conversational Agent was able to provide alternatives, while others did not have such a positive experience. Most respondents felt that the conversational agent was able to handle errors effectively and maintain a coherent conversation.

Negative Aspects. The negative aspects correspond to the drawbacks and areas for improvement of the conversational agent, focusing on critical areas of the users' experience with the technological tool.

Some users expressed difficulty in fully understanding the scope and purpose of the conversational agent. This lack of clarity can lead to confusion and affect the user's perception of the functionality of the conversational agent. Several people experienced confusion when using the mobile application and the conversational agent. This suggests that there may be aspects of the conversational flow that need improvement. When asked about the usefulness and appropriateness of the conversational agent's responses, the results show a mix of opinions. Some users found the responses useful and appropriate, while others had a less satisfactory experience.

After careful analysis of both positive and negative aspects, users show a positive perception of the usability of the Conversational Agent, but areas for improvement are identified, particularly in (i) explaining the scope and purpose of the Conversational Agent, (ii) the ability to handle errors effectively, and (iii) maintaining a coherent conversation. The average overall usability score obtained was 77.27/100, indicating acceptable overall user satisfaction.

General comments and suggestions were also collected during the evaluation. Some users expressed the need for more personalized responses or the inclusion of more food products contextualized to the Ecuadorian market.

3.2   Expert Judgment

This technique is used to gather information and knowledge from individuals who have experience or are experts in a particular field in order to evaluate quantities or parameters that are unknown or uncertain [13]. In the context of the conversational agent, expert evaluation was used to validate conversational agent responses in situations that simulated real-world interactions. Four scenarios were created by two healthcare professionals, covering both preventive and informative situations related to the interactions. Due to space limitations, it is not possible to describe the four scenarios in detail; however, Table 1 illustrates one of them.

Four experts with the following profiles were involved in testing the responses provided by the conversational agent in the scenarios: a pharmaceutical chemist with a Ph.D. in interaction management, a doctor with experience in the treatment of patients with diabetes, a nutritionist with experience in the management of food-drug interactions, and a clinician with daily experience in medical consultations. In addition, two raters were involved to compare the experts' responses with those of the recommendation system using a questionnaire designed on the basis of the proposed scenarios. The results for each scenario are presented below.

Table 1. Scenario-1: To detect drug-drug and drug-food interactions.

SCENARIO 1		
Interaction Case	Drug-Drug and Drug-Food	
Sex	Male	Age 56
Medical History	Type 2 diabetes, with recent cholesterol complications	
Current Medication	Metformina and Simvastatina	
Current Situation	Patient with type 2 diabetes, on treatment with Metformin for 5 years, started taking Simvastine since 15 days ago for high cholesterol levels. He has since experienced muscle pain with no apparent cause after consuming grapefruit. This muscle pain persists since a few days with mild to moderate intensity	
Questions for the Expert	¿Is there any interaction between Metformin and Simvastine? ¿Should additional precautions be taken when combining Metformin and Simvastine in this patient? ¿Are there any possible side effects if these two drugs are taken in addition to grapefruit?	

In Scenario 1, the evaluators gave positive ratings to the system's recommendations for identifying drug-drug and drug-nutrient interactions. In Scenario 2, there was a high level of agreement with the system's ability to identify interactions, particularly between Insulin and Enalapril. In scenario 3, ratings were mixed, with uncertainty in the identification of interactions related to apple and beer. In Scenario 4, there was general agreement on the identification of interactions and the usefulness of the recommendations.

Although there is room for improvement, overall the evaluators acknowledged the usefulness and accuracy of the system in most scenarios, supporting its effectiveness in providing safe and effective guidance to the user. Future improvements could include the inclusion of more food and drug information and the customization of recommendations to further increase the usefulness and accuracy of the system in different cases.

4   Conclusions and Future Work

This work presents a conversational agent that alerts users with diabetes about potential drug-drug and drug-food interactions. For this purpose, a database was designed that contains relevant information about drug-drug interactions as well as food characteristics, nutritional composition and position in the food pyramid. The conversational agent developed has an algorithm that provides users with personalized information about drug-food interactions. This algorithm not only provides information about specific interactions, but also offers food consumption alternatives using content-based filtering. Furthermore, the integration of the conversational agent into the mobile application not only allows for a more intuitive and accessible interaction for the user, but also gives the user the option to receive information via voice. This makes it easier for the user to ask questions and receive recommendations in a simple and convenient way, without having to read long texts or navigate through multiple options, which can benefit vulnerable groups such as older adults by making it easier to use technology.

The application was tested on university students, rather than directly on people with diabetes, because the tool needs to be as accurate as possible in its recommendations and easy to use before it goes into production or is used by the general diabetic population. This would prevent any malfunctioning of the application from causing confusion and bad experiences with the use of technology in patients who are vulnerable and looking for reliable sources or devices to manage their disease. The next version of the tool will consider evaluation and use in diabetic patients, including bioethical protocols for confidentiality of information, including informed consent of participants for use of anonymised data, and data protection according to the Organic Law on the Protection of Personal Data in force.

In terms of future work, it is advisable to consider including more information in the database used to provide more accurate and contextual results. The addition of data such as detailed nutritional composition of specific foods and regional details would allow for more accurate and personalized information for users. In the current version, a database of generic foods was used for testing and evaluation. However, given the diversity and richness of Ecuadorian foods, it would be beneficial to expand the database to include fruits and foods typical of the region. In addition, it is important to emphasize that an exhaustive collection of data from reliable and updated sources should be carried out, with the aim of guaranteeing the accuracy and relevance of the information provided by the application. Collaboration with nutrition experts and validation of the information collected will also be key aspects to consider.

Acknowledgements. This work is part of the research project "VIUC_II INV-VINC_2022_15_ABRIL_VICTORIA", supported by the Vice-Rectorate for Research of the University of Cuenca.

References

1. Altamirano, L.C., et al.: Prevalencia de la diabetes mellitus tipo 2 y sus factores de riesgo en individuos adultos de la ciudad de cuenca-ecuador. Avances en Biomedicina **6**, 10–21 (2017). https://www.redalyc.org/articulo.oa?id=331351068003
2. Bressan Martin, G.S.: Interacción fármaco - nutrientes. Technical report, Facultad de Ciencias de la Nutrición. Universidad Juan Agustín Maza (2020). Tesina de grado
3. Das, S.K., Maheshwari, R.A., Chakraborty, J., Deb Roy, S., Shil, D.: Enhancing drug related problem (DRP) management in Indian healthcare through AI integration: an insight view. Intell. Pharm. **1**(4), 175–178 (2023). https://doi.org/10.1016/j.ipha.2023.08.006. https://www.sciencedirect.com/science/article/pii/S2949866X23000655

4. Díaz SM, X., Neri D, D., Moraga M, F., Rebollo G, M.J., Olivares C, S., Castillo D, C.: Análisis comparativo de la canasta básica de alimentos, pirámide alimentaria y recomendaciones nutricionales para preescolares y escolares chilenos: a comparative analysis. Revista chilena de pediatría **77**, 466 – 472 (2006)

5. Holmes, S., Moorhead, A., Bond, R., Zheng, H., Coates, V., Mctear, M.: Usability testing of a healthcare chatbot: can we use conventional methods to assess conversational user interfaces? In: Proceedings of the 31st European Conference on Cognitive Ergonomics, ECCE 2019, pp. 207–214. Association for Computing Machinery, New York (2019). https://doi.org/10.1145/3335082.3335094

6. IDF Diabetes Atlas, 10th edn.: IDF Diabetes Atlas 2021. International Diabetes Federation, Brussels (2021)

7. Laranjo, L., et al.: Conversational agents in healthcare: a systematic review. J. Am. Med. Inform. Assoc. **25**(9), 1248–1258 (2018). https://doi.org/10.1093/jamia/ocy072

8. Meneses, K.: Tabla de Alimentos. Indice Glucémico y Carga Glucémica (2020). https://d-medical.com/2020/06/nueva-tabla-de-alimentos-indice-glucemico-y-carga-glucemica/

9. Montastruc, J.L., et al.: Pharmacovigilance, risks and adverse effects of self-medication. Therapies **71**(2), 257–262 (2016). https://doi.org/10.1016/j.therap.2016.02.012.   https://www.sciencedirect.com/science/article/pii/S0040595716000317

10. Montenegro, J.L.Z., da Costa, C.A., da Rosa Righi, R.: Survey of conversational agents in health. Expert Syst. Appl. **129**, 56–67 (2019). https://doi.org/10.1016/j.eswa.2019.03.054.   https://www.sciencedirect.com/science/article/pii/S0957417419302283

11. Navarrete-Mejía, P.J., Velasco-Guerrero, J.C., Loro-Chero, L.: Automedicación en época de pandemia: Covid-19. Revista del Cuerpo Médico Hospital Nacional Almanzor Aguinaga Asenjo **13**(4), 350–355 (2021). https://doi.org/10.35434/rcmhnaaa.2020.134.762.   https://cmhnaaa.org.pe/ojs/index.php/rcmhnaaa/article/view/762

12. Patajalo Villalta, S.J., et al.: Automedicación en la región interandina norte del ecuador: una práctica usual. Revista de la Facultad de Ciencias Médicas (Quito) **43**(2), 78–85 (2018). https://doi.org/10.29166/rfcmq.v43i2.2824

13. Ryan, J.J., Mazzuchi, T.A., Ryan, D.J., Lopez de la Cruz, J., Cooke, R.: Quantifying information security risks using expert judgment elicitation. Comput. Oper. Res. **39**(4), 774–784 (2012). https://doi.org/10.1016/j.cor.2010.11.013. https://www.sciencedirect.com/science/article/pii/S0305054810002893. Special Issue on Operational Research in Risk Management

14. Wishart, D.S., et al.: DrugBank 5.0: a major update to the DrugBank database for 2018. Nucleic Acids Res. **46**(D1), D1074–D1082 (2017). https://doi.org/10.1093/nar/gkx1037

15. Xiong, G., et al.: DDInter: an online drug–drug interaction database towards improving clinical decision-making and patient safety. Nucleic Acids Res. **50**(D1), D1200–D1207 (2021). https://doi.org/10.1093/nar/gkab880

Author Index

M. Botto-Tobar et al. (Eds.): ICAT 2023, CCIS 2049, pp. 277–279, 2024.
https://doi.org/10.1007/978-3-031-58956-0

Printed in the United States
by Baker & Taylor Publisher Services